Longman modular texts in business and economics
·····················

Series Editors
Geoff Black and Stuart Wall

Other titles in this series:

Marketing
Elizabeth Hill and Terry O'Sullivan

Business Economics
Win Hornby, Bob Gammie and Stuart Wall

Management Accounting
David Wright

Financial Accounting
Christopher Waterston and Anne Britton

Introducing Human Resource Management
Margaret Foot and Caroline Hook

The macroeconomic environment

Andrew Dunnett

LONGMAN

London and New York

Pearson Education Limited,
Edinburgh Gate,
Harlow,
Essex CM20 2JE,
England
and Associated Companies throughout the world

Visit us on the World Wide Web at:
http://www.pearsoneduc.com

*Published in the United States of America
by Addison Wesley Longman Inc., New York*

First published 1997
Second impression 1999

ISBN 0 582 30581 0 PPR

British Library Cataloguing-in-Publication Data

A catalogue record for this book is
available from the British Library

Library of Congress Cataloging-in-Publication Data

Set by 30 in Stone Serif 9/12pt
Transferred to digital print on demand, 2006
Printed and bound by CPI Antony Rowe, Eastbourne

Contents

Preface   XI

1 The macroeconomic environment   **1**
  1.1   It's the economy, stupid!   1
  1.2   What macroeconomics is about   2
  1.3   The whole ... and the sum of the parts   2
  1.4   The objectives of macroeconomic policy   3
  1.5   Conflicts in objectives   3
  1.6   The French have a word for it   3
  1.7   Full employment   3
  1.8   Inflation   4
  1.9   Economic growth   5
  1.10 The balance of payments   6
  1.11 Other macroeconomic objectives   7
  1.12 The ranking of objectives   7
  1.13 Data: a window on the world   8
  1.14 Using the data to tell a story   9
  1.15 Getting a feel for the data   9

2 Measuring the rate of inflation   **14**
  2.1   The price index and inflation   14
  2.2   Comparing series using index numbers   16
  2.3   Every picture tells a story ... or a lie   17
  2.4   Changes in relative prices   19
  2.5   A weighted average of price rises   21
  2.6   Changes in quality   22

3 The determination of national income   **26**
  3.1   A model of the economy   26
  3.2   Specialisation and exchange   27
  3.3   One man's spending is another's income   27
  3.4   Stocks and flows   28
  3.5   A two-sector model   29
  3.6   Equilibrium in the circular flow   30

3.7   The government can manipulate the level of spending   32
3.8   Savings and investment   35
3.9   The multiplier   36
3.10 The multiplier in practice   39
3.11 Fine tuning   40

4   **Measuring output: GDP**   **44**
4.1   Measuring output   44
4.2   The money value of output   45
4.3   Nominal output and real output   46
4.4   The national accounts   46
4.5   Current-price and constant-price estimates   49
4.6   Is the growth of GNP a suitable way of assessing the performance   50
      of an economy?

5   **The inflationary process**   **56**
5.1   The history of inflation   56
5.2   Demand-pull inflation   57
5.3   Cost-push inflation   59
5.4   Wage-push inflation   59
5.5   A wage–price spiral   59
5.6   How to calculate the growth of real earnings   60
5.7   The policy response   61
5.8   Rebasing the index   62
5.9   The Phillips curve   64
5.10 Expectations   69

6   **Money**   **73**
6.1   The development of money   73
6.2   Cigarettes in prisons   75
6.3   Credit creation   76
6.4   The control of the money supply   79
6.5   Narrow money and broad money   79
6.6   The transmission mechanism   80
6.7   The quantity theory of money   80
6.8   Say's Law   81
6.9   Objections to the quantity theory of money   81
6.10 The velocity of circulation of money   82
6.11 Is the stock of money an instrument which can be controlled? 84
6.12 Say's Law revisited   85
6.13 Monetarists and Keynesians   86
6.14 Problems in defining the money supply   86
6.15 Alternative views of the transmission mechanism – Keynes   88
6.16 Modern views of the transmission mechanism – portfolio balance   89

7   **Trade, the exchange rate and the balance of payments**   **95**
7.1   The gains from trade   95
7.2   Specialisation and comparative advantage   97

7.3	Exchange rates	99
7.4	The determination of the exchange rate	99
7.5	The current and capital accounts	102
7.6	Flexible and fixed exchange rates	102
7.7	Internal and external purchasing power	105

8 Policies to correct balance of payments deficits — **111**

8.1	Debits and credits	111
8.2	The current account	112
8.3	The capital account	113
8.4	The balance for official financing (change in reserves)	113
8.5	Autonomous and accommodating transactions	114
8.6	Interim summary	114
8.7	Current and capital account balances	115
8.8	Is a current account deficit 'a bad thing'?	116
8.9	Interest rates	117
8.10	Deflation (by fiscal means)	117
8.11	Tariffs and quotas	118
8.12	Devaluation	118
8.13	The elasticities approach	118
8.14	The relative profitability approach	121
8.15	Competitiveness	122

9 Unemployment and the labour market — **130**

9.1	Historical perspectives	130
9.2	Problems of definition	132
9.3	Types of unemployment	134
9.4	Frictional unemployment	134
9.5	Structural unemployment	135
9.6	Demand-deficient unemployment	135
9.7	'Classical' unemployment	136
9.8	The effect of a minimum wage	138
9.9	The emasculation of the trade unions	141
9.10	The labour market and inflation	142
9.11	Discovering statistical regularities – correlation	143

10 Public spending ... and taxing — **151**

10.1	Public spending	152
10.2	Transfer payments	152
10.3	Spending on goods and services	154
10.4	Analysis by department	154
10.5	Debt interest	154
10.6	The budget deficit and the PSBR	155
10.7	The PSBR and the national debt	156
10.8	How big is the public sector?	157
10.9	The denominator of the expression	159
10.10	Historical trends	159
10.11	An international comparison – taxes	160

10.12 The financing of government spending   162
10.13 Direct and indirect taxes   162
10.14 Progressive, regressive and neutral taxes   163
10.15 Who pays the tax?   164
10.16 The structure of the tax system: an international comparison   165
10.17 The rationale for public spending   166
10.18 Public goods   166
10.19 The redistributive argument   169

11 Changes in the structure of the UK economy   173
11.1   The dog that didn't bark   173
11.2   The causes of structural change   175
11.3   The rationale for supply-side policies   177
11.4   Supply-side policies   178
11.5   Labour market policies: weakening the power of trade unions   178
11.6   A flexible labour market?   179
11.7   Changes in the structure of taxation and social security   181
11.8   The impact on the distribution of income   183
11.9   Privatisation and liberalisation   189
11.10 Competition: a panacea?   191
11.11 Closing the productivity gap   192

12 The international monetary system   200
12.1   The Gold Standard   200
12.2   Bretton Woods   202
12.3   Problems of liquidity, confidence and adjustment   202
12.4   The Smithsonian Agreement   204
12.5   The pros and cons of fixed versus floating rates   204
12.6   European monetary integration   206
12.7   The Werner Report   207
12.8   The European Monetary System   208
12.9   Black Wednesday   209
12.10 Speculative selling on foreign exchange markets   210
12.11 Maastricht   210
12.12 Rationale for the convergence criteria   211
12.13 A two-speed Europe   213
12.14 Just do it   213

13 The macroeconomic environment and business   218
13.1   Business cycles   218
13.2   The volatility of investment   220
13.3   The accelerator   221
13.4   Exogenous spending   222
13.5   Forecasts and indicators   223
13.6   Investment and the rate of interest   224
13.7   Net present value   225
13.8   The internal rate of return   227
13.9   What determines market interest rates?   228

13.10   The impact of inflation on business   231
13.11   The exchange rate and business   232
13.12   The single European currency   234

Answers to activities and review questions   **240**

A guide to statistical sources   **265**

Index   **269**

Preface

Everything should be made as simple as possible . . . but not simpler.

Albert Einstein

This textbook is designed for students who are taking a one-semester course in macroeconomics on business studies or similar programmes. It will also be useful, however, for students on other programmes who require a text of manageable proportions which nevertheless provides an accessible yet thorough introduction to applied macroeconomics.

Pedagogic style

The pedagogic approach adopted is designed not only to be user-friendly, but to elicit a proactive response from the reader. That is, it sets out deliberately to *engage* rather than simply to inform. Thus the text is interspersed with questions and exercises which you are invited to complete. These are integrated into the text so as to encourage you to tackle them, though of course if they are omitted entirely the text will still make sense. However, as with any other form of human endeavour, the more you put into an activity the more you get out of it, and the full benefit will only be derived if you work conscientiously through the questions and exercises.

How to use this book

Special features in this book are designed to help you to get the most out of it. Most of these features are self-explanatory, but for others it may be helpful if the reasoning behind them is explained.

- Each of the thirteen chapters is divided into sections (numbered 1.1, 1.2 and so on). Regard the numbers merely as navigational aids. Think of yourself as on a motorway, heading in a purposeful way in a particular direction. You can leave the motorway at any point to go for a coffee (for example, at junction 1.2), but you have to rejoin the motorway at the same point afterwards.
- A list of section headings appears at the beginning of each chapter (it helps if you have a map of the motorway).
- In addition, at the beginning of each chapter there is a list of objectives to be achieved by reading the chapter.

XII THE MACROECONOMIC ENVIRONMENT

➤ When key concepts appear for the first time they are printed in **bold type**.

➤ The concepts are explained in the text at this point.

➤ These key words are listed at the end of the chapter in which they first appear. Page numbers refer the reader back to the page where they are to be found. You may find these key concepts particularly useful for revision purposes.

➤ A summary appears at the end of each chapter.

➤ When *italics* appear in the text they are used for *emphasis*.

➤ In most textbooks when a figure (a diagram) is referred to in the text, it is sometimes difficult to know whether to look at the figure straight away or continue reading and look at the figure afterwards. You may find that you have to stop reading because the text begins to be incomprehensible without the figure and you realise you could have saved time by looking at the figure earlier. To avoid this problem a convention is used in this book as follows. If a figure (diagram) being referred to in the text is printed in bold italics (for example, ***Figure 1.1***), it means 'stop reading the text and look at the figure now'. If it is printed in normal type (for example, Figure 1.1), it means 'carry on reading the text and look at the figure afterwards'. The same convention applies to tables.

➤ Activities appear within each chapter. Answers and suggestions are given at the back of the book.

➤ Review questions appear at the end of each chapter. Answers to these questions are given at the back of the book.

➤ Sources you can use to give you access to up-to-date information and data are provided at the end of relevant chapters.

A note to teachers

For those involved in the teaching of macroeconomics on business programmes, the title of the book requires some explanation. The initial proposal was for a book called *The Business Environment*. The use of the term 'business environment' rather than 'macroeconomics' was intended to convey to teachers that the approach adopted here is less theoretical than that found in texts aimed at subject specialists – for example, those students on Economics degree programmes – and that is indeed the case. It is important to emphasise, however, that the approach adopted here is not 'watered-down macroeconomics,' since that would imply that the essence of macroeconomics consists of esoteric abstractions and models with little relevance to policy issues in contemporary society. This is a view to which I do not subscribe. Rather I take the view that the study of macroeconomics cannot be divorced from the world to which it relates and that as macroeconomists we perceive that world through the empirical data. At one time it was fashionable to use the term 'applied macroeconomics' to describe such an approach, though this is open to the same objection as that raised above. More recently, the term 'business environment' has been used to identify courses which essentially teach macroeconomics in a context deemed appropriate for business studies students. This is unfortunate for four reasons. First, it is an ungainly expression. Second, it conveys little meaning in itself. Third, it smacks of an educational philosophy – now thankfully on the wane – which believed that students on vocational courses should not be exposed to academic disciplines, such as economics, either because those disciplines were not 'relevant' (to use the jargon) or because such students lacked the motivation or ability to cope with a conceptual approach. These views seem to me to be both patronising and demeaning – and they are also wrong. The overriding reason for eschewing the use of the term 'business environment' for this text, however, is the belief that we should say what we mean. Economists should not be embarrassed or defensive about their discipline. Rather than trying to sneak their subject into business courses under the guise of calling it something else, they should proclaim a fundamental truth: namely, that the study of macroeconomics provides a perspective on business – and indeed on society generally – which is quite simply indispensable. Thus the title *Business Environment* was dropped in favour of a title which included the key word 'macroeconomics', since in essence this is the subject matter of the book. The word 'environment' was retained to indicate, hopefully, the approach adopted.

The book is divided into thirteen chapters. It is reasonable to expect that the material contained therein can be assimilated and understood within a normal semester consisting of approximately twelve teaching weeks. The ordering of the material is not critical and teachers who prefer a slightly different order of presentation can use the book accordingly.

The book sets out to provide a framework through which economic events can be analysed. Although written in a UK context, the text also provides a European and – where appropriate – a global focus. This reflects the increasing internationalisation of business, a theme which appears frequently in the text. In essence the book has a simple objective. By the choice of material and by its approach it sets out to provide the reader with an understanding of the macroeconomic events which shape our everyday lives.

I would like to thank colleagues at Thames Valley University for their support in the writing of this text. My particular thanks go to Michael Simpson, who read through the entire manuscript with his usual attention to detail.

Andrew Dunnett
Holland on Sea

CHAPTER 1

The macroeconomic environment

Objectives

This chapter will enable you to:
- distinguish between microeconomics and macroeconomics
- appreciate that, if we focus on the economy as a whole rather than on individual parts, we may get a clearer overall picture
- list the key objectives (targets) of macroeconomic policy
- appreciate the primary importance of economic growth which (provided it outstrips population growth) is synonymous with an increase in living standards
- appreciate that objectives often conflict and that differing views exist regarding the relative importance of the various objectives
- understand the importance of statistical data in the process by which we perceive the world
- appreciate the importance of getting a feel for the data.

1.1 It's the economy, stupid!
1.2 What macroeconomics is about
1.3 The whole ... and the sum of the parts
1.4 The objectives of macroeconomic policy
1.5 Conflicts in objectives
1.6 The French have a word for it
1.7 Full employment
1.8 Inflation
1.9 Economic growth
1.10 The balance of payments
1.11 Other macroeconomic objectives
1.12 The ranking of objectives
1.13 Data: a window on the world
1.14 Using the data to tell a story
1.15 Getting a feel for the data

1.1 It's the economy, stupid!

You probably think you've heard this somewhere before. In fact it was the slogan used by the Democratic Party in America when Bill Clinton was elected in 1992. Its meaning and significance are obvious – as in most political campaigns the world over, it is the performance of the national economy and the government's handling of that economy that is at the top of the political agenda. Moreover, voters generally understand this – hence the use of the word 'stupid'. Americans are a trifle direct.

In every country the performance of the economy has a most dramatic and fundamental effect on the lives of each and every citizen. It influences not only their material standard of living – the amount of goods and services they can afford to buy – but more importantly whether they work at all. It determines the quality and quantity of public services available to them. It influences the choices open to them and the life chances they enjoy. In short, it affects the well-being of every citizen in the widest possible sense.

But at some stage in their lives, most individuals are also involved as producers of wealth as well as consumers, and it is here that the impact of the economy on their lives is perhaps the most obvious and the most direct. Changes in interest rates, tax rates and the exchange rate will have a direct effect on the success or failure of individual firms, as will the state of the labour market, the level of inflation and the rate of economic growth.

An understanding of the macroeconomic environment within which firms operate is therefore of vital importance for all those engaged in business. This textbook sets out to provide a framework which will foster such an understanding.

1.2 What macroeconomics is about

The academic discipline of economics is conventionally divided into **microeconomics** and **macroeconomics**. In microeconomics the focus is the individual elements which make up the economy. Thus microeconomics studies the price of individual products (such as the price of petrol), the activities of individual companies (such as the prospects for Eurotunnel) and the behaviour of individual markets (such as the housing market). In contrast, in macroeconomics the focus of study is the economy as a whole. Thus it concerns itself not with individual prices, but with the price level as a whole; it attempts to explain not the output of a *specific* good or service, but the output of *all* goods and services; and it attempts to explain employment not in a specific firm or industry, but in the whole economy. Macroeconomics therefore has a broad focus.

1.3 The whole ... and the sum of the parts

In a logical sense, of course, the whole is simply the sum of the parts. But if we were to concentrate on the individual parts we might – as the saying goes – lose sight of the wood for the trees. Although the macroeconomy is clearly made up of individual markets and individual prices, if we were to attempt to explain the workings of the whole economy simply by adding up all these myriad pieces of information, we would fail to appreciate the picture as a whole. We need to step back in order to see things in perspective. By analogy, if you study a newspaper photograph under a magnifying glass, you can see that it is made up of thousands upon thousands of individual dots – black, white and various shades of grey. However, it is impossible to understand what is going on – to make sense of what we are seeing – by concentrating on these myriad individual dots. Rather you have to stand back to see the picture as a whole before it makes any sense. The dots transform themselves into something which is meaningful when they are viewed as a whole. This is what macroeconomics does.

1.4 The objectives of macroeconomic policy

It is conventional to identify four major macroeconomic **objectives** or **targets**. These are: the control of inflation, the control of unemployment, the promotion of economic growth and the avoidance of balance of payments difficulties. Macroeconomics consists of trying to achieve acceptable levels of each of these four targets. This is achieved – or not achieved – by the use of **instruments** such as tax rates, interest rates and so on. The policy-maker (in the UK, the Chancellor of the Exchequer) has control over certain policy variables (such as tax rates) and he can use these to affect the four targets in a way that he deems desirable. The aim of macroeconomic management is to achieve a satisfactory level of each of these four target variables.

1.5 Conflicts in objectives

The four targets that we have identified may **conflict** with one another. For example, a particular policy that brings about an improvement in, say, the rate of inflation may at the same time lead to a worsening in the level of unemployment. The policy-maker's task therefore involves not just a technical competence – that is, an understanding of the impact that a particular instrument will have on a particular target. Rather, it also involves making **value judgements** about the compromises that have to be reached when these various targets conflict with one another.

1.6 The French have a word for it

Successful macroeconomic management thus involves achieving the 'best' combination of the four targets – a high rate of growth, but not so high as to cause inflation or balance of payments problems, and high enough to prevent unacceptable levels of unemployment. Clearly this is a complicated juggling act where the juggler – in this case the Chancellor – needs to keep his eye not just on one ball, but on all four. The French have a word for this – *la conjuncture*. The Germans have a word for it too – *Konjunkturpolitik*. In fact the word is used in almost every European language except English. Although there exists a word **conjuncture** (literally, 'joining together'), the phrase in English which is always used when referring to this activity is 'short-term macroeconomic management'.

We now consider each of the four major macroeconomic objectives in turn.

1.7 Full employment

In the immediate post-war period – that is, in the 1950s and 1960s – in western Europe **full employment** would have been regarded as the most important macroeconomic objective. This resulted from the experience of many western countries, including the United States, during the inter-war period. In the Great Depression of the 1920s and 1930s, high and persistent levels of unemployment caused social unrest and misery for millions. The emphasis on the control of unemployment also results, however, from the influential writings of one man, John Maynard Keynes, who is widely regarded as the most important single influence on the way we now think about the workings of the macro-economy and the role of government. He is the founding father of modern macroeconomics who demonstrated in his famous book *The General Theory of Employment, Interest and Money* (1936) that unemployment could be reduced – that is, employment could be stimulated – by government action: namely, by government spending.

The importance attached to full employment as an objective has, however, declined dramatically in the 1980s and 1990s. As the actual level of unemployment has risen in most western countries, governments have attached less and less importance to reducing the amount of unemployment. For the last fifteen years or so, the level of unemployment in most western economies has been around 10 per cent – that is, one individual in ten who would actually like to take up paid employment has been unable to find a job. Note, however, that unemployment tends to be a localised phenomenon so that even within a particular country some prosperous regions may be experiencing low unemployment (and rapidly rising wages) whereas other less fortunate areas may be experiencing levels of recorded unemployment of 50 per cent or more. Finally note that, as one British Labour Prime Minister once remarked, 'For the man who is unemployed, unemployment is 100 per cent.'

1.8 Inflation

In many ways the decreasing importance attached to the control of unemployment has been mirrored by an increasing concern with controlling the rate of **price inflation**. In the 1950s and 1960s moderate levels of price inflation of 2–4 per cent per annum were the norm in most western countries. This was known as 'creeping inflation'. But in the 1970s inflation rates in a number of western countries increased dramatically and for brief periods, for example, following the oil price shock of the mid-1970s, inflation exceeded 20 per cent in some western countries.

In the late 1970s and early 1980s, governments throughout the West, but particularly in the United States and the UK, began to attach the greatest importance to controlling the rate of inflation. President Reagan described inflation as 'public enemy number one' and in the UK Mrs Thatcher saw the control of inflation as a prerequisite for any sort of economic success. In western Europe by the mid-1990s, the rate of inflation had been reduced to rather modest levels – typically less than 5 per cent per annum. In central and eastern Europe in this period, however, the newly 'marketised' economies such as those of the former Soviet Union experienced high rates of inflation. Moreover, these high rates of inflation were coupled with high levels of unemployment as the rigours of a market system began to bite.

1.9 Economic growth

Despite the importance attached to the control of unemployment and inflation by many politicians, it is **economic growth** which is viewed by most economists as being the most important of all the objectives of macroeconomic policy. Other things being equal, economic growth – by which we mean an increase in incomes – is synonymous with an improvement in the **living standards** of the citizens of the country. It gives them the ability to consume a greater volume of goods and services. Not only does it improve their *material* standard of living, however, but by making them 'better off' it also gives them more choice, and this choice includes the possibility of rejecting the consumer society and all its trappings if they so wish.

Note that economic growth is synonymous with an increase in living standards only if there is no population growth. If not, we should distinguish between income and **income per capita** (that is, income per head of the population). In most industrialised countries the size of the population is stable so that it is unnecessary to make this distinction. In developing countries the high rate of population growth is, however, a significant factor in depressing the growth of income per capita.

CASE
ILLUSTRATION

Living standards double each generation

Note that we are talking here about the rate of economic growth measured in **real terms** – that is, once an allowance has been made for a fall in the purchasing power of the money used to measure income and output; or in other words, once the effects of inflation have been taken into account. In *real* terms most economies in the West grow at a modest rate of 2–3 per cent per annum on average. Table 1.1 shows the average annual growth rate for the period 1976–95 for the so-called Group of Seven (or G7) countries.

Overlaid on the long-term trend growth rate of 2–3 per cent per annum, there are substantial fluctuations in economic activity. So, for example, in some years the economy will be growing at 4 per cent and in other years it will actually be shrinking. A positive though modest rate of economic growth ensures, however, that on average people become 'better off' through time. In broad terms, living standards double each generation – today's children can expect a material standard of living which is twice as high as that of their parents. In other words, over a 25–30-year period there will be a doubling of the real level of income per capita. Indeed, the vertical bar chart (Figure 1.1) shows how rapidly real incomes per head have grown in the UK over time. Using constant 1990 prices, we can see that in 1995 the standard of living was almost four times higher than it had been in 1948.

table 1.1

Average annual growth rates, Group of Seven countries, 1976–95

UK	2.0
Canada	1.4
Italy	2.3
Germany	2.3
Japan	3.6
France	2.1
USA	2.7

Source: OECD.

Figure 1.1

UK income[1] per capita (£ per year)

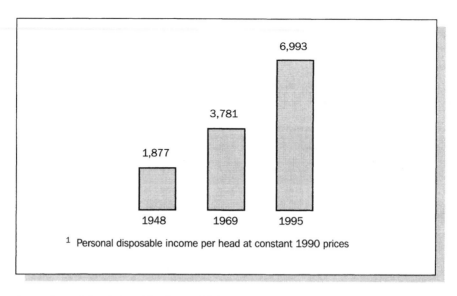

1 Personal disposable income per head at constant 1990 prices

Source: *Economic Trends Annual Supplement*, 1996/97.

This, of course, is a broad approximation that applies to the economies of western Europe and North America. In some of the newly industrialising countries (NICs) of Asia the rate of economic growth is substantially faster. At one stage during the 1970s the Japanese economy was growing at a rate of more than 10 per cent per annum (which implies a doubling of income every seven years), though the rate has slowed substantially and is now nearer western levels. Rapid rates of economic growth are currently being experienced by the 'Asian tigers' – those fast-growing economies of countries such as Korea, Hong Kong, Taiwan and Malaysia. The newly marketised economies of central Europe have grown rapidly but erratically.

1.10 The balance of payments
....

The balance of payments, or the balance of trade, is not an objective in itself. Rather the *avoidance* of **balance of payments problems** is a means towards an end. If balance of payments difficulties occur, the policy-maker will have to tackle those immediate problems in a way which is likely to have a detrimental effect on other domestic policy objectives. Thus a country with a large balance of payments deficit may be forced to raise interest rates as a short-term palliative and this may adversely affect domestic investment. In short, it is the avoidance of balance of payments problems that can be seen as an objective.

ACTIVITY **1**
....

The largest balance of payments deficit in recent times was in 1989, when the current account of the balance of payments showed a deficit of £22.5 billion. In that year the size of national income (as measured by GDP at market prices) was about £516 billion. Calculate the size of the current account deficit as a proportion of GDP.

Check with answer/suggestions at the back of the book.

1.11 Other macroeconomic objectives
....

In addition to the four main objectives that we have considered, policy-makers will wish to influence a number of other variables in the economy. For example, they may be concerned about **regional imbalance** within a country – in Britain, for example, the south-east is comparatively affluent with low levels of unemployment, whereas the north is characterised by higher levels of unemployment and lower wages. In Italy the reverse is true – the predominantly agricultural south is poorer than the more affluent industrialised north. Thus the policy-maker may be concerned not just with the macroeconomic impact of his policies, but also with the way in which they impact on various regions, or sectors, of the economy.

The policy-maker may also be concerned with the **distribution of income** between individuals (or as economists say, between *households*). Policies which raise taxes – on goods and services or on incomes – cannot fail to have some impact on the distribution of real incomes, and the policy-maker may wish to take this into account in assessing the desirability of his policies. Most people would agree that large inequalities in income and wealth are socially divisive and undesirable – the disagreement lies in how one defines 'large inequalities'. In the UK over the last fifteen years, the distribution of income has become more unequal as a result of various government policies on taxation and public spending.

The policy-maker may also be concerned to some extent with the impact of his policies on the **environment** – for example, in considering ways in which taxation can be raised to finance expenditure, he may consider that it is legitimate and indeed desirable to impose high taxes on polluting activities. So, for example, high taxes may be levied on petrol to discourage people from using their cars. It may also be considered sensible to impose high taxes on tobacco, the consumption of which is harmful to health.

Most importantly, a key area of disagreement among economists and political parties involves the appropriate **balance between the private and public sectors** and in particular the implications that this has for what is known in the UK as the **welfare state** – that is, the range of goods and services that are provided free of charge out of general taxation. The most important of these services are health care, education, and environmental services such as public parks and libraries. Also included under the heading of the welfare state would be **income maintenance programmes** such as state retirement pensions, unemployment benefit and invalidity payments.

1.12 The ranking of objectives
....

It is worth noting that the relative importance attached to each of these objectives will vary from one person to another, and in particular from one political party to another. Different individuals or parties will **rank** them differently. For example, parties on the right of the political spectrum would tend to emphasise the importance of 'sound money' (and thus attach a rather high priority to the control of inflation), regarding high unemployment as a 'price worth paying' to get inflation down. On the left of the political spectrum, the priorities would be reversed, inflation being regarded not as public enemy number one, but as a necessary social evil preferable to the worse social evil of unemployment.

All political parties, with the possible exception of the Greens, would agree on the desirability of economic growth, but the most major disagreements of all would arise regarding the *composition* of that growth – in other words, whether resources should flow into the private or the public sector. Right-wing parties tend to favour a small – in some cases, a minimalist – state sector, whereas liberal, social democratic and socialist parties favour a larger state sector (together with the increased tax burden that this involves).

1.13 Data: a window on the world

As macroeconomists we perceive the world in a number of different ways. One of these is by simply looking at the world around us. For example, we may notice that there seems to be an increasing number of cars on the road when we drive to work in the morning; or that one's friends always go abroad on holiday; or that the person in front of you at the checkout in Sainsbury's is buying a lot of junk food; or that most of the houses in your road have 'for sale' notices. This way of perceiving the world is known as **casual observation**. There is no particular structure to the way in which we note certain things and not others. Casual observation is an important part of the way we perceive the world. It is, however, *impressionistic* and somewhat *subjective*. Moreover – and this is the principal criticism that one can level against it - it is based on a very *small sample* of experiences which may not be representative. Perhaps the perceived increase in the volume of traffic is due to road works – when the road works are completed the traffic is able to flow more freely and hence the volume seems less – and perhaps the tourist exodus is caused by exceptionally poor weather at home.

Because casual observation may be an unreliable guide, it is important that as macroeconomists we consult statistical sources which are based not just on a very small number of personal observations, but on a very large number of objective observations. This large number of objective observations we shall refer to as **statistical data** (or simply **data** or **statistics**). For example, the Department of Transport publishes statistical data on the number of new cars sold, the number of vehicle registrations, annual expenditure on petrol and sample statistics on traffic volumes. Each of these will give us some information which can help us to assess whether the particular things which we observe by casual observation are representative of a more general trend.

It is worth noting that some published statistics count *all* of the observations (for example, the number of new cars sold), whereas others take a *sample* (for example, traffic volumes, since we cannot record every car journey made every day by every person in the UK). However, both types of data can be reliably used to check our subjective impression that there seems to be an increasing number of cars on the road – indeed, we can use these statistics to *quantify* the actual increase.

1.14 Using the data to tell a story

There is no shortage of published statistical data. To derive meaning from it, however, it is necessary to ask a number of simple questions, such as:

➤ What is actually being measured?
➤ How could the data have been collected?
➤ What trends or changes do the data help us identify?
➤ What is the point of collecting the data?

The last question is perhaps the most important. There is no point in collecting data just for the sake of it. For example, we could collect statistics on the number of purple T-shirts sold in Manchester. But this is not very interesting (unless you happen to be a retailer of T-shirts). However, if we collected statistics on the number of hours per week spent playing video games by fifteen-year-old boys, this would be moderately interesting. What would make it more interesting would be to compare the figure for boys with that for fifteen-year-old girls (casual observation suggests that boys spend more time than girls playing video games), or to compare the figure now with the comparable statistic for five years ago.

In other words, the data start to become meaningful and to be worth collecting when we have an interest in the thing being discussed (as in the case of the T-shirt manufacturer) or when they help us to identify and investigate social phenomena. We can then use the data to tell a story – albeit a rather short story. And we can test to see whether our casual observation is in fact borne out by the statistical evidence.

PAUSE FOR THOUGHT *Why might the number of red T-shirts sold in Manchester be more than the number sold in comparable cities, particularly during the football season?*

1.15 Getting a feel for the data

A man wins £20 million on the National Lottery. For most of us our annual income and our wealth is measured in thousands of pounds rather than millions, so it is difficult to imagine what a million pounds is like. A million is one thousand thousand (1,000,000), but for British people the number of noughts is already becoming confusing – though not for Italians, since they are used to paying several *mille lire* (thousand lire) for a cup of coffee. Whatever currency you are used to, however, you can only get a feel for what a million pounds is like if you compare it with something that you are familiar with. For example, suppose the price of an exclusive house set in its own grounds in the town where you live is £250,000 (a quarter of a million pounds), then you can begin to appreciate that a million pounds is equivalent to four such houses.

However, aggregate statistical data (that is, data which relate to the whole economy) are often expressed in units of measurement which do not relate at all to our everyday experience – for example, billions of pounds or millions of tonnes of steel. We may not even know what a billion is. (In fact, the old British (and French) billion, which was one million million, has now been almost universally overtaken by the **American billion**, which is one thousand million (one and nine noughts) and that is the sense in which it is used here.

To get a feel for the magnitudes used to measure aggregate statistical data, we must again make comparisons. But we cannot compare a billion pounds with anything that is meaningful to us personally. So what we have to do is to make comparisons with the past, with other countries and by calculating ratios.

Consider the following example.

➤ Public spending (by central and local government) in the UK in 1995 was £300 billion. Total output (gross domestic product at market prices) was £713 billion. How could the size of public spending be expressed in a more meaningful way?

➤ Only by comparing the size of public spending with the total output of the economy (GDP) can we begin to judge how large public spending is. Clearly we would here calculate public spending as a *proportion* of total output: that is,

$$\frac{300}{713} = 0.42 = 42\% \text{ (i.e. } 0.42 \times 100)$$

Public spending is equivalent to about 42 per cent of output (rather more than two-fifths).

And now consider a further example.

➤ When the effect of inflation is removed, consumers' spending rose from £197,980 million in 1982 to £269,347 million in 1992. What was the rise in consumers' spending?

➤ First, the numbers in the question need to be simplified if we are to get any sort of feel for the data. £197,980 million is £198 billion (to the nearest billion) and £269,347 million is roughly £269 billion.

Second, if you were to answer the question by saying that the rise in consumers' spending was £71 billion (269 minus 198), this would be correct, but you would not be able to get a feel for how large the rise was. To do this you need to calculate the *percentage change* (otherwise known as the proportional change). The percentage change (here an increase) is calculated as follows.

$$\text{Percentage change} = \frac{\text{New value} - \text{Original value}}{\text{Original value}} \times 100$$

$$\frac{(269 - 198)}{198} \times 100 = 0.358 \times 100 = 35.8\%$$

PAUSE FOR THOUGHT   **A note on the use of calculators.** *The calculation above requires a minimum of seventeen keystrokes on the calculator – and therefore seventeen possibilities of hitting the wrong key. It is easier – and therefore there is less chance of making a mistake – if you simply calculate*

$$\frac{269}{198}$$

in your calculator and then in your head *subtract 1 from the answer, before multiplying by 100. In other words 1.358 – 1 gives 0.358 which, when multiplied by 100, gives 35.8 per cent. The result is the same and it involves only seven rather than seventeen keystrokes.*

Question: *why is the result the same?*

Note that we can express our earlier formula for percentage change *as:*

$$\left(\frac{\text{New value}}{\text{Original value}} - \frac{\text{Original value}}{\text{Original value}}\right) \times 100$$

$$= \left(\frac{\text{New value}}{\text{Original value}} - 1\right) \times 100$$

A note on accuracy. *The figure for consumers' spending for 1982 is given as £197,980 million. In fact it is not possible to measure these things with complete accuracy. The figures shown are* **estimates**, *which will moreover be subject to subsequent* **revisions** *when more data or more accurate data become available. These revisions may increase or decrease the original estimate by 1 or 2 per cent (or in some cases by more than this). It is therefore sensible to round the estimate to the nearest billion. However, when calculating percentages or percentage changes, the rounding should ideally be done only at the end of the process. Thus we should calculate*

$$\frac{269,347}{197,980} = 1.3604$$

(that is, a 36 percent increase, so that in this case it makes no difference to the answer).

REVIEW QUESTIONS

At the end of each chapter in this book you will find some 'Review questions'. The answers to these are given at the end of the book.

Here are some numbers questions that you should try to work out for yourself. You will need a calculator.

1. In 1995 GNP in the UK was about £567 billion. The population of the UK was about 58 million. What was GNP per capita?

2. The number of *households* in the UK (as distinct from the number of individuals) is about 23 million (since some households contain two, three or more individuals). What was average household income?

3. How do these figures compare with your income?

4. Cedric Brown, the former Chief Executive of British Gas, was awarded a pay increase in 1995 which brought his annual salary up to £475,000. Average weekly earnings (in 1994) varied between £415 in Greater London and £265 in Cornwall. How did Mr Brown's income compare with average earnings?

Summary

In macroeconomics the focus of study is the whole economy rather than the individual parts. Thus in macroeconomics we gain insights into the workings of the economy which would not be apparent if we simply regarded the economy as a collection of individual markets, individual firms and individual consumers. The whole is more than the sum of the parts.

Macroeconomic policy consists of trying to achieve the best possible levels of certain targets (objectives) using the instruments available. The main targets are: economic growth, the control of inflation and unemployment, and avoiding balance of payments problems. The most important of these is economic growth, since it is this which improves living standards. There are also subsidiary objectives relating to regional balance, the distribution of income, the environment and the welfare state. These targets may be in conflict with one another and the ranking attached to them will vary from one side of the political spectrum to the other.

This chapter has also explained that economists perceive the world through casual observation, but more importantly through the analysis of published data. The reader is encouraged to develop a feel for the data and to appreciate that they can be used to 'tell a story'. The data sections of subsequent chapters will develop this theme.

Key concepts

The following key concepts have been introduced in this chapter. Make sure you understand the meaning and significance of each of them. They are listed here in the order in which they first appear, and the page number where they appear is also given. You will find these key concepts in section headings or in **bold** in the text. Each chapter contains a list of key concepts and you may find these particularly useful for revision purposes.

microeconomics	(p.2)
macroeconomics	(p.2)
objectives	(p.3)
targets	(p.3)
instruments	(p.3)
conflicts in objectives	(p.3)
value judgements	(p.3)
conjuncture	(p.3)
full employment	(p.3)
inflation	(p.4)
economic growth	(p.5)
living standards	(p.5)
income per capita	(p.5)
real terms	(p.5)
balance of payments	(p.6)
regional imbalance	(p.7)

distribution of income   (p.7)
environment   (p.7)
balance between private and public sectors   (p.7)
welfare state   (p.7)
income maintenance programmes   (p.7)
ranking of objectives   (p.7)
data: a window on the world   (p.8)
casual observation   (p.8)
statistical data   (p.8)
billion   (p.10)
estimates   (p.11)
revisions to the data   (p.11)

CHAPTER 2

Measuring the rate of inflation

Objectives:
....

This chapter will enable you to:

➤ distinguish between a *price index* and the *rate of inflation*

➤ understand that the Retail Price Index is based on a *basket* of goods and services

➤ appreciate that index numbers can be presented in a way which is misleading

➤ understand that the RPI is a *weighted average* of individual prices

➤ compare price indices for different items to estimate changes in *relative prices*

➤ appreciate that, if wages rise more than prices (for people in employment), prices can be said to have fallen 'in real terms'.

2.1 The price index and inflation
2.2 Comparing series using index numbers
2.3 Every picture tells a story ... or a lie
2.4 Changes in relative prices
2.5 A weighted average of price rises
2.6 Changes in quality

2.1 The price index and inflation
....

We begin our more detailed analysis of the targets of macroeconomic policy by looking at **price indices**. There are two reasons for this choice. First, the concept and the experience of inflation are familiar to everyone and comprehensible to all. Second, price indices can be used to illustrate the use of **index numbers**, a technique used extensively throughout this book.

Table 2.1 shows an index of retail prices in the UK. The index refers to a **basket of goods and services** – the same basket that would be purchased by the typical household in the UK. The interpretation of the index is straightforward. A basket of goods which cost £10 in 1985 would have cost £10.34 a year later in 1986, and the same basket would have risen again in price to £10.77 in 1987. Over the entire period consumers would find themselves paying more than 'half as much again' for the goods and services they bought (in fact, the increase was 58 per cent).

It is important to note that the **rate of inflation** is not the same thing as the price index, but that one can be calculated from the other without too much difficulty. The rate of inflation is normally expressed as the **percentage change in the price index** on an annual basis. Thus if the index increases from 100 in 1985 to 103.4 in 1986, it is easy to see that over that twelve-month period the rate of inflation was 3.4 per cent.

table 2.1

Retail Price Index,

1985–95

1985	100.0
1986	103.4
1987	107.7
1988	113.0
1989	121.8
1990	133.3
1991	141.1
1992	146.4
1993	148.7
1994	152.4
1995	158.0

Source: *Economic Trends* (various).

However, in the following twelve-month period (when the index rises to 107.7), the rate of inflation is *not* 7.7 per cent and nor is it 4.3 per cent (that is, we cannot simply take the difference between 107.7 and 103.4, which would give us a figure of 4.3 per cent). The reason for this is that the rate of inflation is the **proportional change** in the price index rather than simply the change in the price index. We calculate this proportional change (or 'percentage change') as follows:

$$\frac{(\text{New index} - \text{Old index})}{\text{Old index}}$$

or in this example

$$\frac{(107.7 - 103.4)}{103.4} = 0.04158$$

which will then be multiplied by 100 and rounded to give 4.2 per cent.

$$\text{Rate of inflation (\%)} = \frac{(\text{New index} - \text{Old index})}{\text{Old index}} \times 100$$

Thus the rate of inflation is 4.2 per cent rather than 4.3 per cent. Note that this is the same procedure that we carried out in Section 1.15 when we calculated the proportional increase in consumption, and that the same considerations concerning the use of calculators and rounding will apply.

In the example we have chosen, the difference between 4.2 per cent (the correct rate of inflation) and 4.3 per cent (the absolute change in the price index) is not large. It will become more important, however, as we move further away from the base year of our index (in this case 1985). For example, in 1992 the rate of inflation would be correctly calculated as

$$\frac{146.4 - 141.1}{141.1} \times 100 = 3.8\%$$

which contrasts with a change in the index of 146.4 – 141.1 = 5.3.

Note: we can express our formula for the rate of inflation in an equivalent but alternative way as:

$$\text{Rate of inflation} = \left(\frac{\text{New index}}{\text{Old index}} - 1 \right) \times 100$$

2.2 Comparing series using index numbers
••

Indices are a useful way of expressing information because we can derive meaning from them simply by inspection (by looking at the numbers). Consider
Table 2.2, where we have reproduced the earlier information from the 'all items'
index, but also added indices for the price of food and the price of housing. As
before the base year of the index is 1985, but here we have extended the index
backwards to include figures for earlier years.

Because each of these series is expressed as an index with the same base
year (in this case, 1985 = 100), it is easy to compare the rise in the price of individual components within the overall basket. We can see, for example, that the
rise in the price of food over the period 1985–95 was less than the rise in the
price of goods and services generally. We could legitimately say, therefore, that
food became cheaper relative to 'all items' over this period. Note carefully what
has been said here. Food increased in price over the period (by 46.5 per cent
between 1985 and 1995), but this increase was less than the increase in prices
generally (which increased by 58 per cent over the same period). Thus food
became *relatively* cheaper.

Similarly, we can see at a glance that from 1985 to 1995 the cost of housing
increased by more (85.4 per cent) than the increase in the overall price index
(58 per cent): housing became more expensive *relative* to other goods and services. Over the whole period 1982–95, the cost of housing more than doubled.
The increase was in fact 134 per cent, since

$$\frac{185.4}{79.2} - 1 = 1.3409$$

table 2.2
Retail Price Index,
1982–95

	All items	Food	Housing
1982	85.8	88.9	79.2
1983	89.7	91.8	81.2
1984	94.3	96.9	88.7
1985	100.0	100.0	100.0
1986	103.4	103.3	105.8
1987	107.7	106.4	114.8
1988	113.0	110.1	125.0
1989	121.8	116.3	150.3
1990	133.3	125.7	181.9
1991	141.1	132.2	178.9
1992	146.4	135.0	177.3
1993	148.7	138.6	173.6
1994	152.4	141.0	177.5
1995	158.0	146.5	185.4

Source: *Department of Employment Gazette* (various) and *Economic Trends* (various). The calculation of price
indices is now the responsibility of the Central Statistical Office. They are reported in *Business Monitor* MM23.

2.3 Every picture tells a story ... or a lie
••

Index numbers are seemingly so straightforward that their interpretation needs almost no explanation. In practice, however, they are widely misinterpreted and misused – increasingly so, since the widespread availability of graphics packages on computers allows data to be displayed in a visual way through bar charts and line graphs. These visual devices are designed to help the reader to understand the story being told by the data, but when applied to index numbers they can be false friends. Take, for example, Figure 2.1 where we have reproduced the data shown in Table 2.2.

The visual impression that we gain from this is that there are three lines on a graph which cross at a certain point in 1985. We are misled into thinking that the three things are in some sense 'equal' at that time – which of course they are not. The figure in fact conveys little information which was not apparent from casual inspection of the numbers themselves.

The problem is not entirely resolved if we start our graph from 1985 = 100, as in Figure 2.2. We can see clearly that in the period 1988–90 the cost of housing rises faster than all items or food, since the curve is much steeper, but this information was already apparent from the indices themselves.

However, the use of line graphs may enable us to pick up some of the detail which we might otherwise have overlooked from a table – for example, we can see clearly that housing costs actually *declined* in the early 1990s after the rapid increase in the late 1980s, whereas there was no such decline in 'all items' or food prices.

The moral of the story is that the presentation of data in a visual form – or in any other form for that matter – is not a mechanistic process. You cannot simply feed numbers into the computer and tell it to draw a graph or produce a histogram without asking yourself these questions:

Figure 2.1
UK price indices: housing, food, all items, 1985–95 (1985 = 100)

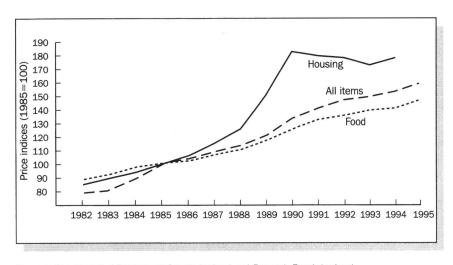

Sources: *Department of Employment Gazette* (various) and *Economic Trends* (various).

Figure 2.2

UK price indices: housing, food, all items, 1982–95 (1985 = 100)

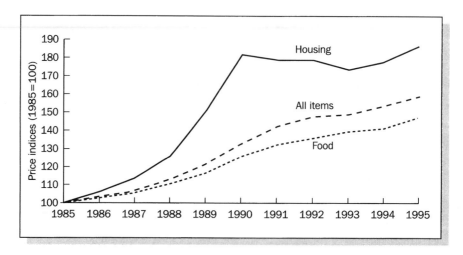

Sources: *Department of Employment Gazette* (various) and *Economic Trends* (various).

➤ Is this an appropriate way to display the data?
➤ If it is appropriate, is the visual impression created misleading in any way?
➤ What is the feature of the data to which I wish to draw the reader's attention?

ACTIVITY **1**
∙∙∙∙∙∙∙∙∙∙∙∙∙

Suppose you have the information on house prices shown in Table 2.3.

table 2.3

Index of house prices, 1982–95

1982	77.1
1983	85.3
1984	93.0
1985	100.0
1986	115.7
1987	133.5
1988	165.1
1989	185.0
1990	202.8
1991	208.5
1992	201.0
1993	195.9
1994	196.1
1995	196.6

Note: This index of house prices is not the same as the index of the cost of housing quoted earlier. The cost of housing will include the cost of rented housing in addition to that of owner-occupation.

(a) From 1982 to the peak in 1991, would it be true to say that house prices doubled, more than doubled, or increased by less than that?
(b) Calculate the increase in prices from 1982 to the peak in 1991.
(c) Calculate the decline in prices which occurred between 1991 and 1993.

Check with answers/suggestions at the back of the book.

2.4 Changes in relative prices
· ·

We shall now explain how such a price index is arrived at in the first place. To do this we need to distinguish **changes in the price level** from **changes in relative prices**. Over the last two decades the price level has been rising – in other words, the value of money has been falling. Notwithstanding this, however, some goods and services have risen in price faster than others, and some goods and services have actually fallen in price. Many electronic products, such as radios and digital watches, are cheaper now than they were twenty years ago.

ASK YOURSELF

What other products (apart from electronic products) can you think of that are now cheaper, not just in relative terms but in absolute terms, than they were, say, ten years ago? You might consider certain foods and you could start in your local supermarket by looking at the poultry department or the fresh fish counter.

The fact that some prices rise faster than others and some actually fall presents the statistician with a problem. Given that there are literally millions of prices in any economy, and that each of these is changing at a different rate, how do we calculate a figure which accurately reflects the *overall* change in the price level – the fall in the value of money – as it affects the average household?

To illustrate the problem, consider a hypothetical economy in which only two types of goods are consumed – sandwiches and beer. Suppose the price of beer rises by only a modest amount but that the price of sandwiches rises substantially. Clearly the fall in the purchasing power of money experienced by teetotallers (those who abstain from alcohol) will be much greater than that experienced by those who spend a large fraction of their income on beer.

Although this may seem a trivial example, the problem for the statistician is a very real one. In practice, low-income households spend a larger fraction of their income on food than do high-income households. Therefore poor households will be affected much more than the rich when there is a rapid rise in the price of food relative to other goods. This is a statistical problem to which there is no straightforward solution.

In practice the Central Statistical Office prepares estimates of the rate of inflation as it affects households of different types – for example, one-person pensioner households (who will spend proportionately more on heating); childless couples; and couples with three children (who will spend proportionately more of their income on video games, a product not much favoured by pensioners). The difficulty here, however, is that the publication of so many indices is confusing. Therefore the media tend to report only an *average* index, known as the Retail Price Index (RPI).

CASE
ILLUSTRATION
· · · · · · · · · · · · · ·

A Mars Bar standard

An enterprising journalist on *The Economist* newspaper once proposed an innovative solution to the twin problems of how to express:

➤ changes in relative prices, and
➤ changes in the general purchasing power of money.

He argued that a few products had kept their value over the years and hence could be used as a yardstick to measure these two phenomena. One such product that was familiar to all was the Mars Bar, and he proposed to use this as a 'gold standard' of purchasing power. Thus the value of a particular good or service could be expressed in terms of so many Mars Bars rather than so many pounds sterling. Moreover, the fall in the value of money could be expressed by looking at the rise in the price of the Mars Bar. Such an index, he argued, would be easier for people to understand than the official Retail Price Index.

This proposal, of course, was an excellent piece of journalistic nonsense which gained publicity for its author. It was, however, fatally flawed. Mars Bars are not a gold standard. Along with other chocolate bars their weight does not stay constant, but is continuously being varied by the manufacturer by small amounts which are usually imperceptible to purchasers.

A similar example of statistical information which should not be taken too seriously is provided in Table 2.4. Although prices rose between 1971 and 1994, so did incomes, so that in 'real terms' goods and services became cheaper. The table shows the length of time necessary for the average person to work so that their net income pays for the various goods listed.

The table shows that almost everything has become cheaper in real terms, but that there have been significant changes in relative prices. Oranges are a bargain. Old potatoes and Ford Escorts are not.

table 2.4
Length of time necessary to pay for selected goods and services[a]

	1971	1994	% reduction
Minutes of work to buy one unit of			
1 lb back bacon	32	19	41
250 g Danish butter	14	7	50
1 lb old potatoes	2	2	0
1 lb oranges	8	2	75
1 lb cod fillets	25	23	8
Chicken	20	8	60
Pint of beer (draught)	14	12	14
20 cigarettes (king size)	22	21	4
Hours of work to buy one unit of			
Ford Escort	2,194	1,787	18
Colour TV licence	19	12	36
Return rail ticket London to Edinburgh[b]	21	9	59

[a] For the purposes of this table, the representative household comprises a married man with a non-earning wife and two children under 11. The original table in *Social Trends* also gives figures for a single female parent with child.
[b] Standard return in 1971. Supersaver in 1994.

Source: *Social Trends 25* (1995).

2.5 A weighted average of price rises

To return to our beer and sandwiches, suppose that the price of beer rises over a twelve-month period by a mere 5 per cent but that the price of sandwiches rises much more – by 25 per cent. In order to calculate the overall rate of inflation, we would need to know how important each of these items was in the spending basket of the average household. If households divided their spending *equally* between beer and sandwiches then the overall rate of inflation would be 15 per cent – a **simple average** of the individual price rises.

$$\frac{(5 + 25)}{2} = 15\%$$

However, if households do not spend half their income on beer and half on sandwiches, the rate of inflation must be calculated by a **weighted average** rather than a simple average. Suppose, for example, that households on average spend one-tenth of their income on beer and the remaining nine-tenths on sandwiches. The weights of beer and sandwiches will therefore be 0.1 and 0.9 respectively.

	Weight in the basket	Price rise
Sandwiches	0.9	25%
Beer	0.1	5%

Note that the weights sum to 1.
The rate of inflation will now be calculated by

$$(0.1 \times 5) + (0.9 \times 25) = 23\%$$

Notice that the calculated rate of inflation is now much higher than our original estimate, since the thing which rose in price the fastest – sandwiches – has such a large weight in the spending basket. This pushes up the rate of inflation experienced by the average household. Check the above calculation for yourself, and also repeat it using weights of 0.5 and 0.5 to verify that, if the products are equally weighted, the calculated inflation rate will again be 15 per cent.

ACTIVITY 2

The discussion of the Mars Bar standard earlier suggests that the fall in the value of money could be measured by looking at the rise in the price of Mars Bars. How large a weight would implicitly be given to Mars Bars and how large a weight to other goods and services if one were to do this?

Check with answers/suggestions at the back of the book.

2.6 Changes in quality

In addition to the problem of changes in relative prices, the statistician also has to cope with an even more intractable problem. Over time there will be **changes in the quality of the products** in the basket.

Consumer products tend to improve in quality, in the sense that their technical specification increases and newer designs are more reliable, safe and energy efficient. This applies most obviously, of course, to electronic products, but it also applies to most other consumer products. For example, even a 'basic' car bought in 1995 will have radio cassette player, heated rear window, windscreen washers, adjustable seats and vastly increased performance, fuel economy and reliability in comparison to one bought 30 years earlier when even the 'luxury' model would have had none of these features.

Some products may decline in quality over time. Arguably some foods which are now cheaper than they were are also of lower quality – they are less nutritious, tasty and wholesome than previously. Services such as foreign package holidays are now very cheap, but are arguably of a lower quality than a similar product purchased when only the rich could afford such expensive 'luxuries'.

On balance, statisticians argue that there has been an overall increase in the quality of the goods and services bought by the average household, but that it is difficult to reflect these improvements in quality in the index of prices. It is sometimes argued that a modest rate of inflation of 1 or 2 per cent per year does not in fact represent a fall in the value of money. Rather it comes about as a result of an improvement in the quality of goods, which is not adequately taken account of by the index.

REVIEW QUESTIONS

1 Suppose you have the following hypothetical information on the price indices for food and 'all items'.

	Index 1985 = 100	
	All items	Food
1985	100	100
1995	140	130

Clearly food has risen in price less than 'all items'. There has been a change in relative prices. But what is the best way of expressing the magnitude of this change? Consider the validity of the following statements:

(a) Over the period the increase in the price of all items is 33 per cent greater than that for food.
(b) Over the period food has gone up 25 per cent less than prices generally.
(c) Over the period the overall rate of inflation was 10 percentage points higher than the rate of increase of food prices.
(d) 'All items' are now 7.7 per cent more expensive than food.
(e) Food is now 7.1 per cent cheaper relative to 'all items' than it was.

Which of these is the most satisfactory (or least unsatisfactory) description of what has happened to relative prices over the period? Justify your answer.

2 Table 2.4 (on page 20) shows that since 1971 oranges have fallen in price in 'real terms' by 75 per cent, whereas the price of Ford Escorts has gone

down by only 18 per cent. Hence it was concluded that oranges are a bargain now whereas Ford Escorts are not. Why might this conclusion be unfair to Ford Escorts?

3 Table 2.5 shows the length of time necessary for a person on average hourly adult earnings to work so that their net income pays for the various goods. However, unlike Table 2.4 which referred to a married couple with two children, this table refers to a single female parent with one child.

You are required to fill in the blanks in the table.

Hint: You can simply calculate the percentage reduction for each good from the table, but there is a short-cut way of doing this. Think about the relationship between the figures in this table and those in Table 2.4.

Note: You will need to look back at Table 2.4 to fill in the second blank for 'potatoes'.

4 Tables 2.4 and 2.5 show the apparent reduction in the real cost of rail travel. Why might this figure not be representative?

5 Suppose the typical consumer spends half their income on food, one-third on housing and the remainder on clothes. What would be the recorded increase in the price level over a twelve-month period if food increased in price by 10 per cent, housing by 30 per cent and clothes by 3 per cent?

table 2.5
Length of time necessary to pay for selected goods and services: single female parent with child

	1971	1994	% reduction
Minutes of work to buy one unit of			
1 lb back bacon	47	22	53
250 g Danish butter	20	8	60
1 lb old potatoes	3	?	?
1 lb oranges	12	2	?
1 lb cod fillets	37	27	?
Chicken	30	10	?
Pint of beer (draught)	20	15	?
20 cigarettes (king size)	33	25	?
Hours of work to buy one unit of			
Ford Escort	3259	2119	?
Colour TV licence	29	15	?
Return rail ticket London to Edinburgh[a]	131	10	?

[a] Standard return in 1971. Supersaver in 1994.

Summary
∙∙∙∙∙∙∙∙∙∙∙∙

A price index such as the Retail Price Index measures the price of a basket of goods and services. Changes in the price of this basket are how we measure the rate of inflation.

The RPI is a weighted average. Individual items within the basket will have different weights attached to them to reflect how important each item is in the spending of the average household.

Different items within the basket will go up in price at different rates. Thus we can speak of a change in *relative prices*. If, for example, the price of petrol rises less than the price of other goods and services, we could describe this as a *fall in the relative price* of petrol. Similarly, if petrol goes up in price but incomes go up more, we could describe this as a *fall in the real price* of petrol.

It is important to distinguish changes in relative prices from changes in the price level.

Key concepts
••••••••••••••••••

The following key concepts have been introduced in this chapter. Make sure you understand the meaning and significance of each of them. They are listed here in the order in which they first appear, and the page number where they appear is also given. You will find these key concepts in section headings or in **bold** in the text. Each chapter contains a list of key concepts and you may find these particularly useful for revision purposes.

price index	(p.14)
index numbers	(p.14)
basket of goods and services	(p.14)
rate of inflation	(p.14)
percentage change in the price index	(p.14)
proportional change	(p.15)
change in the price level contrasted with change in relative prices	(p.19)
simple average contrasted with weighted average	(p.21)
changes in the quality of products	(p.22)

Sources of information
••••••••••••••••••••••••••

Data on the rate of inflation are reported on a regular basis in the media. However, one month's figures are unlikely to prove very useful to you. You may need to get a series for specific price indices over a period of time. Such series, comprising both monthly and annual data, can be found in *Economic Trends*, published monthly with an *Annual Abstract* containing annual data going back over several decades. Monthly data in less detailed form appear in the *Monthly Digest of Statistics*. The Blue Book, *UK National Accounts*, contains annual figures.

Until quite recently, the work of compiling the Retail Price Index rested with the Department of Employment. The RPI and other price indices were therefore published in the monthly *Employment Gazette*. However this responsibility has now passed to the Office for National Statistics (formerly the Central Statistical Office) and as a result the information is now published in *Business Monitor* MM23.

More information on these and other sources is to be found in the **Guide to Statistical Sources** at the back of this book.

Some or all of this data may be available to you in electronic form – for example, on *Datastream* or other commercial services – although it is more difficult to check exactly what you are getting with this medium, since the numbers often appear without the necessary definitions, footnotes and explanations that appear in the printed sources.

CHAPTER 3

The determination of national income

Objectives:
•••••••••••••••

This chapter will enable you to:

➤ understand that in a closed economy the flows of spending income and output are equal

➤ distinguish between the stock of money and the flow of spending

➤ understand that the size of the flow (of spending, income and output) is influenced by leakages from and injections into the circular flow

➤ appreciate that the government can influence the level of economic activity (spending, income and output) as a deliberate act of policy by its fiscal stance

➤ identify three types of injection and three types of withdrawal, and assess whether they will reduce or increase the level of activity in the economy

➤ understand what is meant by the multiplier process and calculate the value of the multiplier in a simple model.

3.1 A model of the economy

3.2 Specialisation and exchange

3.3 One man's spending is another's income

3.4 Stocks and flows

3.5 A two-sector model

3.6 Equilibrium in the circular flow

3.7 The government can manipulate the level of spending

3.8 Savings and investment

3.9 The multiplier

3.10 The multiplier in practice

3.11 Fine tuning

3.1 A model of the economy
•••••••••••••••••••••••••••••••••••

In Chapter 1 we noted the size and complexity of economies in the real world. This complexity makes it impossible to study them unless we can simplify them in some way. This we do by constructing a **model** which allows us to concentrate on the important features while ignoring irrelevant detail. Of course, in practice deciding *which* features are important and which are irrelevant calls for judgement on the part of the modeller. Moreover, different models will stress different features of the real world. However, the model which we are about to present here is more or less a*xiomatic*. That is, it introduces certain key concepts which all economists would regard as being true by definition.

3.2 Specialisation and exchange

Suppose the economy consists of only three individuals – Tom, Dick and Harry. These individuals live in a community which is completely isolated from all outside influences. There is no trade with other communities. Hence this is known as a **closed economy**. Moreover, in this model there is no government sector to which the inhabitants pay taxes or from which they receive benefits.

Each of the individuals concerned is capable of being self-sufficient. That is, each of them can grow his own food, make his own clothes, build his own house and so on. However, each of them finds it preferable to engage in what economists call **specialisation** and **exchange**. That is, each of these individuals specialises in producing the thing that he is best at, and then exchanges his surplus with his neighbours.

Tom happens to be an expert gardener. He therefore specialises in producing food. Dick is good at designing and making clothes, and Harry, who describes himself as a master builder, specialises in building and repairing houses. By concentrating on what they are best at, they find that each of them can enjoy a larger quantity of goods and services than would be possible if each of them were forced to do everything for themselves.

However, in order for each of them to benefit from the specialisation and exchange, it is necessary for there to be a **double coincidence of wants**. It is then possible for **barter transactions** (where goods are exchanged for goods) to take place. In other words, if Tom has spare food and wants clothes, it is necessary for Dick to have spare clothes and want food. But if Dick has spare clothes but needs his house painted, there is a problem. He wants to buy from Harry and sell to Tom.

This problem – the absence of a double coincidence of wants – can be overcome by the **use of money**. The existence of money allows Tom to sell his food to Dick in exchange for money and then to use the money to buy from a third person – in this case, Harry. Without money the only trade that is possible is barter trade. Money allows the full benefits of specialisation and the **division of labour**. A vastly increased flow of goods and services is therefore made possible.

Suppose for the purposes of our example that a stock of money exists in the economy – £10 say – and that this money belongs to Tom. Suppose that he uses this money to buy clothes from Dick. Dick has therefore received an income of £10. Suppose then that Dick spends all this income on paying Harry to paint his house. Harry in turn will thus receive an income of £10, which he then uses to buy cabbages from Tom. Tom's income is thus also £10.

3.3 One man's spending is another's income

Let us suppose that all these transactions take place over a twelve-month period. Notice that income and spending have flowed around the economy in a circular fashion. One person's spending becomes another person's income. If we add up all the incomes received, we find that the sum of all the incomes must be the same as the sum of all the expenditures. Thus in our example total income (Tom's income plus Dick's income plus Harry's income) equals £30 per year and total spending will also be £30 per year. Note that the value of the output is also £30. In our example, what has been produced is £10 worth of cabbages, £10 worth of clothes and £10 worth of services (painting services). Thus the output of goods and services in the economy is £30 per year.

We can therefore write that

Total spending = Total income = Total output

But note that this is true only because we are dealing with a closed economy. As we shall see later, if foreign trade were to be introduced, this equality would no longer hold.

Since we have assumed that Tom, Dick and Harry constitute the whole economy, we could relabel spending, income and output as **national expenditure**, **national income** and **national output** (or **national product**). The last is particularly important. It is the output of goods and services in the economy – normally referred to as **gross national product** or **GNP**.

3.4 Stocks and flows

Furthermore, it is extremely important to distinguish between the **flow** of spending that has taken place during the year in question and the **stock** of money that financed it. The stock of money was and remains at £10. It has financed a flow of spending of £30 per year, in effect because each pound has changed hands three times during the year. We say that the **velocity of circulation of money** is (in this case) three times per year. To reiterate: **money is a stock. Spending, income and output are flows**.

Figure 3.1
The circular flow of income and spending

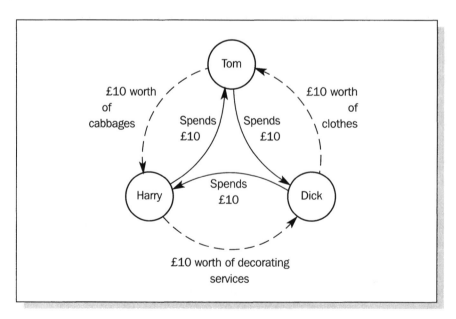

This model of the **circular flow of income** illustrates a number of concepts which are fundamental to the study of macroeconomics. Notice how the model simply assumes away all of the detail of a real-world economy, so that it can concentrate on certain key features such as the equality (in a closed economy) of spending, income and output; and the distinction between the stock of money and the flow of spending. The features which the model illustrates will be common to any model of the circular flow of income.

ACTIVITY **1**
············

In Mytown a single company, Dairies Inc., supplies all of the milk consumed by the inhabitants. This it does by a system of door-step deliveries of milk, using glass bottles which are then returned by the consumers for reuse. Each of the bottles contains 1 pint and bottles are never broken or lost. No one in Mytown buys their milk from the supermarket or from any other source. The total stock of milk bottles owned by Dairies Inc. is 60,000. The company's sales amount to some 360,000 pints of milk per month.

What is the velocity of circulation of milk bottles? Why are you being asked this question?

In bad winters the doorsteps of the houses in Mytown are covered in snow, so that empty milk bottles often lie buried for days on end. What happens to the velocity of circulation of milk bottles and what problems does this cause for Dairies Inc?

Check with answers/suggestions at the back of the book.

3.5 A two-sector model
·····························

Our second model of the economy contains not three individuals but **two sectors** – a household sector and a firm sector. Suppose we make the following simplifying assumptions:

➤ Households spend all their income: that is, there is no saving or, for that matter, dissaving.
➤ Firms sell everything that they produce: that is, they neither build up nor run down their stocks of finished goods.
➤ There is no government sector or foreign trade.
➤ The firms are owned by the households as shareholders. Firms can be seen as transforming **factor inputs** (labour, land and capital) into **outputs** (goods and services), which they then sell back to households. Any profits which result from this process accrue to the owners of the firms – the shareholders – who are in the household sector.

Looking at Figure 3.2, you will note that the right-hand part of the diagram represents the *consumption* side of the model: each year households buy £100 million worth of goods and services produced by the firm sector. The left-hand side of the diagram represents the *production* side of the model: each year firms buy in factors of production, all of which are owned by the households.

In return for the use of these factors of production, households receive income. For example, when they sell their labour, they receive a return in the form of labour income (wages). Similarly, when they lease out land and buildings

Figure 3.2

A two-sector model of the circular flow

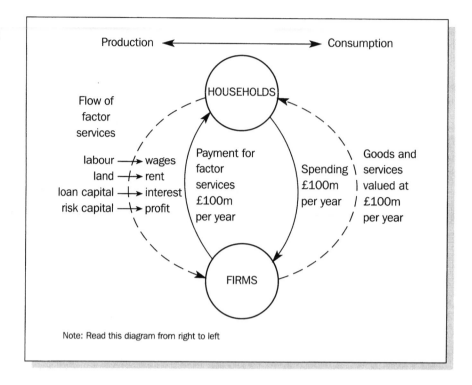

to firms, households receive a rental income for so doing. Likewise when they lend money to firms, households will receive a return in the form of interest. And finally any surplus which is left over from sales revenue after all the costs have been paid will accrue to the owners of the firm (themselves in the household sector) in the form of profits. Thus we say that wages, rent, interest and profits are the rewards respectively to labour, land, loan capital and risk capital.

It is important to note that the total value of factor services purchased must also be equal to £100 million per year in our example. This is ensured by the assumptions that we have made – particularly by the assumption that any residual (i.e. profit) accrues to the owners of firms, who are themselves in the household sector. Thus we see that in Figure 3.2 the magnitude of the circular flow of income, spending and output is £100 million per year.

3.6 Equilibrium in the circular flow

Provided nothing happens to disturb it, the size of the circular flow of income, spending and output will continue to be £100 million per annum. That is, in each and every year, households will sell £100 million worth of factors to firms, and in return households will receive an income of £100 million which they spend in purchasing £100 million worth of output from firms. Thus, as before we note that

Total income = Total expenditure = The value of total product

What could happen either to increase or to reduce the size of the income flow? Suppose we relax the assumption that there is no foreign trade and suppose further that households develop a liking for imported consumer goods. Thus rather than spending all of their income on goods produced in the domestic economy, they spend part of it – say, £10 million – on imported goods. This spending we can say 'leaks out' of the circular flow.

Spending on domestically produced goods and services will fall from £100 million to £90 million per annum. Domestic firms will find that they can no longer sell £100 million worth of goods and services. They can only sell £90 million worth. Rather than produce things that cannot be sold, firms will cut back their production. If they are to produce fewer goods they will need fewer factors. Whereas previously they required £100 million worth of factors, they now need only £90 million worth. Thus in the following time period, household income will fall from £100 million to £90 million per annum. Equilibrium income thus falls to £90 million as in **Figure 3.3**.

What could then cause the value of equilibrium income to rise again? Well, suppose now that an additional export order of £20 million is received. Firms will now be able to sell £110 million of goods and services (£90 million domestically plus £20 million abroad). To produce this they will need additional factors of production – in fact they will need £110 million of factors. They will need more labour, more land, more capital – and presumably this expansion in activity will result in higher profits as well. Household income therefore rises to £110 million as in **Figure 3.4.**

Figure 3.3
Spending leaks out

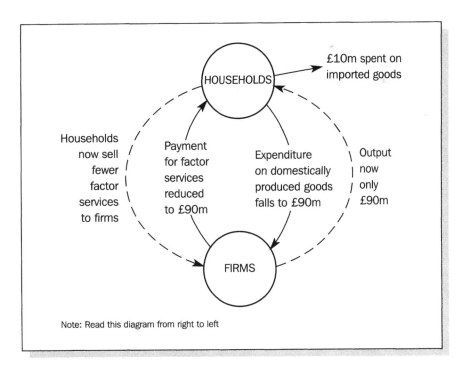

Figure 3.4

An injection of spending

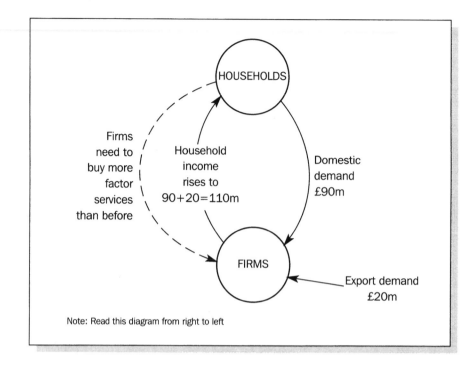

Note: Read this diagram from right to left

Spending on imports represents a **leakage** – sometimes called a **withdrawal** – of spending from the circular flow. Additional export demand represents an **injection** of spending into the flow. In the real world, we would expect both imports and exports to be continuously occurring. We could argue therefore that if the **volume of injections exceeds the volume of withdrawals, the overall level of spending in the economy will rise** (and therefore income and output will rise too). Conversely, if the volume of withdrawals is greater than the volume of injections, then spending, income and output will fall.

3.7 The government can manipulate the level of spending

We saw above how changes in the level of spending in an economy occur as the unintended consequence of the excess of imports over exports (or exports over imports). However, it is also possible for the government to bring about changes in the overall level of spending by *deliberately* reducing or increasing the ability of households and firms to spend. This is achieved through **taxation** and **public spending**. The changes in these variables, taken together, constitute **fiscal policy**. Taxation reduces the post-tax incomes (known as **disposable incomes**) of households and firms, and thus reduces their ability to spend. Public spending puts purchasing power into the hands (and wallets) of households and firms by increasing their incomes.

In our simple model, it makes no difference what form this public spending takes. Suppose, for example, that the household sector contains retirement pensioners and that the government decides, generously, to increase the state retirement pension, giving an extra £10 million in total to this group. The effect will be to increase the incomes of those households, and therefore in all probability to increase their spending by an equivalent amount.

The impact on the economy would be the same if the government decided to spend an extra £10 million on road building. The construction companies would receive an additional £10 million. They would hire an additional £10 million of factors of production from households whose income would therefore rise by £10 million.

In both cases the level would be raised by the injection brought about by the additional government expenditure.

DID YOU KNOW?

The 1920s was a period of rapid economic expansion. However, the impression of rising affluence was partly a mirage caused by over-inflated stock market prices, particularly in the USA. This came to a sudden end in 1929 with the Great Crash on Wall Street. This event ushered in a period which came to be known as the Great Depression. In Britain in 1932 the level of unemployment reached 22 per cent, with even higher levels in America.

It was increased public spending that finally brought an end to the Great Depression, which lasted throughout most of the 1930s. The main reason for this was that western governments began to spend large amounts on rearmament in the face of the growing threat from Nazi Germany, which had the unintended but desirable consequence of helping to lift the economy out of recession. Additionally, governments responded to the work of economists such as John Maynard Keynes, who argued that the government could spend its way out of a recession by injecting spending into the economy. In the short term, he argued, it mattered little how this spending was financed. The important thing was that the shortfall of demand on the part of households should be made good by extra spending on the part of government.

To summarise: the government can manipulate the level of spending in the economy. By increasing taxes (a withdrawal) it will bring about a reduction in the level of spending. By increasing public spending (or by reducing taxes) it will increase the level of spending in the economy. These policy changes form the basis of the government's **Budget** (normally conducted once a year, but sometimes more frequently). We define a **budget deficit** as a situation where government spending exceeds revenue from taxation. Budget deficits therefore represent a net addition to spending in the economy. They boost demand (that is, they boost spending). In contrast a **budget surplus** is defined as a situation where the government takes out of the economy in taxation more than it injects back in again in the form of state spending, thus reducing the overall level of demand in the economy.

There is a certain amount of jargon which must be understood here. A Budget is said to be **deflationary** if it reduces the level of economic activity (spending, income and output). It is said to be **reflationary** if it is designed to increase the level of activity. And finally a **neutral Budget** is one which leaves the overall level of spending, income and output unchanged. The (perhaps unhelpful) term **fiscal stance** refers to whether a Budget is deflationary, reflationary or neutral.

Why is the Budget important for firms in the economy?

The Budget influences the overall level of spending in the economy. This in turn will affect the demand for the products of individual firms. When spending in the economy as a whole is rising rapidly, each individual firm is likely to experience an increase in demand for its products. Conversely, when spending nationwide is falling, individual firms will suffer a decline in sales.

Some firms will suffer more than others, however. In particular, those firms producing **consumer durables** such as cars, furniture and camcorders will be hit harder than those producing **non-durables** such as chocolate bars or toothpaste. This is because consumers can delay the purchase of consumer durables – or simply decide not to buy at all – but they are unlikely to economise on the use of toothpaste, and to cheer themselves up (because they cannot afford a new car) they will continue to buy sweets.

DID YOU KNOW?

When the Chancellor delivers his Budget speech to Parliament each year, the event is saturated with media coverage. It is broadcast live on radio. BBC1 television runs a Budget Special in which pundits in the studio give 'instant' (but carefully prepared) reactions to the Chancellor's words. It is pure theatre.

The more technical details of the Budget are published in the **Red Book** (Financial Statement and Budget Report). This is embargoed until the Chancellor has finished delivering his Budget speech, but thereafter goes on sale at HMSO shops. Officially it is available for purchase from 'the moment he sits down' – the act which signifies the end of his Budget speech. Queues form at the London branch of HMSO in High Holborn of people anxious to get access to the detailed information as soon as possible.

Some information is also available on the Internet. This too is put on the Internet 'the moment he sits down', though exactly how this is achieved is unclear. One theory is that he has a micro-switch sewn to the seat of his trousers, activated when he sits down, which automatically sends the information directly to the World Wide Web.

The Internet address is:-

http://www.hm-treasury.gov.uk

It is important to note that our analysis does not – at least for the moment – concern itself with the question of how a budget deficit is to be financed. Clearly, if the government spends more than it receives in tax revenue, the shortfall must be made good in some way or other. What we are concerned with here, however, is the impact that the budget has on the overall level of spending in the economy. In this model – and remember it is just a model – everything else is an irrelevant detail which, for the moment at least, we can ignore.

Economists use the term *ceteris paribus* ('all other things being equal') to describe this approach. In effect what this means is that we recognise the vastly complex nature of real economies and that our answers cannot possibly take into account all of the possible ramifications of any particular policy. What we do, therefore, is to imagine that everything stays the same apart from the policy variable whose effects we wish to study. In this way we conduct a kind of thought experiment to see what the most immediate and most important effect of the policy will be.

3.8 Savings and investment
....

So far we have seen that spending on imports represents a leakage from the circular flow and that export demand represents an injection. Similarly, taxation is a leakage and government spending an injection. Now we introduce a third 'pair' – **savings and investment**. It is easy to see that, if households save part of their income, this will act very much like spending on imports or increased tax payments – it will constitute a leakage of spending from the circular flow. Note that we assume *ceteris paribus*. We do not concern ourselves with the question of what households do with their savings. They may put their savings in the bank, purchase some financial assets or simply stuff their savings underneath the mattress. It makes no difference to our analysis, since we are assuming *ceteris paribus*.

The impact that investment has on the size of the circular flow is less obvious, mostly because the word 'investment' can take on a number of different meanings. For our present purpose, however, it is best to think of investment as an injection of additional expenditure into the economy brought about, for example, by a firm building a new factory or installing additional capital equipment in an existing factory. Again we leave aside the question of how that new expenditure is financed and just study the immediate impact on the economy.

PAUSE FOR THOUGHT

Suppose the government decides to increase expenditure on armaments such as tanks, and to destroy them all by driving them over the nearest cliff and into the sea. Would this boost incomes and employment and thus be good for the economy?

If we assume *ceteris paribus* – in the sense that the increased expenditure on armaments was not financed by spending less on other things such as education and health care – then the answer to the above question is an unequivocal 'yes'.

John Maynard Keynes advocated something rather similar. He suggested that, if the government were to pay people to dig holes and fill them in again, this would be beneficial to the economy. The newly employed hole-diggers would spend their new incomes on beer and ham sandwiches and in so doing would create income for others.

Keynes was emphasising that, even if the activity of the newly employed workers was futile and pointless, it would nevertheless be beneficial in a *macroeconomic* sense. Think how much more beneficial it would be if the activity were not so futile.

Thus to summarise:

➤ Saving, tax payments and spending on imports all constitute a leakage or a withdrawal of spending from the circular flow.
➤ Investment, government spending and exports constitute an injection into the circular flow.

If total injections exceed total withdrawals, the level of equilibrium income will rise. Similarly, if total withdrawals exceed total injections, the level of equilibrium income will fall.

We can summarise this using symbols instead of words:

$$W = S + T + M$$

Total withdrawals equals savings plus taxation plus spending on imports.

$$J = I + G + X$$

Total injections equals investment plus government spending plus export demand.

➤ If $W = J$, the economy is in equilibrium and there will be no tendency for the level of income (spending and output) to rise or fall.
➤ If $W > J$, the net withdrawals from the circular flow will cause the level of income to fall.
➤ If $J > W$, the net injection will cause the level of income to rise.

3.9 The multiplier

The task of manipulating the level of aggregate demand in the economy is made easier by the fact that any injection of new spending will eventually create a rise in income which is larger than the initiating rise in spending. This is known as the **multiplier** phenomenon. It works, of course, both ways – a withdrawal of spending also leads to a fall in incomes, which is some multiple of the original withdrawal.

Suppose, for example, that a large steel works in a particular area is closed down. The former steelworkers – who are now unemployed and whose incomes have therefore fallen – will have to curtail their spending in the local shops. The incomes of the shopkeepers will fall so that they in turn will have to reduce their own spending at the local hairdressers, car showrooms and estate agents. Since hairdressers, car salesmen and estate agents suffer a fall in income, they too reduce their spending. Since one person's spending is another person's income, the eventual loss of spending and income is much greater than that which set the process in motion.

Similarly, an injection of spending – perhaps by the building of a new retail park – creates jobs for new sales assistants, who then spend their incomes on goods and services, creating employment for others locally. The rise in the income of the community as a whole is greater than the rise in income of the sales assistants.

These two events – the closure of a steelworks and the opening of a retail park – are presented here as if the impact on spending were symmetric. But are they really equal and opposite events in terms of their impact on local incomes, even if the number of additional jobs in retailing were the same as the number of jobs lost in steel making?

The answer is that, unless the retail parks are selling only locally produced goods, a greater proportion of spending in these retail parks will 'leak out' of the local economy. It will also leak out of the national economy if the goods being sold are imports from foreign countries.

The size of the multiplier effect depends upon the proportion of any extra income which is passed back to the circular flow. The higher the proportion which is passed back, the higher the value of the multiplier.

Suppose, for the purpose of exposition, that we assume a closed economy with no government sector. Therefore the only way in which spending can leak out of the circular flow is if households decide to save their extra income rather than spend it. The higher the proportion of any extra income saved, the more spending will leak out of the flow and the lower will be the multiplier effect.

Notice here that we are considering *extra* income, increments over and above what they had before. Economists refer to this as **marginal** income. The proportion of their extra income that households choose to save is known as the **marginal propensity to save** (abbreviated to *mps*) and the proportion of any extra income that they choose to spend is the **marginal propensity to consume** (*mpc*).

Figure 3.5
The multiplier process

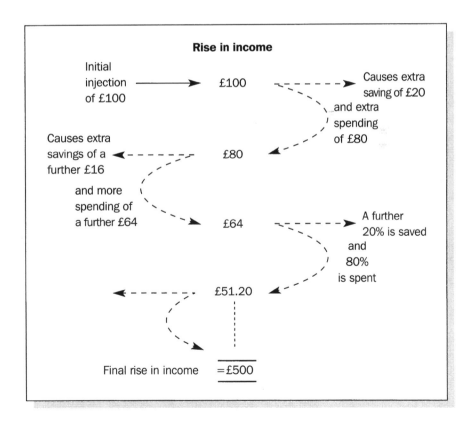

Suppose as in ***Figure 3.5*** that households have a marginal propensity to consume of 0.8 (and therefore a marginal propensity to save of 0.2). An initial injection of spending of £100 will cause a second round rise in spending of a further £80. This will cause a third round rise in spending of £64 (that is 0.8 × £80). The fourth round will produce a further rise of £51.20 (0.8 × £64).

The multiplier process will take many rounds before it is complete. However, we can work out mathematically how large the eventual rise in incomes will be. In this hypothetical example, an injection of spending of £100 will eventually produce a rise in income of £500. The multiplier effect here has produced a fivefold increase in income. The mathematical proof of this is given in the illustration below.

CASE
ILLUSTRATION
• • • • • • • • • • • •

Derivation of the value of the multiplier

We assume a closed economy with no government sector. Therefore there are only two categories of spending: consumption (C) and investment (I). In other words, total expenditure $E = C + I$.

Assume that consumption depends upon income according to the equation

$$C = 0.8Y$$

where Y is income. This **consumption function** illustrates that the *mpc* in this example is 0.8.

Suppose initially that investment spending = 100. Since, in equilibrium, income and expenditure are equal, we can write

$$Y = E = C + I$$

and therefore

$$Y = 0.8Y + 100$$

Solving this equation, we have

$$0.2Y = 100$$
$$Y = 500$$

Equilibrium income is therefore 500 (of which 400 is consumption and 100 is investment).

Suppose now that an injection of additional investment occurs: that is, investment rises by 10 to 110. The new equilibrium value of income will be

$$Y = 0.8Y + 110$$

$$0.2Y = 110$$

$$Y = 550$$

Equilibrium income has risen by 50 following a rise in injections of 10. Therefore, the value of the multiplier is 5 since

$$\text{Value of multiplier} = \frac{\text{Change in equilibrium income}}{\text{Change in injections which brought it about}} = \frac{50}{10}$$

In a closed economy model, the multiplier will be

$$\frac{1}{mps} \left(\text{here } \frac{1}{0.2} = 5 \right)$$

which is the same as

$$\frac{1}{(1 - mpc)} \quad \left(\text{here } \frac{1}{(1 - 0.8)} = 5 \right)$$

which the reader can verify.

ACTIVITY **2**
....

Repeat the example in the illustration above using a value for the *mpc* of 0.6. How large will equilibrium income be if investment = 100?

If investment rises to 110, what will the new level of income be? What therefore is the value of the multiplier? Is this confirmed by the 'multiplier formula' (1/*mps*)?

Check with answers/suggestions at the back of the book.

3.10 The multiplier in practice
....

The textbook account of the simple multiplier produces values which are quite large – 2, 3, 5 or even 10. These improbably large values are produced because the simple multiplier is based on a closed economy model where the only way in which spending can leak out is in the form of saving. In practice, in an open economy spending also leaks out in the form of spending on imports. Moreover, the introduction into the model of a government sector provides an additional channel through which spending can leak out – that of tax payments.

These additional leakages mean that in practice the value of the multiplier will be quite small. The Keynesian view, however, is that it is always more than 1. The multiplier effect remains an important plank in the Keynesian platform.

DID YOU KNOW?
The two major schools of thought in macroeconomics are known as Keynesians and monetarists. These two schools disagree in a most fundamental way on the question of how the economy works – or should work – which will become increasingly apparent to the reader as we proceed. The Keynesians follow much of the pioneering work of the then Cambridge-based economist, John Maynard Keynes. The monetarists owe much to the work of the Chicago-based economist Milton Friedman.

Monetarists tend to question the validity of the multiplier effect, or at least to question how large the effect is. Some suggest that if the government tries to raise demand by an injection of additional public spending, this will displace or 'crowd out' an equivalent amount of private sector investment. This is the **crowding out hypothesis**. It is based on the idea that there exists a fixed amount of loanable funds. If the government pre-empts these funds for its own purposes, fewer funds will remain for private firms to borrow and use. Moreover, high levels of government borrowing allegedly drive up interest rates, which in turn discourage firms from borrowing for investment purposes.

Most economists now agree that, although crowding out exists as a theoretical possibility, there is little if any empirical support for the hypothesis. At one time it was quite fashionable, but then so, at one time, were flared jeans.

3.11 Fine tuning
·····················

In general, Keynesians advocate **fine tuning**. That is, they believe that the government has the ability and the responsibility to manipulate the level of demand, often by quite small amounts, so that it is neither too great (thereby causing inflation) nor too little (thereby causing unemployment). Rather they believe that the skilled policy-maker can bring about a level of demand which, like baby bear's porridge, is 'just right'.

Monetarists, in contrast, believe that our understanding of the workings of the economy is insufficiently precise, and our skill in controlling it insufficiently great, to enable us to produce a beneficial outcome. Active intervention, they argue, is just as likely to make things worse as to make things better. Therefore it is preferable to adopt a 'hands-off' approach rather than attempting to fine tune the economy.

REVIEW QUESTIONS

1 State whether each of the following constitutes an injection into the circular flow of income or a withdrawal from it:
   (a) government spending on building a new motorway
   (b) saving part of one's income
   (c) an increase in spending on imports
   (d) increased export sales
   (e) an increase in taxation imposed by the Chancellor
   (f) spending on infrastructure financed by the government
   (g) spending on infrastructure by private firms financed by borrowing from households.

2 State what impact the following will have on the demand for UK-produced goods and services (assume *ceteris paribus* throughout and briefly explain your answer)
   (a) a decrease in spending on defence as a result of the ending of the Cold War
   (b) an increase in income tax personal allowances
   (c) greater penetration into the UK car market by Volkswagen
   (d) Sainsbury's builds a new superstore
   (e) sales by British Aerospace of aircraft to Saudi Arabia.

3 What will be the likely effect on the Florida economy of a hurricane hitting the Florida coast?

4 Japanese households save a larger proportion of their incomes than do British households. Why isn't this bad for the Japanese economy – does the Paradox of Thrift not apply in Japan?

5 We can calculate the *mpc* by the ratio

$$\frac{\text{Change in consumption}}{\text{Change in income}}$$

This *mpc* has to be less than 1 because otherwise the multiplier process will never converge. In fact the process would be unsustainable.

Table 3.1 gives data on consumption and disposable incomes for the period 1985–95 from which the value of the *mpc* can be inferred. Using these data, calculate a value for the *mpc* for the period 1985–95. In other words, calculate

$$\frac{\text{Change in consumption}}{\text{Change in income}}$$

Then inspect the value of the *mpc* for individual years: for example, 1985–86, 1990–91 and 1993–94. What is strange about the result? And why is this irreconcilable with the simple model of the consumption function?

table 3.1

Disposable income and consumption, 1985–95 (£bn, 1990 prices)

	Disposable income	Consumption
1985	309.8	276.7
1986	323.6	295.6
1987	334.7	311.2
1988	354.6	334.6
1989	371.6	345.4
1990	377.6	347.5
1991	377.1	339.9
1992	385.8	339.5
1993	392.3	348.4
1994	395.5	358.9
1995	408.1	364.0

Source: *Economic Trends*.

Summary

Spending and income flow around the economy in a circular fashion – from households to firms and back again to households. In a closed economy, the flow of spending is equal to the flow of income. Spending and income are also equal to the value of output (gross national product).

Spending, income and output are all flows. Money is a stock.

Saving part of one's income, spending on imports, and paying taxes all represent leakages. These withdraw spending from the circular flow. In contrast, additional spending can be injected into the economy as a result of new investment, additional export sales and government spending.

Equilibrium in the circular flow of income results when the spending which leaks out of the economy is offset by an exactly equal volume of injections. The size of this equilibrium flow can be reduced or increased as a result of government policy. A budget deficit will add to demand and hence raise income and output. A budget surplus does the opposite – it reduces spending income and output below what they would otherwise have been.

Spending is subject to a multiplier effect. Since one person's spending is another's income, an increase in spending will lead to an increase in incomes, which will in turn lead to a further increase in spending. However, not all income is spent and thus passed back into the circular flow. Some leaks out in the form of saving, spending on imports and paying taxes. The size of these leakages determines the value of the multiplier. The larger the propensity to save, to buy imports and to pay tax, the smaller will be the multiplier effect.

Key concepts
••••••••••••••••••

The following key concepts have been introduced in this chapter. Make sure you understand the meaning and significance of each of them. They are listed here in the order in which they first appear, and the page number where they appear is also given. You will find these key concepts in section headings or in **bold** in the text. Each chapter contains a list of key concepts and you may find these particularly useful for revision purposes.

model	(p. 26)
closed economy	(p. 27)
specialisation and exchange	(p. 27)
double coincidence of wants	(p. 27)
barter transaction	(p. 27)
use of money	(p. 27)
division of labour	(p. 27)
one man's spending is another's income	(p. 27)
national expenditure	(p. 28)
national income	(p. 28)
national output (national product)	(p. 28)
gross national product (GNP)	(p. 28)
stocks and flows	(p. 28)
velocity of circulation of money	(p. 28)
money is a stock	(p. 28)
spending is a flow	(p. 28)
circular flow of income	(p. 29)
two-sector model	(p. 29)
factor inputs	(p. 29)
outputs	(p. 29)
equilibrium in the circular flow	(p. 30)
leakage (withdrawal)	(p. 32)
injection	(p. 32)
the government can manipulate the level of spending	(p. 32)
taxation	(p. 32)
public spending	(p. 32)
fiscal policy	(p. 32)
disposable income	(p. 32)
budget	(p. 33)
budget deficit	(p. 33)

budget surplus (p. 33)
deflationary budget (p. 33)
reflationary budget (p. 33)
neutral budget (p. 33)
fiscal stance (p. 33)
consumer durables (p. 34)
non-durables (p. 34)
Red Book (p. 34)
ceteris paribus (p. 34)
savings and investment (p. 35)
$W = S + T + M$ (p. 36)
$J = I + G + X$ (p. 36)
multiplier (p. 36)
paradox of thrift (p. 37)
marginal propensity to save (*mps*) (p. 37)
marginal propensity to consume (*mpc*) (p. 37)
consumption function (p. 38)
crowding out hypothesis (p. 39)
fine tuning (p. 40)

Sources of information

The material in this chapter forms the central core of Keynesian economics. Keynes' most famous work is J. M. Keynes, *The General Theory of Employment, Interest and Money* (1936). Galbraith's account of the 1929 stock market crash is a good read: J. K. Galbraith, *The Great Crash: 1929* (1954).

More information on these and other sources is to be found in the **Guide to Statistical Sources** at the back of this book.

CHAPTER **4**
· · · · · · · · · · · · ·

Measuring output: GDP

Objectives:
· · · · · · · · · · · · · ·

This chapter will enable you to:

➤ appreciate that in an open economy the level of spending will not be the same as the level of income and output

➤ appreciate that a figure for aggregate output can be expressed only in *value* terms, not in terms of physical quantities

➤ distinguish between changes in *nominal* output and changes in *real* output

➤ be aware of the three methods of calculating national output

➤ understand how to calculate output (GNP) by the expenditure method

➤ distinguish between current-price and constant-price estimates

➤ convert data measured in current prices to constant prices using an appropriate deflator

➤ appreciate some of the limitations of the use of GNP per capita to measure the standard of living.

4.1   Measuring output
4.2   The money value of output
4.3   Nominal output and real output
4.4   The national accounts
4.5   Current-price and constant-price estimates
4.6   Is the growth of GNP a suitable way of assessing the performance of an economy?

4.1 Measuring output
· ·

The previous chapter explained that in a closed economy the terms *spending, income* and *output* could be used synonymously – or, more correctly, that the *value* of these three magnitudes would be the same. We showed how, for example, an increase in state retirement pensions of £10 million would lead to an increase in consumer spending of the same amount, provided of course that all of the increased income were spent purchasing the output of domestic firms (rather than saved or spent on imports). It followed that the output of domestic firms would rise also by £10 million. Factor incomes – wages, rent, interest and profit – would rise by the same amount as well.

In this chapter we shall be concerned with how we measure these magnitudes. Before we come to this, however, it is necessary to point out a very important caveat. The example that we gave in the previous chapter related to a *closed economy* – there were no imports or exports. That is, the equality between spending, income and output holds only for an economy where consumers must spend their income purchasing the output of domestic firms. If they are able to devote part of their income to buying the output of non-resident

44

firms (i.e. imports) we need to distinguish between, on the one hand, **total domestic spending**, and on the other, **total spending on domestically produced goods and services**.

In an open economy, these two magnitudes will not be the same, unless of course consumers choose to buy no imports at all (and there is no export demand), or the spending by foreigners – say foreign tourists – exactly offsets the spending of domestic consumers on imported goods.

ACTIVITY **1**

The previous paragraph used the phrase 'an open economy'. Some economies are more open than others. Consider the following three countries – Britain, the United States and the Netherlands. Which would you expect to be the most open and which the least open, and why?

Check with answers/suggestions at the back of the book.

Since in an open economy the three magnitudes – spending, income and output – will not in general be the same, we need to ask ourselves which of the three is the most important. Clearly all three are important, but if we wish to answer the question 'How well is the economy performing?' the answer will be found in its ability to provide goods and services for its citizens. Thus *output* is the magnitude that we should be primarily interested in measuring.

4.2 The money value of output

Before we proceed to show how this can be measured, we need to talk about a second major caveat. All of the magnitudes that we have been discussing are **measured in money terms**. There is no alternative to this. If output consists of cars, cabbages, computers and concert tickets, the only way in which we can aggregate (or add up) these magnitudes to arrive at a total is by measuring them in terms of their **value** (prices) – that is, the value of cars produced, the value of cabbages sold and so on. This is necessary because the products are *heterogeneous* – they are all different – and the only way that we can compare a car with a cabbage is in terms of its value.

Note also that, even within a particular class of goods, there will be differences in size and quality which will be reflected in the price (the value). Large luxury cars are worth more than small cars, and cabbages with brown shrivelled leaves will fetch less in the market than freshly picked green ones. In short, the value of all goods and services, in a market economy, is measured in terms of prices.

It is worth noting in passing that, in the **command economies** of the former Soviet Union, prices were not used to measure value. The price of a cabbage was fixed so that the same price would be paid for a clean, freshly picked cabbage as for a slug-infested, rotten one. Thus – as is now recognised – there was no incentive for producers to strive to increase the quality of the goods and services they produced, because higher-quality products would not command a higher price.

4.3 Nominal output and real output
• •

Money therefore serves as a yardstick – a measuring rod which we can use to assess the value of a particular good or service. However, there is one major problem with the use of money as a measuring rod: namely, the measuring rod keeps shrinking. In other words, money loses its value. Inflation erodes the value of money, so the standard which we use to measure things is not fixed.

It follows, therefore, that we need to take account of the fall in the value of money when we measure the growth of output. To use the economist's jargon, we need to distinguish between **nominal output** and **real output**. Later on in this chapter we shall show how the money value of output (that is, nominal output) can be adjusted to take account of the fall in the value of money. In other words, we can adjust our figures to take account of the effect of inflation.

It is worth highlighting that in the previous chapter we implicitly assumed that the value of money was constant: that is, an increase in expenditure called forth an increase in output in both real and nominal terms. In practice, of course, an increase in spending will by definition lead to an increase in the money value of output, but part of this increase in output will simply be because prices have risen. In other words, the increase in output will be – in part at least – an increase in nominal output rather than in real output.

Sellers will take advantage of the increased demand for their cabbages – or whatever – to increase prices. Their incomes will rise, and by definition the value of their output will rise, but the *quantity* of cabbages sold may have remained the same. In practice, an increase in demand may lead either to an increase in prices or to an increase in real output; or – most likely – to a bit of both.

For the time being, however, and to simplify our discussion, let us assume that prices are constant.

ACTIVITY **2**
• • • • • • • • • • • •

Look back at the data on income per capita shown in Figure 1.1 on p. 6. Is income in this diagram measured in real or nominal terms? Why is it measured in this way?

Check with answers/suggestions at the back of the book.

4.4 The national accounts
• •

Most western countries now adhere to a standardised system of national accounting, so that the format in which the information is presented and the magnitudes which are measured are basically the same everywhere. As we noted earlier, the most important statistic is the measurement of the *output* of the economy – the output of goods and services available to the citizens of the country.

There are three basic approaches used to measure output – the **income method**, the **output method** and the **expenditure method**. Note, however, that all three methods are ways of measuring *output*. Each of these approaches should give the same result, though of course errors and omissions will cause the three results to differ slightly.

The expenditure approach, which is perhaps the most important and the one we shall illustrate here, calculates **total expenditure on domestically produced goods and services**. By definition, the total amount of money spent on purchasing these goods and services must be equal to the total value of the goods and services sold – in other words, to the total value of output.

Total domestic spending is made up of consumers' spending (*C*), investment spending (*I*) and government spending (*G*). Thus

$$\text{Total domestic spending} = C + I + G$$

Consumers' spending represents all of the spending of households on food, cars, holidays and so on. Investment spending is undertaken by firms rather than households, and is made up mostly of **fixed capital formation** (that is, spending on buying new machines or building new factories). However, **stockbuilding** (that is, the building up of stocks of raw materials and finished goods) is also treated as a form of investment. Finally **government spending** relates to expenditure by central and local government on things such as education, roads, defence and health care.

Note, however, that some of the expenditure undertaken by consumers, firms and the government will be on imported goods. This therefore will not create an income for domestic firms, and there will be no domestic output that corresponds to this. If our objective is to get an estimate for the output of domestically produced goods and services, we should therefore subtract total **spending on imports** (*M*) from total domestic spending. In addition, however, some goods and services will be produced domestically, but will be sold directly to foreigners rather than being sold domestically. These are **exports** (*X*) and we should add them back to our equation in order to arrive at an estimate for total spending on domestically produced goods and services. Thus

$$\text{Total spending on domestically produced goods and services}$$
$$= C + I + G + X - M$$

This will be equal to the **value of the output of the economy**, and is the basic magnitude that we sought to measure. Notice how, by combining various *spending* magnitudes in a particular way, we arrive at a measure for *output*.

Consider the following example based on figures for the UK economy in £bn:

1	Consumers' spending	350
2	Government spending (excluding capital spending)	110
3	Gross fixed capital formation (firms and government)	105
4	Stockbuilding	−5
5	*equals* Total domestic expenditure at market prices	560
6	*plus* Exports	135
7	*minus* Imports	−145
8	*equals* Gross domestic product	550
9	Net property income from abroad	5
10	*equals* Gross national product at market prices	555

Lines 1 to 8 correspond exactly to our equation. The total in line 8, however, is described as **gross domestic product**, and to arrive at our figure for **gross national product** we have to add **net property income from abroad**.

In any one year, UK households and firms will receive income in the form of interest payments and dividends from abroad, which accrue to them by virtue of their ownership of foreign assets. Similarly, British firms will have to make interest and dividend payments to foreign shareholders and banks. These inward and outward flows are very large, but they approximately cancel each other out, so that the *net* flow is very small.

The same is true for most countries, the exception being countries like Kuwait where the net flow of property income from abroad is a large positive amount (in 1989 Kuwait's GNP exceeded her GDP by some 35 per cent). Ask yourself why this should be the case. Newly marketised economies tend to have a negative net property income from abroad, so that in those countries GNP is less than GDP. Again, ask yourself why this should be the case.

Two further adjustments can be made to the totals we have calculated, as follows:

10	Gross national product at market prices	*555*
11	*less* Taxes on expenditure	*–80*
12	*plus* Subsidies	*5*
13	*equals* GNP at factor cost	*480*
14	*less* Capital consumption (depreciation)	*–60*
15	*equals* Net national product ('national income')	*420*

In lines 11 and 12 we perform a **factor cost adjustment**. The total shown in line 10 has been calculated at market prices – that is, we have used the prices actually paid by consumers to arrive at our total. But these market prices will include sales taxes, such as VAT, and other indirect taxes, such as excise duties on tobacco and alcohol. Such taxes will be not be received by the sellers of the goods in question, but will be passed on directly to the government. The value of the output that these firms have produced should therefore be shown net of these tax payments, which is why we subtract them in line 11. Subsidies, if there are any, are like negative taxes, so we have to add them back (line 12).

Finally, note that in line 14 we subtract **depreciation** (officially known as **capital consumption**). This is because the investment spending shown in line 3 is shown 'gross'. That is, no allowance was made for the fact that part of the investment spending shown in line 3 served merely to replace machines and other equipment that had simply 'worn out' as a result of their use. A notional figure for this is shown in line 14. It is subtracted from gross national product to arrive at a figure for **net national product** (NNP).

NNP is sometimes labelled 'national income' to denote that this comes closest to our notion of the amount of 'income' available to the citizens of the country. The figure for depreciation, however, is purely notional – there are no actual expenditures which correspond to this magnitude – and therefore GNP rather than NNP is often taken to be a more objective indicator.

This concludes our explanation of how GNP is calculated by the expenditure method.

4.5 Current-price and constant-price estimates

In addition to being interested in the composition of output at any particular time, we are also interested in how GNP grows through time. As we noted earlier, however, a difficulty that arises is that the price level also changes over time. Part of any observed increase in GNP will thus be due to the effects of inflation.

In order to work out the *real* increase (or decrease) in output, we therefore have to remove the effect of inflation from the figures. This procedure is known as **deflating,** and the estimates thus produced are known as **constant-price estimates**. They are the figures that would have been produced if the value of money had stayed constant – in other words, if there had been no inflation. To illustrate the procedure involved, consider the data in Table 4.1.

The figures for GNP are known as **current-price estimates**: that is, the figure for 1977 is measured in 1977 prices, the figure for 1978 in 1978 prices and so on. Prices are measured by the Retail Price Index (RPI), which is an index of prices paid by the 'average' household. In our example, 1980 = 100. As we can see, prices increased by 12 per cent in 1981, by a further 8 percentage points in 1982 and so on.

Over the period, GNP more than doubled. In fact the rise was 121 per cent, which is calculated as follows:

$$\frac{(323 - 146)}{146} = 121\%$$

However, prices also increased more than twofold over the period (the index rose from 65 to 132), an increase of 103 per cent, since

$$\frac{(132 - 65)}{65} = 103\%$$

Therefore, most of the increase in GNP was as a result of inflation. It did not represent an increase in the real volume – that is, the quantity – of goods and services being produced.

We need to adjust the current-price estimates to remove the effect of inflation. This can be done using the RPI as a **deflator**.

Suppose you were asked to produce a series for GNP at constant 1980 prices – that is, you were asked to fill in the blanks in Table 4.2.

What should the figure for 1981 be? That is, what would GNP have been if prices had stayed the same as they were in 1980? Well, if prices had doubled between 1980 and 1981 (i.e. the index had risen from 100 to 200), we would have to divide the figure of £255 billion by 2 (i.e. we would have to halve it because money is only worth half what it was). If prices trebled (index 100 → 300), we would have to divide £255 billion by 3. And if prices increased by 50

table 4.1
Uk output and prices, 1977–84

	1977	1978	1979	1980	1981	1982	1983	1984
GNP (£bn)	146	167	198	230	255	278	303	323
Prices (RPI)	65	73	83	100	112	120	126	132

table 4.2
**Deflating current-
price estimates using
the RPI**

	1977	1978	1979	1980	1981	1982	1983	1984
RPI	65	73	83	100	112	120	126	132
GNP (£bn, current prices)	146	167	198	230	255	278	303	323
GNP (£bn, constant 1980 prices)	*	*	*	230	*	*	*	*

per cent (index goes from 100 to 150), we would have to divide £255 billion by 1.5. It follows that if prices increase by 12 per cent (index 100 → 112), we need to divide £255 billion by 1.12 to arrive at the estimate of what GNP would have been in 1981 if prices had stayed the same as they were in 1980. Since 255/1.12 = 228 (which is less than 230), we can see that in 1981 there was a *fall in real output*.

Similarly, the 1979 figure for GNP (measured in 1980 prices) would be 239 (i.e. 198/0.83).

The completed table is shown is Table 4.3.

Thus we can now see that in real terms output declined between 1979 and 1982 – the economy was in recession – even though in money terms output was growing.

4.6 Is the growth of GNP a suitable way of assessing the performance of an economy?

So far in this chapter we have explained why and how output is measured, and demonstrated how an adjustment can be made to take account of the effects of inflation. Finally, we turn to the question of whether GNP is a 'good' measure to use if we wish to evaluate the performance of the economy.

As we have seen, GNP measures the output of goods and services. If we divide this by the total population, this will give us a figure for **GNP per capita**, which can be taken to be a measure of the **standard of living** of the average citizen. The *growth* of real GNP per capita can similarly be taken as an indication of how the standard of living is improving. Many economists, however, are unhappy with the use of GNP per capita as an index of economic welfare, for a number of reasons.

First, GNP per capita tells us nothing about how incomes are distributed in a country. Statistics show that the country with the highest per capita income is not the United States, or any of the major industrialised countries. Rather the oil-rich states of the Middle East have the highest income per capita – though the wealth is concentrated in the hands of the ruling élites and the average citizen is not particularly affluent by western standards.

table 4.3
**Deflating current-
price estimates using
the RPI**

	1977	1978	1979	1980	1981	1982	1983	1984
RPI	65	73	83	100	112	120	126	132
GNP (£bn, current prices)	146	167	198	230	255	278	303	323
GNP (£bn, constant 1980 prices)	225	229	239	230	228	232	240	245

Second – and this is a more serious objection to the use of GNP as a measure of welfare – GNP tends to mix up 'goods' and 'bads' indiscriminately and to treat them as if they were the same. For example, suppose an airport (which produces a useful service to the travelling public) is also responsible for intolerable noise levels which force local residents to install double-glazing in their homes to reduce noise levels inside their houses. The smoke from the aircraft exhausts also soils the clothes of the householders (so they have to wash them more frequently), and the air pollution also causes chronic bronchitis, which necessitates expensive medical treatments.

Clearly, in this example the expenditure which goes on purchasing the output of the double-glazing firms, the washing powder manufacturers and the local hospital is in the nature of 'defensive' expenditure – it is necessary only because of the pollution caused by the airport. Logically, it should be subtracted from the output of the airport (the value of its travel services) when calculating the total output. GNP, however, just lumps everything together and treats it as if it were of equivalent value – a pound spent must represent a pound's worth of output, no matter what it is spent on.

Third, many transactions go unrecorded. Because individuals may wish to conceal certain activities, they deliberately fail to report them. The transactions involved may be illegal – such as those involving drugs or prostitution – or more likely the activities themselves are legal but the individuals involved wish to avoid paying tax on such transactions (both income tax and VAT). These are invariably cash transactions, thus making them much more difficult to trace than those involving cheques or credit cards.

The sum total of these transactions is known as the **cash economy** or **black economy**. Estimates of the size of the black economy vary, but it is widely believed to be larger in countries such as Italy (mostly because of the influence of the Mafia in the south) than in countries such as Germany, thought to be a more law-abiding and ordered society.

REVIEW QUESTIONS

1 Using the following information, prepare a set of national accounts showing GDP and GNP. You may not need all the information shown.

Government spending on goods and services	90
Exports of goods and services	75
Imports of goods and services	81
Gross domestic fixed capital formation	45
Consumers' spending	115
Tax revenue	85
Net property income from abroad	–6
Privatisation proceeds	7
Value of physical increase in stocks and work-in-progress (stockbuilding)	–4

2 Using the data in Question 1, calculate:
   (a) the balance on the current account of the balance of payments
   (b) the fiscal stance (budget balance).

3 Table 4.4 shows estimates of consumption spending and government spending (both in current prices) for the UK. It also shows what happened to prices over the period.

table 4.4

UK consumption, government spending and prices, 1981–95

	Consumption	Government spending	RPI (1985 = 100)
1981	155.4	55.3	79.1
1982	170.6	60.4	85.9
1983	187.1	65.8	89.8
1984	200.3	69.8	94.3
1985	218.9	73.8	100.0
1986	243.0	79.3	103.4
1987	267.5	85.3	107.7
1988	302.0	91.7	113.0
1989	330.5	99.0	121.8
1990	350.4	109.9	133.8
1991	367.8	121.9	141.1
1992	383.5	131.9	146.9
1993	406.4	138.1	149.3
1994	427.3	144.1	152.9
1995	447.3	149.5	158.0

Calculate the growth of C and G over the period (that is, calculate the percentage change in each variable over the period). Which grew faster, and why?

These estimates are measured in *money terms* – that is, the 1981 figures are measured in 1981 prices, the 1982 figures in 1982 prices and so on. Prices, of course, increased over the period. Use the RPI as a *deflator* to convert these estimates in money terms to estimates in *real terms*. In other words, construct a series for C and G in terms of *constant 1985 purchasing power*.

Having done this, calculate the growth in real terms of C and G over the period.

4 Prepare a list of some of the expenditures that are part of GNP which seem to be 'bads' rather than 'goods'.

5 In the UK in 1981, GNP was about £220 billion. In 1995 it was about £604 billion. Which of the following statements are correct:
(a) People were almost three times as well off in 1995 as they were in 1981.
(b) The increase in living standards is of the order of 175% (that is, living standards were two and three-quarter times as high in 1995 as in 1981).
(c) It is impossible to say by how much living standards rose if one only has this information.
(d) On average and other things being equal, we can say that people were spending around two and three-quarter times as much as fourteen years previously.

6 Suppose that everyone became more risk-averse and as a result decided to increase the insurance cover on their belongings. *Ceteris paribus* would this increased expenditure on insurance constitute an increase in GNP? If the same money were spent on gambling, would this also be part of GNP? Is the same true if the same money were spent on illegal black-market drugs?

Summary
....

In an open economy the spending that takes place in the economy is not the same as the output of the economy. We need to take into account the additional demand for UK goods which comes from exports, and the fact that some consumption and investment spending will be on imported goods. Therefore we distinguish between total domestic spending, on the one hand, and total spending on domestically produced goods and services, on the other.

$$\text{Total domestic spending} = C + I + G$$

(the sum of consumer spending, investment spending and government spending), whereas

$$\text{Total spending on domestically produced goods/services} = C + I + G + X - M$$

(we need to add export demand (X) and subtract the spending of UK consumers on imported goods (M)).

The latter (that is, $C + I + G + X - M$) is how we calculate the output of the economy by the expenditure method. This is because it follows by definition that the total amount of money spent purchasing the goods and services produced by the UK economy must be equal to the total value of the goods and services produced. This will also be equal to the total income received by the sellers of those goods/services.

Money acts as a yardstick by which we measure the value of output, the size of incomes and the amount of spending. However, this yardstick is continually shrinking as inflation erodes the value of money. If the price level doubles, the value of money is halved. Thus, following a doubling of the price level, £100 worth of goods represents only half the *amount* of goods that it did before the rise in prices.

When looking at changes in output (spending and income) through time, we therefore distinguish between changes in *real* output (that is, after making due allowance for changes in the value of money) and changes in *nominal* output (that is, ignoring the fact that prices have altered). Real changes are measured using *constant-price estimates* (of output, spending and incomes). If we wished to measure *nominal changes*, they would be measured using *current-price estimates*. The process of converting current-price estimates into constant-price estimates is known as *deflating*.

There are three ways of calculating the output of the economy – the expenditure method, the income method and the output method. Note, however, that all three are methods of calculating output (GNP).

GNP – or, more precisely, GNP per capita – is often taken as a measure of the standard of living. However, this measure says nothing about how output is distributed among the population. Moreover, it ignores the fact that some spending is in the nature of *defensive* expenditure – spending necessary to counteract the bad effects of the production and consumption of some of the goods and services in the economy.

Key concepts

· · · · · · · · · · · · · · · · ·

The following key concepts have been introduced in this chapter. Make sure you understand the meaning and significance of each of them. They are listed here in the order in which they first appear, and the page number where they appear is also given. You will find these key concepts in section headings or in **bold** in the text. Each chapter contains a list of key concepts and you may find these particularly useful for revision purposes.

output measured in money terms	(p. 45)
output measured in value terms	(p. 45)
command economies	(p. 45)
nominal output and real output	(p. 46)
Three methods of calculating output	(p. 46)
income method	(p. 46)
expenditure method	(p. 46)
output method	(p. 46)

$$Y = E = C + I + G + X - M$$

Value of output = Value of expenditure on domestically produced goods and services

where $C + I + G$ = Total domestic spending

	(p. 47)
fixed capital formation	(p. 47)
stockbuilding	(p. 47)
government spending	(p. 47)
spending on imports	(p. 47)
exports	(p. 47)
value of the output of the economy	(p. 47)
gross domestic product	(p. 48)
gross national product	(p. 48)
net property income from abroad	(p. 48)
factor cost adjustment	(p. 48)
depreciation (capital consumption)	(p. 48)
net national product	(p. 48)
current price and constant price estimates	(p. 49)
deflating the current price estimates	(p. 49)
deflator	(p. 49)
GNP per capita	(p. 50)
standard of living	(p. 50)
cash economy	(p. 50)
black economy	(p. 50)

Sources of information

The principal source of information on the output of the UK economy is the Blue Book, *UK National Accounts*, published annually in the autumn (that is, the September 1996 edition has annual data up to 1995). The Blue Book contains information in both current prices and constant prices, and price deflators so that you can, if necessary, convert from one to the other.

More recent quarterly data are to be found in *Economic Trends*, published monthly.

More information on these and other sources is to be found in the **Guide to Statistical Sources** at the back of this book.

CHAPTER **5**

The inflationary process

Objectives:

This chapter will enable you to:
- distinguish between *demand-pull* and *cost-push* inflation
- understand how the two interact
- understand what is meant by *real wages* and calculate them
- rebase an index
- be aware of the Phillips curve and its implications
- understand the monetarist critique of the Phillips curve
- appreciate the importance of expectations in the inflationary process.

5.1 The history of inflation
5.2 Demand-pull inflation
5.3 Cost-push inflation
5.4 Wage-push inflation
5.5 A wage–price spiral
5.6 How to calculate the growth of real earnings
5.7 The policy response
5.8 Rebasing the index
5.9 The Phillips curve
5.10 Expectations

5.1 The history of inflation

Inflation is as old as money itself. For example, Ancient Rome was plagued by inflation and the Roman Emperor Diocletian is alleged to have issued a wage decree in AD 301. Those who breached it were sentenced to death.[1]

Sixteenth-century Spain experienced rapid inflation as a result of an influx of gold from the New World. In the inter-war period many central European states experienced bouts of **hyperinflation**, with rates of inflation of over 500 per cent per month, often resulting in a total loss of confidence in the currency and its enforced replacement by a new one.

In the UK in the post-war period, the history of inflation has been characterised by certain key features which can be seen in Figure 5.1.

Until the 1970s, the rate of inflation was well below 10 per cent. In common with other countries, however, Britain then experienced the effects of two oil-price hikes – the first in 1973–74, the second in 1979–80. These brought rapid domestic inflation in their wake. After 1980 the rate of inflation declined, partly as a result of the emphasis placed upon the control of inflation by the

[1] The policy was abandoned as a failure after thirteen years.

Source: quoted in R. Layard, S. Nickell and R. Jackman, *Unemployment: Macroeconomic Performance and the Labour Market.*

Figure 5.1
UK annual rate of inflation, 1960-95 (%)

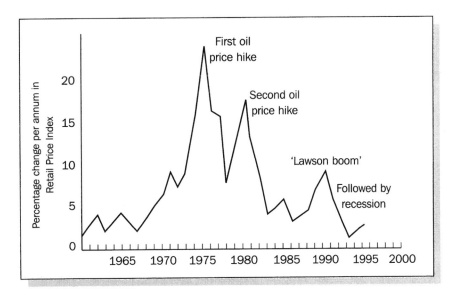

Source: Derived from *Economic Trends Annual Supplement.*

government and partly as a result of external factors. However, the boom of the late 1980s brought renewed inflation. The severity of the recession which followed the boom brought inflation down again to a low level.

5.2 Demand-pull inflation

To see why inflation occurs, we need to understand the mechanism by which prices are set. Microeconomics teaches us – and common sense confirms – that the price which an individual product can command is determined by its **scarcity**. Goods which are in scarce supply relative to the demand for them will command a high price. Goods which are in plentiful supply and for which there is little demand will command only a low price. These are the so-called **laws of demand and supply**.

ACTIVITY **1**

Consider the data on oil prices given in Table 5.1.

table 5.1
Oil price (US$ per barrel: OPEC average)

1983	29.2
1984	28.6
1985	28.0
1986	15.6
1987	17.1
1988	13.5
1989	16.1
1990	21.0
1991	17.9
1992	17.5
1993	15.2

Source: *National Institute Economic Review*, Statistical Appendix.

As can be seen from the table, in the mid-1980s the price of oil dropped suddenly by almost 50 per cent. Were demand or cost factors responsible for this?

Check with answers/suggestions at the back of the book.

If there is an increase in demand for something which is in fixed supply, there will be shortages – some of those who would like to have bought at the pre-existing price will be unable to do so. They would be prepared to pay slightly more in order to satisfy their requirements, and sellers will be very happy to accept a higher price if it is offered. Thus it makes no difference in this analysis whether it is the buyer or the seller who first quotes the higher price. Both buyer and seller are party to the bargain and it is assumed that each of them is free to trade or not to trade.

To summarise, in this analysis if supply is fixed or is unable to respond, an increase in demand will inevitably lead to an increase in prices. The inflation that results is called **demand-induced inflation** or **demand-pull inflation**.

However, the assumption that supply is fixed is not very realistic in most instances, except possibly in the case of land, and even in this case there are some countries – such as Holland and Japan – which have made strenuous efforts to increase the supply by reclaiming land from the sea. Generally, however, a firm faced with an expansion in demand has two options – either it can increase output or it can maintain its pre-existing output but charge a higher price for it. Both strategies obviously lead to higher profits.

The choice of strategies will depend upon the ease with which the firm is able to increase output without incurring significantly higher costs. In the short run, if the firm is operating at or near the **full capacity level of output**, a further increase in output can normally be achieved only with an increase in unit costs. For example, if all the firm's workers are fully employed, labour input can be increased only by paying the workers to work overtime, which will lead to an increase in unit costs. These cost increases are likely to be passed on to the consumer as higher prices.

In the longer term, however, the firm can hire additional workers, and it can even build a larger – and probably more efficient – factory. In the long run, that is, there is no reason to suppose that an increase in demand cannot be met by an increase in supply without involving the firm in higher unit costs.

5.3 Cost-push inflation
....

It is possible, however, for the firm to experience an increase in costs which is not associated with an increase in the demand for its product. For example, the price of a raw material – say, aluminium – used by the firm may have increased not because of any extra demand from the firm itself, but because of an increase in the world market price of this commodity. Moreover, British firms will be importing this material from abroad, and a fall in the value of the pound on foreign exchange markets (a devaluation of the pound) will result in an increase in the price of imported aluminium (when measured in sterling terms) even though prices measured in dollars may not have risen.

Economists describe these as **autonomous increases in costs** – they are increases which are not associated with an increase in demand for the product. The inflation that results from them is known as **cost-push inflation**.

5.4 Wage-push inflation

There is one category of factor inputs deserving of special attention: namely, labour. The demand for labour is derived from the demand for the final product which that labour helps to create. It follows, therefore, that an increase in the demand for the *product* will result in an increase in demand for the *labour* which produces it. As with anything else, an increase in demand tends to cause upwards pressure on prices – in this case, the price of labour (wages). But in this case the increase in wages has resulted from demand pressure in the labour market, which in turn resulted from high demand for the product.

However, it is possible to imagine a situation in which labour costs rise not as a result of demand pressure in the labour market, but as a result of militant trade union activity which pushes up wage costs in the absence of any excess demand for labour. In such a situation this increase in wages would be called **pure wage-push inflation**.

5.5 A wage–price spiral

Pure wage-push inflation is comparatively rare. What is much more common is a situation in which unions take advantage of a situation of buoyant demand in the product market to pursue their wage claims. In such a situation, demand and cost inflation reinforce one another in an inflationary spiral.

Characteristic of such a situation is the fear on the part of employees that the increase in prices will lead to a decline in their **real earnings**. Employees – particularly unionised employees – will try to maintain the purchasing power of their earnings by securing increases in money wages which are at least as large as the increase in the price level which they are experiencing. If they succeed in securing relatively large wage rises, unless there is an offsetting increase in labour productivity this will result in an increase in labour costs to the firms involved (wage-push inflation) and a further tightening of the wage–price spiral.

5.6 How to calculate the growth of real earnings

Calculating the growth of real earnings may seem simple enough. If earnings increase by 6 per cent and prices increase by 4 per cent then common sense tells you that the growth of real earnings is 2 per cent (that is, 6 minus 4).

Common sense is wrong here, though in this example it is not far out because the numbers involved are quite small.

To see what the correct answer is, consider the hypothetical data in Table 5.2, which shows (as an index) money earnings in the first column, prices in the second column and, in the third column, real earnings: that is, earnings in constant 1995 prices. How are we to calculate the missing figure – the index of real earnings for 1996?

Using the same reasoning as in section 4.5 (which you may need to re-read), we use the price index as a deflator. That is, we *divide* the increase in money earnings by 104/100, or equivalently by 1.04. Thus the index of real earnings for 1996 is

$$\frac{106}{1.04} = 101.9$$

Therefore, the increase in real earnings is 1.9 per cent, not 2 per cent.

Although in this example the difference is very small, it will clearly be much more significant over a longer series. Consider Table 5.3 where we present an index of average earnings (in money terms) and an index of consumer prices for the UK. Both indices are based on 1980 = 100.

As can be seen, earnings increased by around 175 per cent whereas prices increased by only around 125 per cent (more than doubling). As we now know, the increase in real earnings is not 175 – 125 = 50 per cent. Using the price index as a deflator, we can calculate the index of real earnings for 1995 as

$$\frac{275.1}{2.246} = 122.5$$

so that the increase in real earnings was roughly 22 per cent. In Table 5.4 we have inserted a third column where we have calculated the index of real earnings for the entire period.

Notice that real earnings were very slack in the period 1980–85, which corresponded to a prolonged recession when demand – in the goods market and in the labour market – was very weak, and hence employees were in a weak bargaining position. Thereafter (in the 'Lawson boom' of 1986 onwards) the growth of real earnings was more rapid, but the growth in real earnings was halted when the boom was brought to an end in 1989, before moving ahead again in the recovery period of the early/mid-1990s. Real earnings growth was, however, still weak in 1994 and 1995.

table 5.2
Calculating the growth of real earnings

	Earnings	Prices	Real earnings (constant 1995 prices)
1995	100	100	100
1996	106	104	?

table 5.3

UK average earnings and consumer price indices, 1980–95

	Average earnings	Consumer prices
1980	100.0	100.0
1981	112.4	111.9
1982	121.7	121.5
1983	131.1	127.1
1984	137.7	133.5
1985	147.8	141.5
1986	159.2	146.3
1987	169.2	152.4
1988	182.4	159.9
1989	197.1	172.4
1990	215.9	188.7
1991	234.1	199.7
1992	250.1	207.2
1993	255.8	211.3
1994	266.0	217.3
1995	275.1	224.6

5.7 The policy response

Earlier we explained that economic theory distinguishes two 'types' of inflation – demand-pull inflation and cost-push inflation. In practice, demand-pull and cost-push inflation tend to coexist, though it is possible in theory at least to distinguish 'pure' demand-pull and 'pure' cost-push. The reason why we go to such great pains to analyse the causes of inflation, however, is straightforward – only if we know the cause can suitable counter-inflationary policies be devised.

If demand-pull inflation is diagnosed, the appropriate policy is one which reduces the level of demand – what is called a **deflationary policy**. If, on the other hand, pure cost-push inflation is diagnosed, deflation would not be appropriate. Rather a policy to restrain cost increases is necessary. In

table 5.4

Uk average earnings, consumer prices and real earnings indices, 1980–92

	Average earnings	Consumer prices	Real earnings (constant 1980 prices)
1980	100.0	100.0	100.0
1981	112.4	111.9	100.4
1982	121.7	121.5	100.2
1983	131.1	127.1	103.1
1984	137.7	133.5	103.1
1985	147.8	141.5	104.4
1986	159.2	146.3	108.8
1987	169.2	152.4	111.0
1988	182.4	159.9	114.1
1989	197.1	172.4	114.3
1990	215.9	188.7	114.4
1991	234.1	199.7	117.2
1992	250.1	207.2	120.7
1993	255.8	211.3	121.1
1994	266.0	217.3	122.4
1995	275.1	224.6	122.5

practice, the appropriate policy would depend upon the nature and source of the cost increases.

Autonomous increases in wage costs ('pure wage-push inflation') could be contained by a policy designed to weaken the strength of militant trade unions, and in effect this was the long-term policy of the Conservative government in Britain in the 1980s and 1990s. If, on the other hand, the cost increases result from an external force such as an increase in the world price of raw materials, there is no straightforward remedy since world prices are beyond the control of the policy-maker in the UK. However, the policy-maker in the UK does have some control over the exchange rate, and this will have an influence on the sterling price of imported goods.

PAUSE FOR THOUGHT   *Deflation, reflation and inflation. Which is the odd one out?*

The terms 'deflation' and 'reflation' both refer to demand. Deflation means a reduction in demand. Reflation is the opposite – an increase in demand. The odd one out is inflation, since it refers to prices. Curiously, or perhaps not so curiously, there is no single word which is the opposite to inflation – we have to use a phrase such as 'a fall in the price level'.

5.8 Rebasing an index (splicing together two series)

This section deals with a problem that you will frequently confront when using indices. You will often be faced with a situation where the information you want is already in the form of an index, but different (or inconvenient) bases are used. For example, part of the series may be based on 1980 = 100, whereas another part from a later edition of the same statistical source is based on 1985 = 100.

Consider, for example, the data shown in Table 5.5. It is easy to see (from the right-hand column) that a basket of goods which cost £10 in 1985 would have cost £10.44 in 1986 and so on. But since the two series have different bases,

table 5.5
Price indices for consumers' expenditure

	From 1986 edition (1980 = 100)	From 1989 edition (1985 = 100)
1975	52.2	
1976	60.4	
1977	69.4	
1978	75.8	54.0
1979	86.1	61.3
1980	100.0	71.3
1981	111.4	79.3
1982	121.1	86.2
1983	127.2	90.5
1984	133.2	95.1
1985	140.2	100.0
1986		104.4
1987		108.4
1988		113.8

Source: *UK National Accounts*, 1986 and 1989.

it is not possible to compare at a glance prices in 1975 with those in 1988. To do this we need to rebase the second series to 1980 = 100 (alternatively, we could rebase the first series to 1985 = 100. It really does not matter which way round we do it). Provided we have at least one year in which the series overlap, this is straightforward.

Suppose we wish to base everything on 1980 = 100. We know that prices in 1986 were 4.4 per cent higher than those in 1985. Thus to get the figure for 1986, we need to multiply 140.2 by 1.044. This gives us 146.4 (146.368 rounded).

Similarly, to obtain the index for 1987, we multiply 140.2 by 1.084 (= 152.0), since prices were 8.4 per cent higher in 1987 than in 1985.

There is an even easier way than this however. Suppose we wished to base everything on 1985 = 100. We would, of course, have to fill in the gaps in the *second* column of Table 5.5 for the years 1975–77. Consider the year 1978, a year where the two series overlap. How could we convert the number 75.8 into 54.0? Well, we have to divide by 75.8 and multiply by 54.0. That is, we multiply by 0.712, where

$$\frac{54.0}{75.8} = 0.712$$

This number in fact becomes a sort of conversion factor which we can use to rebase *all* the figures in the first column. In fact, it does not matter which year we choose to calculate our conversion factor. All we need is one year where the series overlap. We could, for example, choose 1982, which would give us a conversion factor of

$$\frac{86.2}{121.1} = 0.711$$

or more obviously we could choose 1980, which would give us a conversion factor of

$$\frac{71.3}{100.0} = 0.713$$

As you can see, apart from the rounding errors, the conversion factors are the same. All you need to do, therefore, is to take one year where the indices overlap, calculate the conversion factor and store it in the memory of your calculator, and you can then rebase the whole series. The index for 1977, for example, will become

$$0.713 \times 69.4 = 49.5$$

(note, however, that the last digit will be subject to a rounding error).

In Table 5.6 we have filled in the gaps in both series (the numbers in bold italics are those we have computed). We can now see (using either series) that between 1975 and 1988 prices increased slightly more than threefold – a 306 per cent increase in fact. (Note that you will get a slightly different figure using the two series because of rounding errors (305.55 as opposed to 305.91).

table 5.6		(1980 =100)	(1985 = 100)
Price indices for			
consumers'			
expenditure	1975	52.2	*37.2*
	1976	60.4	*43.0*
	1977	69.4	*49.4*
	1978	75.8	54.0
	1979	86.1	61.3
	1980	100.0	71.3
	1981	111.4	79.3
	1982	121.1	86.2
	1983	127.2	90.5
	1984	133.2	95.1
	1985	140.2	100.0
	1986	*146.4*	104.4
	1987	*152.0*	108.4
	1988	*159.5*	113.8

5.9 The Phillips curve
· ·

In the 1950s 'the cause of inflation' was being hotly disputed between the demand-pull school of thought and the cost-push school. The demand-pull school saw the cause of inflation as being excess demand, whereas the cost-push school blamed autonomous increases in costs, particularly wage costs. A. W. Phillips, then a professor at the London School of Economics, supported the demand-pull interpretation. Although he recognised the importance of the labour market in the inflationary process, he argued that rises in wages were caused by excess demand for labour rather than arising spontaneously as a result of autonomous forces.

However, it was not possible to test this interpretation, since the amount of excess demand for labour could not be directly measured. He argued, however, that another variable, the level of recorded unemployment, could be used as a proxy for the excess demand for labour. The two things would be negatively correlated – when the labour market was slack and the demand for labour was low, unemployment would be high; and when the demand for labour was high, unemployment would be low.

His hypothesis therefore was that one would expect to see an inverse relationship between the level of unemployment and the rate of change of wages. With low unemployment, the buoyant demand for labour would force up wages and these wage rises would feed through into price rises. In contrast, when the demand for labour was slack, there would be high levels of unemployment and wage increases would consequently be low, as would price increases.

Figure 5.2 illustrates in schematic form the technique used by Phillips. The diagram shows a scatter of points, each one representing an observation on the rate of inflation (on the vertical axis) and the level of unemployment (on the horizontal axis). The data which Phillips used to test this hypothesis actu-

Figure 5.2
**Derivation of the
Phillips curve**

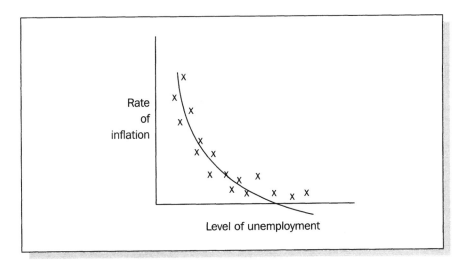

Note: Each cross represents an annual observation on the rate of inflation and the level of unemployment.

ally covered a period of almost a hundred years. Throughout this time there appeared to have been a stable relationship between the level of unemployment and the rate of inflation. It was the discovery of this (supposedly) stable relationship which was to make the Phillips curve so famous.

If a stable inverse relationship did indeed exist between unemployment and inflation, it demonstrated the existence of a **trade-off** between these two policy variables, as ***Figure 5.3*** illustrates. The Phillips curve suggested that it was possible to reduce inflation, but only at the cost of higher unemployment. That is, by suitable deflationary measures it was possible to move from point *A* on the Phillips curve to point *B*, securing lower inflation, but suffering higher unemployment as a consequence. Conversely, reflationary measures would

Figure 5.3
**The 'trade-off' which
the Phillips curve
illustrates**

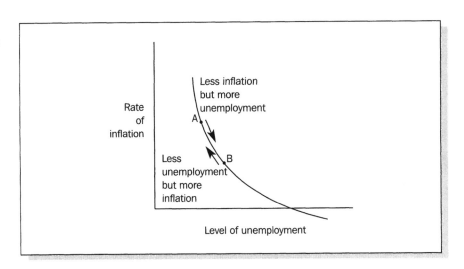

increase demand, pushing the economy from *B* to *A*, thus reducing unemployment but causing higher inflation.

ACTIVITY **2**
············

(a) Give two examples of a deflationary fiscal policy capable of pushing the economy from *A* to *B*.
(b) Give an example of a reflationary monetary policy which would push the economy from *B* to *A*.

Keynesian economists had long believed in the existence of such a trade-off. The Phillips curve seemed not only to confirm its existence, but also to make it possible to quantify the **terms of the trade-off**. It gave policy-makers a **menu of choice,** enabling them to predict exactly *how much* extra unemployment would be required to reduce the rate of inflation by a given amount.

Phillips' work was therefore immensely influential and seminal inasmuch as it sparked off a huge amount of subsequent research. However, far from settling the debate between competing schools of thought, Phillips' work provoked yet more controversy.

First, the cost-push school argued that Phillips' findings were equally compatible with an explanation which cited trade union militancy as the cause of inflation. Militancy, they argued, will itself be correlated with the level of economic activity. When the labour market is buoyant, unions are able to be more aggressive in their wage bargaining. Hence when unemployment is low, a higher rate of wage inflation will result, not from demand pressure directly, but as a result of trade union militancy. And in contrast when unemployment is high, trade unions become more docile and wage inflation moderates. This is illustrated in ***Figure 5.4.***

Figure 5.4
**Wage increases
linked to trade union
militancy**

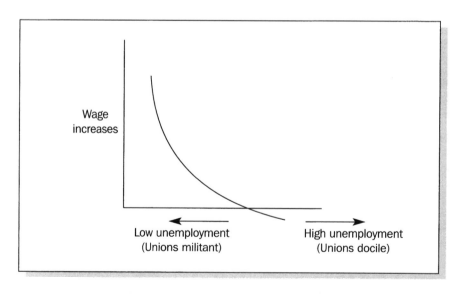

However, it was from the monetarists that the fiercest criticism of Phillips was to come. It was argued, most cogently by Friedman (1968) and Phelps (1967) that Phillips had been wrong to consider the rate of change of money wages. The variable which responded to demand pressure in the labour market was *real wages* not money wages. Although wage negotiations are normally conducted in terms of money wages, both parties implicitly bargain in real rather than money terms. The higher the rate of price inflation, the higher the rate of money wage rises that employees will try to secure.

Real and nominal oil prices

To illustrate the distinction between real and nominal values, consider the price of oil shown in Table 5.1 earlier (page 57). This price is measured in dollars. What would you expect to happen to the price of oil if the dollar falls in value?

For example, suppose the price of oil initially is $20 a barrel, and suppose that the dollar falls in value by 10 per cent *ceteris paribus* (that is, it falls by 10 per cent *vis-à-vis* all other currencies and *vis-à-vis* all goods and services). Would the dollar price of oil be affected by this, and if so by how much?

To gain some insight into this question, consider what would happen if the price of oil remained at $20 a barrel. This would mean that the amount of goods and services that could be bought with a barrel of oil would fall by 10 per cent. That is, the *real price* of oil would have fallen despite the fact that the nominal price had not changed. To preserve the real price of oil, the nominal price would have to rise – by 10 per cent to $22 a barrel.

Suppose that demand conditions in the labour market were such that increases in real wages would be restricted to the rate of increase in labour productivity – say, $2\frac{1}{4}$ per cent per year. If price inflation were zero, then money wage rises would be $2\frac{1}{4}$ per cent and **wage costs per unit of output** would remain unchanged. Monetarists argue that this will occur at what they call the **natural level of unemployment**, shown as U_n in ***Figure 5.5.***

Suppose now that reflationary policies push the economy up the short-run Phillips curve (labelled I in Figure 5.5). Initially such policies will indeed have the intended effect of reducing unemployment, but the induced rise in money wages quickly feeds through into prices. As the rise in prices catches up with the rise in wages, the rise in *real wages* drops back to that level consistent with the natural level of unemployment, U_n. Thus the economy returns to the same (natural) level of unemployment, but with higher increases in money wages and inflation – at point *B* in Figure 5.5.

Further reflationary policies are now necessary to reduce unemployment. If pursued, these policies reduce (temporarily) the level of unemployment as the economy is pushed along the short-run Phillips curve (labelled II). As soon as

Figure 5.5
The vertical Phillips curve

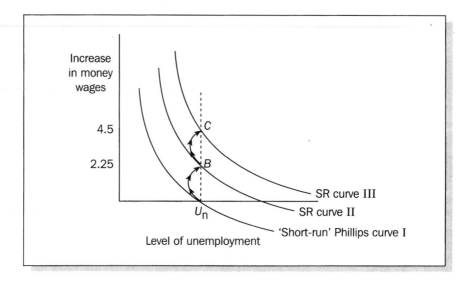

prices catch up with wages, however, the rise in real wages again becomes no more than that consistent with the natural level of unemployment, so that the level of unemployment returns to U_n (at point C in Figure 5.5).

Successive attempts at reducing unemployment trace out a vertical line – the **long-run Phillips curve** or **vertical Phillips curve**. The trade-off between inflation and unemployment exists only in the short run. In the long run it disappears and the policy-maker is faced with a very restricted menu of choice, one which offers the natural rate of unemployment coupled with low inflation, or the natural rate of unemployment coupled with high inflation. That is, a choice exists as to how high a rate of inflation to accept, but the level of unemployment cannot be altered.

PAUSE FOR THOUGHT *Why do you think that parties on the right of the political spectrum might endorse the views embodied in the vertical Phillips curve?*

If it can be demonstrated that unemployment cannot in fact be permanently reduced by government action, the existence of high unemployment cannot be ascribed to a failure of economic management. The responsibility for reducing unemployment no longer rests with the policy-maker if it can be shown that such things are beyond the ability of any government to control. This fits in well with the non-interventionist or *laissez-faire* approach favoured by parties on the political right.

5.10 Expectations

There is a final piece in this jigsaw. It concerns the way in which economic agents form their expectations about future movements in prices. Economic theory had traditionally asserted that people base their expectations about future price movements on what has happened in the recent past. Expectations are slow to adjust to changed circumstances, so unanticipated actions on the part of the policy-maker can often fool people into under-predicting or overpredicting the rate of inflation that actually occurs. This **adaptive model of price expectations** thus gave the policy-maker some scope for reducing unemployment – albeit temporarily – if people's expectations of price inflation were slow to adjust.

In the 1980s, however, a different and revolutionary model of expectations formation gained support. This was known as **rational expectations** (to contrast it with the former model, which was deemed to be 'irrational'). The rational expectations hypothesis argued that, although some people will overpredict and some underpredict the rate of inflation, on average people will guess correctly. They will learn from their mistakes and modify their behaviour accordingly. This curtails the ability of the policy-maker to generate continuously the sort of surprises necessary to reduce the level of unemployment – even temporarily – since wages and prices always increase *pari passu* in response to reflationary policies. Thus the policy-maker cannot reduce the level of unemployment, even in the short run.

This conclusion is, of course, the complete antithesis to the belief embodied in the Keynesian paradigm. Keynesians believe that the policy-maker has the ability and the responsibility for controlling the level of demand in order to prevent demand-deficient unemployment.

REVIEW QUESTIONS

1. Which of the following could *ceteris paribus* be responsible for an increase in the price of houses in Ealing, a suburb of West London? Explain in each case the nature of the causal mechanism, stating whether the mechanism is of the demand-pull or the cost-push type.
(a) a reduction in house prices in Wembley (a neighbouring borough)
(b) a reduction in interest rates
(c) relaxation of local authority planning controls
(d) an increase in the cost of timber.

2. 'In the UK in 1980 the rate of inflation exceeded 20 per cent but three years later it was down to less than 5 per cent thanks to Margaret Thatcher's strict monetary policy'. What is wrong with this statement?

3. 'If wages go up, prices go up. It's as simple as that.'
Use the following concepts to show that it is not as simple as that:
➤ the distinction between wages and *wage costs* (per unit of output)
➤ productivity
➤ ability of firms to absorb cost increases
➤ incentive for them to do so
➤ market conditions.

4. Table 5.7 shows indices for average earnings and consumer prices for the UK, France and Germany. Calculate an index which measures the growth of real earnings in each of these countries. Which country had the highest growth of real earnings in the period 1984–94?

table 5.7

Average earnings and consumer price indices: UK, France and Germany, 1984–94

	Average earnings			Consumer prices		
	UK	France	Germany	UK	France	Germany
1984	80.2	86.7	90.4	87.6	89.4	97.7
1985	86.3	92.4	93.2	92.9	94.8	99.9
1986	93.3	96.4	96.7	96.1	96.7	99.7
1987	100.0	100.0	100.0	100.0	100.0	100.0
1988	108.2	104.4	103.2	104.9	102.9	101.3
1989	117.8	109.3	106.2	113.1	106.1	104.1
1990	129.0	115.3	111.4	123.8	109.3	106.9
1991	139.7	120.8	118.1	131.1	112.7	110.6
1992	147.7	126.2	124.9	135.9	115.7	115.0
1993	153.2	129.7	128.6	138.1	118.7	119.7
1994	157.6	132.3	131.8	141.5	120.9	123.4

Source: *National Institute Economic Review*, Statistical Appendix, 1995 Q3.

Summary
• • • • • • • • • • •

Economists define two types of inflation (or two models of the inflationary process). These are demand-induced (demand-pull) inflation and cost-induced (cost-push) inflation.

Demand inflation results when the level of spending is too high. Prices are driven up by scarcity – that is, the level of demand in comparison to the supply available. In contrast, cost inflation results from autonomous increases in costs. These might be the cost of raw materials or more often the cost of labour. The latter would therefore be described as wage-push inflation. Pure demand-pull or pure cost-push inflation is rare. Normally the two combine in a wage–price spiral. However, a successful counter-inflation policy needs to identify the cause before appropriate remedial action can be taken.

The Phillips curve illustrates the trade-off between inflation and unemployment. The monetarist critique of the Phillips curve is that real wages rather than money wages are the key variable, and that once this is recognised there is no trade-off in the long run. The Phillips curve is therefore vertical at the 'natural level' of unemployment. This implies that the government cannot permanently reduce unemployment by reflationary policies.

This conclusion follows *a fortiori* if economic agents are assumed to form their expectations 'rationally'. The rational expectations hypothesis suggests that changes brought about by reflationary government policy will already have been taken into account by economic agents. Such policies are therefore ineffective in reducing unemployment even in the short run.

This chapter has also explained how to calculate the growth of real earnings and how to rebase an index.

Key concepts
••••••••••••••••

The following key concepts have been introduced in this chapter. Make sure you understand the meaning and significance of each of them. They are listed here in the order in which they first appear, and the page number where they appear is also given. You will find these key concepts in section headings or in **bold** in the text. Each chapter contains a list of key concepts and you may find these particularly useful for revision purposes.

hyperinflation	(p.56)
scarcity	(p.57)
the laws of demand and supply	(p.57)
demand-induced (demand-pull) inflation	(p.58)
full capacity level of output	(p.58)
autonomous increases in costs	(p.59)
cost-push inflation	(p.59)
pure wage-push inflation	(p.59)
wage-price spiral	(p.59)
real earnings	(p.59)
deflationary policy (demand reducing policy)	(p.61)
rebasing an index	(p.62)
Phillips curve	(p.64)
trade-off between inflation and employment	(p.65)
terms of the trade-off	(p.66)
menu of choice	(p.66)
wage costs per unit of output	(p.67)
natural level of unemployment	(p.67)
long-run Phillips curve	(p.68)
vertical Phillips curve	(p.68)
adaptive expectations	(p.69)
rational expectations	(p.69)

Sources of information
•••••••••••••••••••••••••••

Business Monitor MM23 has detailed information on price indices. However, you may not find this in the library you are using. *Economic Trends* contains most of the information you need on prices. Data on earnings can be found in the *Employment Gazette* (monthly), which contains a statistical appendix.

The *Employment Gazette* contains a small amount of comparative data on other countries, but for more comprehensive coverage of other countries you will need to consult sources such as *OECD Main Economic Indicators* (which has data on prices and earnings for OECD countries) and *International Financial Statistics* (which covers almost every country in the world).

More information on these and other sources is to be found in the **Guide to Statistical Sources** at the back of this book.

CHAPTER 6

Money

Objectives:

This chapter will enable you to:

➤ answer the question 'What is money?' by tracing the evolution of money from primitive times to the present day

➤ understand how banks create credit money by the process of multiple credit creation

➤ appreciate that money can be defined either narrowly or broadly so as to include various types of credit money as well

➤ understand how the central bank attempts to control the amount of credit money created

➤ appreciate the debate about the transmission mechanism between the stock of money and the flow of spending

➤ be aware of the quantity theory of money and the shortcomings of the theory

➤ appreciate those aspects of the debate between monetarists and Keynesians which relate to the importance of money in the economy

➤ understand the portfolio balance view of the transmission mechanism.

6.1 The development of money
6.2 Cigarettes in prisons
6.3 Credit creation
6.4 The control of the money supply
6.5 Narrow money and broad money
6.6 The transmission mechanism
6.7 The quantity theory of money
6.8 Say's Law
6.9 Objections to the quantity theory of money
6.10 The velocity of circulation of money
6.11 Is the stock of money an instrument which can be controlled?
6.12 Say's Law revisited
6.13 Monetarists and Keynesians
6.14 Problems in defining the money supply
6.15 Alternative views of the transmission mechanism – Keynes
6.16 Modern views of the transmission mechanism – portfolio balance

6.1 The development of money

One of the questions most often asked of economists relates to the nature of money itself. *What exactly is money?* Banknotes and coins are obviously money. But most people are aware of alternative means of payment in modern financial systems – things such as cheques drawn on bank or building society accounts. What does the balance shown on a bank statement actually signify? Does the bank have this money stored away in a vault somewhere, waiting for you to collect it? And are plastic cards, such as credit cards and debit cards, also money? And if so, how much money do they represent?

To understand what money is and what **functions** it performs, we need to travel back in time to a period in history before money was invented. In these primitive times the only transactions which took place were *barter* transactions. As we saw earlier, these were extremely impractical because they depended upon a *double coincidence of wants*. However, certain goods such as cattle were universally acceptable and people would often sell their products in exchange for cattle, even though they did not have any use for the cattle themselves. They knew that they could sell these cattle to a third party in exchange for the goods that they did want. Thus cattle became the first **medium of exchange**. Moreover, the value of other goods could be expressed in terms of cattle, which therefore became a measuring rod to gauge the worth of something or some-one. They became what we now call a **unit of account**.

However, the use of cattle was very inconvenient. They were very difficult to carry around, there were different sizes and types (large cows, small cows, old bulls and so on), they could not be used for small transactions and they tended to wander off or die if they were not looked after properly. Thus – and this rep-resents one of early man's greatest achievements – someone had the idea of using **tokens** which would stand for the real thing. Because this development occurred at a time when the skills of metal smelting were just being mastered, it was natural to use small pieces of metal bearing the picture of an animal. These small pieces of metal became the first coins. They served both as a *medium of exchange* and a *unit of account*. They also served as an excellent **store of value** – you could store up purchasing power to use later.

Since these early times, the development of money has proceeded apace. Coins were infinitely more convenient than cattle. They had certain desirable characteristics – namely, that they were portable and durable – but they still had the disadvantage that if you wanted to make a large purchase they were rather heavy. And they could be stolen by thieves. Thus goldsmiths who had secure premises which could not be raided by thieves began to accept deposits for safekeeping. In return they issued notes (or receipts) to the depositors. The notes represented **claims** to a certain quantity of coins and they were the fore-runners of modern banknotes.

PAUSE FOR THOUGHT

Look at any British banknote. You will find that it bears the words: I promise to pay the bearer on demand the sum of … five pounds *(or whatever). The origins of this date back to the time when goldsmiths issued receipts for the coins deposited with them.*

People soon discovered that the notes themselves were acceptable as a means of payment, and there were considerable advantages in using notes. Paper was much lighter and a single piece of paper could stand in the place of several sackfuls of coins.

Later still, cheques were used to take the place of banknotes because cheques were much less susceptible to theft. But the processing of millions of cheques each day was a laborious and wasteful procedure. The invention of computers enabled the processing of cheques to be automated, but it was still necessary for these pieces of paper to be moved around the country and around the globe. It came to be realised that the printing and physical conveyance of cheques from one location to another was itself a wasteful procedure. Money transfers could be made electronically along telephone lines – there was no longer a need for the pieces of paper themselves to be transported.

Thus in contemporary society, if 'money' has any physical existence, it is now in the form of tiny electrical impulses or a piece of binary code on a magnetised storage medium in a computer. This has replaced the use of cheques drawn on bank accounts, themselves a form of money, which in turn replaced the use of an earlier form of money – banknotes. These in turn replaced the use of coins, which at one time were the only form of money. Coins in their turn replaced the use of acceptable physical objects such as cattle, which again, in their time, were the only form of money. Each of these forms of money can be seen as *claims* – they give the holder an entitlement to real resources.

DID YOU KNOW?

The word 'pecuniary' (which means relating to money or consisting of money) comes from a Latin word pecudes *meaning cattle. Someone who is 'impecunious' has no money – and probably no cattle either.*

To summarise the discussion above, we can see that money, in whatever form it exists, must be capable of fulfilling three functions. It must be:

➤ a medium of exchange
➤ a unit of account
➤ a store of value.

Anything which does not fulfil *all three* functions cannot be regarded by the economist as money. Thus we can see that many of the things that in everyday language are referred to as 'money', such as 'plastic money', are not in fact money, since they fulfil only the first of these three functions. Credit cards, debit cards and even cheques are not in themselves money. They are only a means of payment (a medium of exchange) – a way of transferring money from one individual to another.

DID YOU KNOW?

The slang term 'plastic money' refers to credit cards and debit cards which can be used as a means of payment. The majority of individuals now hold such a card, though the most widely held plastic card is still the cashpoint debit card (which is not, of course, 'plastic money').

6.2 Cigarettes in prison

One can gain further insights into the nature of money by looking at the use of cigarettes as money in prisons. Cigarettes have been used extensively as money, particularly in prisoner-of-war camps in the Second World War and in prisons in peacetime. Because currency was and is not allowed in prisons, the only transactions which could be undertaken by the prisoners were barter transactions, and the use of cigarettes as money developed naturally out of their use in barter.

Prisoners would buy and sell goods for cigarettes even if they themselves were non-smokers because they knew they would be able to trade the cigarettes

table 6.1		
Percentage of	ATM debit card	62
persons aged 16 or	Debit card	52
over holding plastic	Credit/charge card	38
cards: Great Britain,	Visa credit card	28
1993	Mastercard	18
	Retailer card	17
	Any plastic card	76

Source: Association for Payment Clearing Services, quoted in *Social Trends*, 1995.

to a third party for whom the cigarettes did have an intrinsic value. In this respect the use of cigarettes as money developed in much the same way as the use of cattle in primitive societies – both cigarettes and cattle had a **value in use** which was the ultimate assurance of their acceptability.

There are certain **desirable characteristics** possessed by good money substances: namely, they should be **portable**, **durable**, **divisible**, **standardised** and above all **acceptable** and **scarce**. Cigarettes in prisons possess all of these characteristics – they are easy to carry around, they last for a very long time (provided the packet is not opened), they can be divided up into very small amounts for small transactions. Moreover, because the monthly cigarette ration was strictly limited, but there was a continuing and steady demand for them by smokers, cigarettes were *scarce* and this scarcity ensured their acceptability, even by non-smokers.

ASK YOURSELF

The word 'salary' comes from another Latin word which literally means salt-money. *In Roman times, salt was a valuable commodity and soldiers were paid in salt. Why should this have been so? Which of the desirable characteristics of money does salt possess?*

What does it mean if someone is described as being 'worth their salt'?

6.3 Credit creation
....

While the discussion about the use of money in prisons can give us valuable insights into the nature of money, prisons are akin to very primitive societies and we cannot use them to illustrate how money is created and used in modern financial systems. To understand this we must investigate the role of the banking system, and in particular the way in which banks create money through the process of **multiple credit creation**.

In contemporary society, the banking system consists of a **central bank** and a number of **commercial banks**. The commercial banks engage in **fractional reserve banking**. Only a small fraction of the cash deposited with the banks at any one time is retained by them in the form of cash. The banks lend out the remainder to other customers, who then make use of these loans to buy goods and services. The sellers of those goods and services receive payment, which they in turn deposit in the banks. Once again the commercial banks retain a fraction of this in the form of cash and lend out the rest.

In Figure 6.1 we assume that the fraction of their total liabilities which the banks retain in the form of cash is 10 per cent. This is known as a 10 per cent **cash ratio**. The banks feel safe in retaining only 10 per cent of deposits in the form of cash, since they know from experience that although a few customers on any one day might want to withdraw all their funds in cash, it is almost inconceivable that all the bank's depositors would wish to do so on the same day – indeed, if they did all decide to do this the bank would be unable to pay them in cash. Although technically it would have sufficient assets to cover its liabilities, these 'assets' would consist mostly of loans to customers and it would take a long time to call in these loans – that is, to convert them into cash. In the interim, the bank would be unable to meet its short term liabilities – to pay back to the depositors the cash that they had lodged with the bank.

CASE
ILLUSTRATION
• • • • • • • • • • • •

Assets and liabilities

If you are confused about assets and liabilities, it might help to recall that, as with any other enterprise, the bank's accounts are based on the principle of **double entry bookkeeping**. Each entry must be recorded twice, so that at the end of the day the bank can check that no arithmetical errors have been made. It does this by checking that

Total assets = Total liabilities

which is a way of checking the arithmetic. It has no other significance.

If Tom deposits £100 cash in the bank, the bank immediately acquires an asset (£100 cash) and a corresponding liability (since it now owes Tom £100).

If the bank then lends £50 to Jerry, it is simply swapping one asset for another. It now has less cash (minus £50), but more money owed to it (plus £50). Total assets will still equal total liabilities.

It may seem curious that banks regard as assets the loans they make to customers – particularly when banks make loans to some Third World countries (and to some students) who seem unlikely ever to repay.

Suppose therefore that in *Figure 6.1* an initial deposit of £100 is made with the commercial bank. These are banknotes, let us say – money issued by the central bank. Adhering to its 10 per cent cash ratio, the commercial bank will retain £10 and lend out £90 to a customer, who uses the loan to buy a car. The seller of the car deposits the proceeds of the sale with the same bank (it could be a different bank, but our example is more straightforward if we assume there is only one commercial bank). From this new deposit, 90 per cent is lent out again – a further £81 – and so on. We could demonstrate that, once this process of *multiple credit creation* has come to an end, the total amount of money deposited with the bank will be £1,000, of which 10 per cent will be the original £100 cash and the remaining £900 will be **credit money** created by the banking system.

Figure 6.1

The process of multiple credit creation

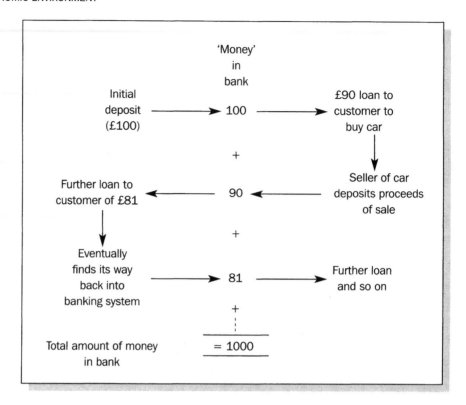

The reader will no doubt notice the similarity here with the multiplier process described in Chapter 3. Indeed, we can talk here about a **bank multiplier**. The total stock of money will be some multiple of the amount of **high-powered money** – the cash issued by the central bank which started the whole process. In our example there will eventually be ten times as much credit money as there is cash, since we assumed that the **reserve requirements** in force consisted of a 10 per cent cash ratio.

ACTIVITY **1**
•••••••••••

What would happen if the reserve requirements imposed by the central bank became more stringent? Suppose, for example, that the central bank now insisted that commercial banks adhere to a reserve ratio of 20 per cent instead of 10 per cent. How would this affect the amount of credit money that could be created by the commercial banks? Would they be able to create more credit money than previously or less than previously? Can you give an inspired guess about how much credit money could now be created from £100 of high-powered money?

Check with answers/suggestions at the back of the book.

6.4 The control of the money supply

The high-powered money created by the central bank is the **cash base** of the system. Although the central bank does not directly control the total money stock, it does control the cash base. If there is always a fixed ratio between the cash base of the system and the amount of credit money created, it follows that the central bank can control the overall money stock by operating on the cash base.

A given reduction in the cash base will cause the process of multiple credit creation to go into reverse – what could be called *multiple credit contraction*. Banks will be forced to call in loans so as not to fall below the 10 per cent cash ratio. The amount of credit money therefore shrinks by ten times as much as the reduction in the cash base, shown schematically in **Figure 6.2.**

6.5 Narrow money and broad money

From the above it is possible to see that the stock of money could be defined either in a very narrow way or much more broadly. Narrowly, we could define it to be equal to the amount of high-powered money issued by the central bank – in other words, the amount of cash (notes and coins) in circulation. This is the **narrow definition** of the money supply which is known as **M0** (pronounced 'M nought').

However, it is also possible to use a much **wider definition** of the money supply which encompasses not only all of the cash in the system, but all the credit money as well. This credit money is the sum total of the credit balances

Figure 6.2
The relationship between the cash base and credit money

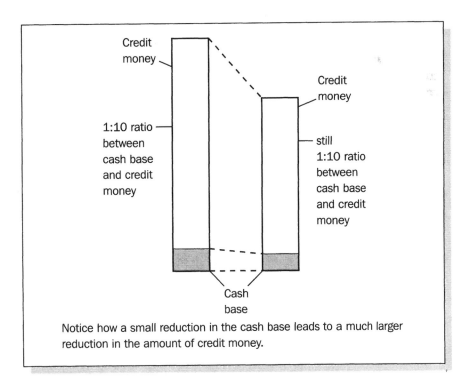

Notice how a small reduction in the cash base leads to a much larger reduction in the amount of credit money.

of the commercial banks' customers, and incidentally those of building societies as well. In other words, when customers receive their statement from the bank at the end of each month, the 'money' shown as being in their account (provided it is in credit!) forms part of the **broad money** aggregate. This broad money aggregate – the wider definition of the money supply – is known as **M4**.

The reader who is wondering what happened to M1, M2 and M3 will have to wait until later in this chapter to find out.

DID YOU KNOW?

Banknotes and coins are issued in various denominations – £1 coins, £5 notes, £10 notes and so on. The amount of each denomination which is issued is more or less determined by demand. For example, there is little demand for £50 notes (except for the payment of black economy transactions such as the 'strictly cash' payments to local builders), and hence relatively few of these large-denomination notes are printed and distributed to banks.

However, the clearest indication that the note issue as a whole is demand determined comes from the realisation that the amount of cash in the economy is seasonal – it is at its maximum in the fourth quarter of the year in the run-up to Christmas, when consumption spending is at its height.

6.6 The transmission mechanism

So far in this chapter, we have discussed what constitutes money in contemporary society. We have shown that the total money stock is made up of the cash base plus some larger quantity of credit money. However, it must be remembered that money itself is a *stock*, while spending is a *flow*. Ultimately, it is the flow of spending which is important, since this flow determines income and output. The stock of money is important only insofar as it affects the flow of spending.

The link between the stock of money and the flow of spending is known as the **transmission mechanism** and this is discussed below.

6.7 The quantity theory of money

The earliest and one of the most straightforward versions of the transmission mechanism is the quantity theory of money. The essence of the theory is embodied in the **equation of exchange**:

$$MV = PY$$

This states that the quantity of money (M) multiplied by its velocity of circulation (V) must be equal to the volume of output (Y) multiplied by the price level (P). The statement is a tautology – something which is true by definition. It is equivalent to saying that the total amount of money spent purchasing goods and services must be equal to the total value of goods and services purchased, and hence is a definition rather than a theory about the role of money in the economy. It can, however, be transformed into such a theory by making certain assumptions.

First and crucially, assume that V, the velocity of circulation, is a constant. From this it follows that the flow of spending is simply some multiple of the stock of money.

Second, assume that the stock of money is an instrument which can be manipulated at will by the monetary authorities. It therefore follows from these two assumptions that prior changes in the stock of money cause changes in spending, which in turn cause equivalent changes in money incomes and the money value of output (both represented in the equation by *PY*). That is, the money supply *determines* money incomes and the money value of output. In symbols:

$$M \rightarrow\rightarrow PY$$

Proponents of the quantity theory then proceeded to make a further assumption, based on the notion of Say's Law (see below). This assumption was that *real output* (*Y*) would be determined independently and not be influenced in any way by purely monetary forces. If this were true then changes in the money supply (*M*) could only affect the price level (*P*). To express the same idea in a slightly different way, the rate of growth of the money supply determined the rate of inflation. Thus we see in this 'strict' version of the quantity theory that the money supply is an enormously important variable, since it single-handedly determines the rate of inflation.

6.8 Say's Law

The French economist Jean-Baptiste Say (1767–1832) was one of the key figures of classical economics. Say's Law is normally stated as: **supply creates its own demand**. His justification for this assertion was as follows. People will not supply goods and services to the market as an act of philanthropy. They will do so only in order to acquire the money necessary to purchase the goods and services that they cannot supply for themselves. The production and sale of goods will generate the incomes – and therefore the expenditures – sufficient to ensure that all those goods are sold. Thus there can never be a shortfall of effective demand.

As a supplementary, we could note that there may be a mismatch between the goods that are produced and the goods that consumers actually want. Along with other classical economists, Say resolved this problem by assuming perfectly flexible prices and wages. The price of the unpopular goods would fall sufficiently to ensure that the market *cleared* (that is, all the unpopular goods would be marked down in price sufficiently to ensure that they were sold), and the price of goods for which there was a high demand would rise sufficiently to choke off the excess demand. Thus changes in *relative prices* would ensure that each market cleared (that is, that demand equalled supply in each market). And in the aggregate there would always be just sufficient demand – no more, no less – to ensure that the total supply of goods and services would be purchased.

ASK YOURSELF *Why has it been argued (only half seriously) that congestion on the M25 motorway is an example of Say's Law in operation?*

6.9 Objections to the quantity theory of money

Today no one accepts that the influence which money has on the economy can be explained in terms of a simple quantity theory. To a lesser or greater extent they would question the three key assumptions necessary to convert the equation of exchange into a theory of the determination of prices. As we have seen, these three key assumptions were:

➤ the velocity of circulation of money is constant
➤ the stock of money is an instrument which can be controlled
➤ Say's Law ('supply creates its own demand') will operate.

The validity of each of these three assumptions is considered in detail below.

6.10 The velocity of circulation of money

It is easy to calculate the velocity of circulation of money, and having done so, it is easy to see that it is not constant.

As explained earlier, we can measure the stock of money either narrowly (MO) or broadly (M4). Both measures of the money stock are shown in **Table 6.2** alongside data for GDP.

In Table 6.2 GDP is measured in current prices. Hence it represents *PY* in the equation of exchange. To calculate *V* we simply rearrange the equation of exchange

$$MV = PY$$

to give

$$V = \frac{PY}{M}$$

ACTIVITY **2**

Calculate the velocity of circulation of narrow money (MO) for 1985 and 1994. Account for the change that has taken place.

Check with answers/suggestions at the back of the book.

The same idea – a rise in the velocity of circulation of money – can also, of course, be expressed as a *fall* in the ratio of the money supply to GDP. This fall in the ratio of MO to GDP is shown in **Figure 6.3**. As can be seen, there is a trend decline in this ratio (that is, a trend increase in the velocity of circulation).

table 6.2
Money stock and GDP, 1985–94 (£bn)

	MO	M4	GDP
1985	14.1	214.7	357.3
1986	14.7	246.2	384.8
1987	15.4	285.6	423.4
1988	16.5	336.2	471.1
1989	17.4	397.9	516.0
1990	18.2	460.0	551.1
1991	18.7	494.7	575.3
1992	19.1	515.1	597.2
1993	20.1	532.5	630.7
1994	21.4	559.9	668.9

Source: *National Institute Economic Review*, Statistical Appendix, 1995 Q3.

Figure 6.3
**The falling ratio of
M0 to GDP, 1963–95**

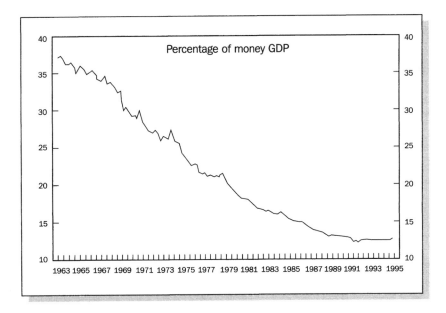

Source: *Financial Statement and Budget Report 1996–97.*

As the reader can check from the data in Table 6.2, the velocity of circulation of broad money has behaved in a completely different way to that of narrow money. Over the period, the increase in money GDP was about 87 per cent while the increase in M4 was about 161 per cent – almost twice as large. This means that the ratio of M4 to GDP has been rising, implying a *fall* in the velocity of circulation of broad money. The rise in the ratio of M4 to GDP is shown in *Figure 6.4*.

Figure 6.4
**The rising ratio of M4
to GDP, 1963–95**

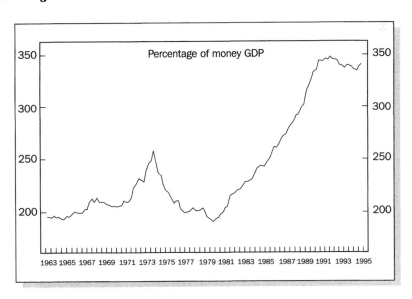

Source: *Financial Statement and Budget Report 1996–97.*

ACTIVITY **3**
．．．．．．．．．．．．

In 1994 the flow of spending (money GDP) was about £670 billion. This was larger than the stock of money (M4), which was about £560 billion. The stock of money has, however, grown faster than GDP. If past trends continue into the future, when will the stock of money exceed the annual flow of spending?

Hint: work out the average annual growth rate of the two variables and in this way forecast their future values.

Check with answers/suggestions at the back of the book.

6.11 Is the stock of money an instrument which can be controlled?
．．．

We saw in the previous section that the velocity of circulation of narrow money has risen and that of broad money has fallen. This leads us to consider the next objection to the crude quantity theory: can the money supply be controlled?

Table 6.3 shows the annual growth rates of MO and M4 for the period 1985–95. As can be seen, in the years leading up to 1989 (known as the 'Lawson boom') the growth of M4 was very rapid indeed, exceeding 18 per cent in 1989, the last year before the Lawson boom was turned into recession.

The erratic growth of MO and M4, and in particular the very rapid growth of M4 in the late 1980s, leads us to question whether the monetary authorities are really capable of controlling these aggregates. Why did they allow such a very rapid growth in M4, far in excess of the real rate of growth of the economy?

These are rhetorical questions, posed merely in order to emphasise that such a rapid growth in M4 calls into question the ability or the willingness of the monetary authorities to exercise control over what is declared to be an important monetary magnitude. In this light, it is difficult to see how a sane policy would have allowed the growth of the money stock to exceed 18 per cent when the trend rate of growth of real output was about $2\frac{1}{2}$ per cent.

table 6.3

Growth of MO and M4, 1985–95

	MO	Annual growth rate	M4	Annual growth rate
1985	14.1	4.5	214.7	13.4
1986	14.7	4.3	246.2	14.7
1987	15.4	4.8	285.6	16.0
1988	16.5	7.1	336.2	17.7
1989	17.4	5.5	397.9	18.3
1990	18.2	4.6	460.0	15.7
1991	18.7	2.7	494.7	7.6
1992	19.1	2.1	514.5	4.0
1993	20.1	5.2	530.3	3.1
1994	21.4	6.6	557.5	5.1
1995	22.7	6.0	599.6	7.5

Source: *Financial Statistics*.

Some economists would go as far as to argue that the supply of broad money is not – as a matter of empirical fact – under the control of the monetary authorities. It is not an **exogenous** instrument capable of being controlled. Rather, the growth of the money supply responds in a passive fashion to changes in money GDP, rising and falling in response to the growth rate of money GDP. That is, the money supply is **endogenous** rather than exogenous.

More simply, the distinction between exogeneity and endogeneity can be characterised as follows: do changes in the money supply lead to changes in money GDP, or do changes in money GDP bring about changes in the money supply?

6.12 Say's Law revisited
....

If we were to assume, however, that the money supply is an exogenous instrument, and also to assume that the velocity of circulation were constant, this would still leave open the question: do changes in the money supply affect prices or real output, or both? And if the answer is both, is the major impact on prices or on real output? The question is illustrated schematically in *Figure 6.5*.

In diagram (a), the major effect of prior changes in the money supply is on prices (*P*) with only a minor impact on real output (*Y*). In diagram (b), we see that the money supply has a large effect on real output with only a minor effect on prices. If Say's Law were to hold, as the quantity theorists suppose, then this would be an extreme version of diagram (a) – the money supply determines the price level and there is no effect on the level of output, which is determined independently by a quite different set of factors.

In very simplistic terms, Figure 6.5 does help to characterise fundamental differences between two competing paradigms in economics – the monetarists and the Keynesians. Although contemporary monetarists do not believe in a crude version of the quantity theory, they would nevertheless tend to support the interpretation shown in diagram (a) – the principal effect which the money supply has is on prices, with only a small effect on real output, perhaps no effect at all in the long run. Keynesian economists, on the other hand, would tend to deny that the money supply has any predictable influence on money incomes. Any influence that it does have, however, will be distributed between real output and prices, but not in equal proportions.

Figure 6.5
The effect of money supply on prices and real output

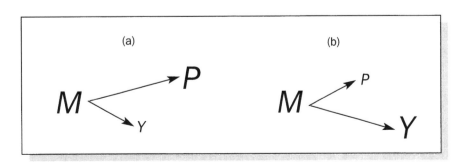

6.13 Monetarists and Keynesians
······································

The money supply has always had a central place in economics. Indeed, at one time the study of the macroeconomy was synonymous with the study of monetary economics. However, in 1936 the publication of J. M. Keynes' *General Theory of Employment, Interest and Money* was to usher in an intellectual revolution – the so-called Keynesian revolution, which was to relegate the role of money from its former position of pre-eminence to a more inferior role.

Keynes emphasised the importance of the *flow* of spending in the economy rather than the *stock* of money. He argued that the two things need not necessarily be closely correlated, and that for governments wishing to control the level of activity in the economy it was more sensible to operate directly on the flow of spending rather than to attempt to influence it indirectly by operating on the stock of money. The Keynesian revolution had a significant and lasting influence on the discipline of macroeconomics, and Keynesian ideas became more or less accepted by governments throughout the western world in the post-war period.

However, among policy-makers in the 1970s there was a resurgence of interest in the money stock as an important instrument of macroeconomic management. Following this, in the 1980s governments became preoccupied with the money supply. Indeed, in the UK in the early years of Mrs Thatcher's administration (i.e. after 1979) it was almost exclusively through the control of the money supply that the target of low inflation was to be achieved.

For a generation the two rival schools of thought – Keynesians and monetarists – strove first of all for intellectual supremacy and then for acceptance by the policy-maker. Undoubtedly for a time in the 1980s the monetarists gained the upper hand, at least in terms of convincing the policy-makers that their view was intellectually credible. Among the economics profession they were always in a distinct though very vocal, and at times very successful, minority. By the end of the 1980s, however, the monetarist experiment can be seen to have petered out and its intellectual shortcomings to have been exposed. Now curiously few economists can be found who would admit to ever having believed it.

Although increasingly sophisticated versions of monetarism were also on offer, crude monetarism, put in its simplest terms, argued that inflation was caused by excessive monetary growth. To cure inflation it was necessary only to restrict the rate of growth of the money supply – say, to 2 or 3 per cent per annum, or whatever was the trend rate of growth of real output. If the money supply expanded faster than this, the excessive money would result in higher prices – that is, inflation. This had the great attraction of simplicity; hence its appeal to politicians and to the general public.

6.14 Problems in defining the money supply
···

There were two main difficulties with the monetarist thesis, neither of which was satisfactorily resolved. First, in an advanced – and, more importantly, an evolving – financial system, it was not possible to define the stock of money in an unambiguous way; or at least there were a number of different but equally valid definitions of the money supply and there was no strong reason for choosing one in preference to any other. As we have seen, money can be defined either *narrowly* or *broadly*. In addition to MO and M4, however, there are or have been within the UK institutional context a number of different definitions of the money supply. The definitions change frequently, as does the popularity of one measure over another, which partly illustrates the difficulty in trying to pin down the concept. The major definitions are listed in ***Table 6.4***.

Notice that the broader the definition of the money supply, the more it will include. Thus M1 comprises all of MO but in addition includes non-interest bearing accounts at banks. Similarly M3 was defined to consist of M1 plus all accounts (including interest-bearing accounts) at banks.

The two principal monetary aggregates now in use are MO and M4. However, in the 1980s the monetary targets were M1 and M3. In fact, in the first half of the 1980s, M3 was seen as the principal means of achieving the government's low inflation objective, though institutional changes have now led to its demise. One such change has been the change in status of building societies.

table 6.4
Definitions of the money supply

MO	Cash. That is, notes and coins in circulation. Also certain balances that commercial banks are obliged to lodge with the Bank of England.
M1	All the above plus non-interest-bearing accounts at banks.
M3	All the above plus interest-bearing accounts at banks.
M4	All the above plus accounts at building societies.

CASE
ILLUSTRATION

What exactly is the difference between a building society and a bank?

The answer to this question, it seems, is 'not very much'.

To put the debate into context: building societies are peculiarly British institutions. However, other countries possess similar institutions with different names which nevertheless perform similar functions. Collectively, such institutions could be called **non-bank financial intermediaries**. Typically, such institutions accept deposits and make loans – which is precisely what banks do. We have already seen how banks create credit money, which forms a major part of the broad definition of the money supply. The control of the money supply is therefore crucially dependent on the amount of credit money created. The multiple credit-creating activities of commercial banks are under the control of the central bank (in the UK, the Bank of England), but non-bank financial intermediaries (although in many ways more restricted in their activities) are typically not subject to banking controls simply because they are not banks. The key question therefore is whether, despite their different legal status, non-bank financial intermediaries do in fact engage in multiple credit creation.

Moreover, if banks are not seen as unique in this respect (that is, they are not the only institutions to create credit), are there other non-bank institutions which also create credit? For example, do life assurance companies create credit? And what about retailers such as Marks and Spencer and Boots, which issue their own credit cards to customers? Does this also contribute to credit creation, so that these retailers are also in effect acting like banks?

There are definitive answers to these questions, but the answers tend to depend upon institutional definitions which are to a greater or lesser extent arbitrary. Thus in the 1980s the monetary aggregate known as M3 was defined so as to *include* all of the money contained in current accounts at banks, but to *exclude* accounts at building societies. In 1989 the Abbey National Building Society, a major financial institution, decided to change its legal status to that of a bank. Therefore with the change in its legal status, all of the 'money' in the accounts of the Abbey National Building Society which previously had been excluded from M3 became included. It was this single event more than any other which led to the demise of M3. It no longer seemed sensible to monitor this monetary aggregate when the change in legal status pointed out the absurdity of excluding the accounts of building societies, which were so similar to banks. As noted earlier, M3 has now been replaced by M4 as the preferred definition of broad money. M4 includes building society as well as bank accounts and cash in the definition of broad money. Two other large building societies, the Halifax and the Woolwich, have now also changed their legal status to that of banks.

And what of Marks and Spencer? Does it also engage in credit creation? It is creating credit money? The answers to these questions are again definitional. Marks and Spencer – along with many other retailers and, indeed, other firms – creates **trade credit**. Trade credit is defined *not* to be part of the money supply. Nevertheless it is an important aggregate which the monetary authorities deem it desirable to monitor, since it may influence spending.

None of these questions is trivial. The amount of spending in the economy will depend *inter alia* on the amount of money – and credit – available for people and companies to spend. The control of spending is therefore dependent on the ability of the monetary authorities to control money and credit.

6.15 Alternative views of the transmission mechanism – Keynes

In a modern financial system with sophisticated methods of payment and sources of credit, the quantity theory of money cannot be regarded as an adequate explanation of the influence that money has on the economy. The extreme Keynesian view, in contrast, is that 'money does not matter', that it has no influence on the economy. However, this too seems untenable. Surely the quantity of money, however defined, has some influence, however difficult it is to discern.

Keynes himself argued that monetary influences would be weak and uncertain, but nevertheless perceptible. His view of the transmission mechanism was that changes in the quantity of money would affect interest rates, and that this would in turn affect investment spending, itself a component of aggregate demand. For example if the money supply were increased, then *ceteris paribus* this would lower interest rates and stimulate investment spending by firms. Conversely, high interest rates would discourage investment spending, dampening down demand in the economy. Note, however, that the effect on the economy which he envisaged would be indirect and rather unpredictable. Better, he argued, for the authorities to operate directly on spending by fiscal means rather than to take an indirect monetary route.

Milton Friedman (1912–) is a rarely talented individual who commands respect as a gifted and creative academic while having an ability as a popular communicator to speak directly to ordinary people. In his working life these two roles made him perhaps the most famous economist of our times.

Born in 1912, he eventually became professor of economics at Chicago University in 1948, where he stayed until his retirement in 1979. He was the leading light in the so-called Chicago School of economics.

In his contributions to serious scholarship, Friedman was prolific. However, it was for his contributions to the more popular media that he will be remembered by many. In the heyday of his proselytising zeal, Friedman was frequently seen on television. The High Priest of Monetarism was in fact a small avuncular figure with a beatific smile, explaining patiently and good-humouredly to his audience that intervention in the workings of the free market was always counterproductive, however well intentioned it might be.

In the early 1980s he made a documentary television series called Free to Choose. *Capitalism and freedom, he argued, were synonymous. The greatest happiness of the greatest number would be promoted if people were left to pursue their own happiness, with minimal intervention by government. These sentiments made him the darling of the right, but were anathema to those – perhaps the majority of the economics profession – who believed that the government had to intervene to correct for the excesses of the market.*

6.16 Modern views of the transmission mechanism – portfolio balance

Contemporary monetarists, of whom Milton Friedman is the best-known spokesperson, have a different and much more sophisticated view of the transmission mechanism. In this view, all individuals possess a **wealth portfolio**, a collection of assets, some of them quite liquid such as cash, others less liquid such as bonds, shares and other financial assets. In addition, they hold real assets which are even more illiquid, such as cars and houses. Each individual will arrange his or her portfolio in such a way as to maximise the psychic and financial return to be derived from it. People strive for balance in their portfolio between the various types of asset holding – hence the name **portfolio balance** given to this view of the transmission mechanism.

An example of such a portfolio is shown in *Figure 6.6*. Note that there is a **liquidity spectrum** which ranges from the most liquid asset (cash) to the most illiquid (such things as houses). As one moves towards the less liquid end of the spectrum, it becomes more and more difficult to convert assets into cash. There are three main classes of asset which are identified: monetary assets, financial assets and real assets.

ASK YOURSELF *Pension rights do not fit readily into this classification. They could be classified as a financial asset, but how liquid are they?*

Each form of asset holding confers benefits on the individual, but each also involves costs. Shares, for example, normally yield a higher return than money put on deposit in the building society, but also involve more risk ('the value of investments can go down as well as up'). Moreover, shares are less liquid than money on deposit, so if you want to use the funds for some unforeseen emergency, converting them into cash may involve a financial penalty.

Suppose you won the National Lottery tomorrow ('it could be you'), and received £1 million. How would you decide to hold your wealth? What proportion would you hold in cash, and what proportion on deposit earning interest? What proportion of the £1 million would you use to buy a house? A car? A new mountain bike? New clothes? In Figure 6.6, consider the costs and benefits *to*

Figure 6.6

A wealth portfolio

		Monetary assets		Financial assets			Real assets	
	Cash	Current a/c	'Deposit' a/c	Bonds	Unit trusts	Shares	Durable goods e.g. cars	Houses
B E N E F I T S		easy access to funds	pays interest but cannot withdraw funds immediately	even higher returns but even less liquid		higher expected return but more risk	stream of services	stream of services
C O S T S	value eroded by inflation	does not pay interest					wasting assets	prices normally keep pace with inflation
								value can go down
*								

More liquid ◄───────────────────────────────────► Less liquid

* = Your preferred holding (percentages must sum to 100%)

you of the various forms of wealth holding and write down (in the space marked *****) the approximate percentages of your total wealth that you would hold in various forms.

You are most unlikely to leave it all in the bank. Some of it will be spent on acquiring other less liquid assets, and some of these 'assets', like clothes or a new bike, will be decidedly short lived because their value depreciates quickly. Nevertheless they yield a rate of return to the owner in the form of the benefits that he or she derives from their possession.

Few people win £1 million on the Lottery, but all individuals have a wealth portfolio – though for the poorest in the land it will be very small indeed. The monetarist view of the transmission mechanism argues that an increase in the money supply will lead to the wealth portfolios of some individuals becoming excessively liquid. Such individuals will no longer be maximising the return from their portfolio because it will have become unbalanced. It is too liquid. They will therefore attempt to re-establish balance in their portfolio by transferring some of this wealth to other forms of asset holding.

The additional liquidity will probably cause an increase in demand for all types of asset. For certain types, particularly those that are in relatively fixed supply, the increase in demand will drive up prices. One could argue that the inflation of house prices that occurred in the period up to 1989 was partly the result of the excessive monetary expansion that had taken place in the preceding few years. Table 6.5 shows the increase in house prices, alongside the rate of growth of broad money.

table 6.5 **Monetary growth and house prices**	M4 (annual growth rate)	House prices (index)	House prices (annual growth rate)
1985	13.4	50.1	–
1986	14.7	56.9	13.8
1987	16.0	66.5	16.9
1988	17.7	84.8	27.5
1989	18.3	101.2	19.3
1990	15.7	100.0	–1.2
1991	7.6	98.5	–1.5
1992	4.0	94.7	–3.9
1993	3.1	92.4	–2.4
1994	5.1	93.8	1.5
1995	7.5	93.7	–0.1

Source: *National Institute Economic Review*, Statistical Appendix, 1996 Q3.

Although the evidence from Table 6.5 seems to suggest a strong link, one should be cautious about accepting simplistic monocausal explanations. Nevertheless it seems sensible to accept that increased liquidity in the economy *will* work its way through to increased spending in some form or another. The monetarist view of the transmission mechanism provides an elegant account of how this happens.

REVIEW QUESTIONS

1. What are the three functions of money?

2. What are the desirable characteristics of a good money substance?

3. In the light of your answer to Q2, consider the extent to which the following could, in certain circumstances, be used as money. Explain the circumstances in which this could happen:
   (a) cigarettes
   (b) cattle
   (c) pieces of metal.

4. 'Plastic money' is not money, at least not according to monetary theorists. Which of the following statements do you agree with?
   (a) You cannot include plastic money in your definition of the money supply because you do not know what to include. Should you include the outstanding balance, the credit limit or what?
   (b) It is not real money. Real money is cash.
   (c) It is not real money. Real money is cash – and possibly cheques as well.
   (d) In the long run your ability to buy on credit depends on the money you have in the bank. So it is correct to include the money in your bank account as part of the money supply, but not to include credit cards.
   (e) Money has three functions (see Q1), and credit cards do not in fact perform all of these three functions.
   (f) This whole debate just goes to emphasise that what is important is the *flow of spending* not the *stock of money*.

5. Are forged notes money?

6. July 1995 was a particularly hot month in the UK. Normally in Britain hot weather causes reservoirs to run dry and railway lines to buckle. In 1995, however, the *Guardian* reported that the weather had been hot enough to distort the money supply statistics. It appears that consumers had been rejecting weekend trips to DIY stores, a recreational pursuit where the preferred method of payment was by plastic, in favour of trips to the seaside, fairgrounds and parks, where the preferred method of payment was cash. The amount of cash in the economy rose by 0.6 per cent in July, equivalent to nearly $7\frac{1}{2}$ per cent on an annual basis.

What light does this shed on the debate about the exogeneity or endogeneity of the money supply?

Summary
••••••••••

Barter transactions are inefficient because they depend for their success on a double coincidence of wants. Money transactions enable people to sell goods for money and to use that money later to buy other goods from a third party. Money serves as a medium of exchange, a unit of account and a store of value. Good money substances have certain desirable characteristics – they should be portable, durable, standardised and divisible, but, above all, acceptable and scarce. Some money substances, such as salt in primitive societies, and cigarettes in prisons, have a value in use. Most money, however, simply represents *claims* to real resources.

Commercial banks create money through the process of multiple credit creation, made possible because banks only keep a fraction of their reserves in the form of cash. The credit money created by the banks is indistinguishable in practice from the high-powered money created by the central bank.

The money supply may be defined to include only the cash (high-powered money) created by the central bank. This narrow definition is called M0. Alternatively, the wider definition, M4, includes, in addition to cash, all the credit money created by commercial banks and building societies.

The central bank directly controls the supply of cash. In theory, it also exercises indirect control over the amount of credit money being created. However, there is a debate about whether the money supply is an exogenous instrument (that is, something which can be controlled) as opposed to an endogenous variable (something which merely responds passively to what is going on in the economy).

Economists use the term 'the transmission mechanism' to describe how changes in the stock of money bring about changes in the flow of spending. A primitive view of the transmission mechanism is provided by the quantity theory of money. A crude quantity theory assumes that the velocity of circulation of money is constant, and hence, by definition, changes in the stock of money lead to equivalent changes in the flow of spending. Keynes rejected this idea. More sophisticated accounts of the transmission mechanism are based on the notion of individuals having a portfolio of assets. If this portfolio becomes too liquid, the individual will exchange some liquid assets (such as money) for some less liquid ones (such as bonds or real assets). In this way, changes in spending spread through the economy.

Key concepts
· · · · · · · · · · · · · · · ·

The following key concepts have been introduced in this chapter. Make sure you understand the meaning and significance of each of them. They are listed here in the order in which they first appear, and the page number where they appear is also given. You will find these key concepts in section headings or in bold in the text. Each chapter contains a list of key concepts and you may find these particularly useful for revision purposes.

functions of money	(p. 74)
medium of exchange	(p. 74)
unit of account	(p. 74)
tokens	(p. 74)
store of value	(p. 74)
claims	(p. 74)
value in use	(p. 76)
desirable characteristics of money	(p. 76)
portable	(p. 76)
durable	(p. 76)
divisible	(p. 76)
standardised	(p. 76)
acceptable	(p. 76)
scarce	(p. 76)
multiple credit creation	(p. 76)
central bank	(p. 76)
commercial banks	(p. 76)
fractional reserve banking	(p. 76)
cash ratio	(p. 77)
double entry bookkeeping	(p. 77)
credit money	(p. 77)
bank multiplier	(p. 78)
high-powered money	(p. 78)
reserve requirements	(p. 78)
cash base	(p. 79)
narrow definition of the money supply (M0)	(p. 79)
wider definition of the money supply (M4)	(p. 79)
broad money	(p. 80)
transmission mechanism	(p. 80)
equation of exchange	(p. 80)
Say's Law	(p. 81)
supply creates its own demand	(p. 81)
exogenous	(p. 85)

endogenous	(p. 85)
monetarists	(p. 86)
Keynesians	(p. 86)
non-bank financial intermediaries	(p. 87)
trade credit	(p. 88)
wealth portfolio	(p. 89)
portfolio balance	(p. 89)
liquidity spectrum	(p. 89)

Sources of Information

Milton Friedman's major academic works are as follows. 'A monetary and fiscal framework for economic stability', *American Economic Review*, 1948, set out his non-interventionist beliefs. *Studies in the Quantity Theory of Money* (1956) reinstated money as an important policy variable. 'Inflation is always and everywhere a monetary phenomenon.' A year later he published his hugely original *A Theory of the Consumption Function* (1957), in which he developed the permanent income hypothesis, still a compulsory part of the syllabus for economics specialists. *Capitalism and Freedom* appeared in 1962. *A Monetary History of the United States 1867–1960*, a monumental work written with Anna Schwartz, followed in 1963. Again the theme was that 'money matters'. His seminal contribution to the debate on the Phillips curve (see Chapter 5) appeared in 'The role of monetary policy', *American Economic Review*, 1968.

Detailed information on the various monetary aggregates and on interest rate, can be found in *Financial Statistics*, published monthly by the ONS, or in the *Bank of England Quarterly Bulletin*. Comparative data for other countries can be found in *International Financial Statistics*.

More information on these and other sources is to be found in the **Guide to Statistical Sources** at the back of this book.

CHAPTER **7**

Trade, the exchange rate and the balance of payments

Objectives:

This chapter will enable you to:

➤ appreciate the reasons for the internationalisation of production and the associated growth of trade
➤ understand that trade and specialisation can partly be explained in terms of the theory of comparative advantage
➤ understand that there are gains from trade and that policies of autarkic development have largely been unsuccessful
➤ understand how market exchange rates are determined
➤ be able to distinguish between the current account and the capital account of the balance of payments
➤ appreciate the distinction between floating and fixed exchange rates
➤ appreciate the distinction between the internal purchasing power of a currency and its external purchasing power and understand how the two are related.

7.1 The gains from trade
7.2 Specialisation and comparative advantage
7.3 Exchange rates
7.4 The determination of the exchange rate
7.5 The current and capital accounts
7.6 Flexible and fixed exchange rates
7.7 Internal and external purchasing power

7.1 The gains from trade

One of the salient features of the world economy in the last 50 years has been the increasing **internationalisation** (or **globalisation**) of production. Improved transport systems and vastly improved communications have made it possible for companies to operate on an international rather than a purely local scale, and many companies – not just the large multinationals – operate on a global scale. It follows from this that individual nation states have become more **open** – that is, an increasing proportion of economic activity is associated with foreign trade. There has been an increase in the fraction of total demand which comes from exports and – the concomitant of this – there has been a similar increase in the share of total spending which goes on imports.

Note that the policy of exposing a country to the full rigours and opportunities of foreign trade contrasts sharply with the policy of **autarky** formerly pursued by those countries of central and eastern Europe which espoused a policy of central planning. 'Autarky' means self-sufficiency and implies separate development. The rationale for this policy was that the eastern European countries, trading only among themselves, would be able to develop in a way which was untainted with the excesses of western (and Far Eastern) capitalism. The policy, as we know, proved unsuccessful. Countries which cut themselves off from foreign trade denied themselves the benefits that trade brings – though it must be admitted that exposure to foreign trade also brings with it certain disadvantages.

Some of the benefits from trade are obvious. By trading, countries can acquire technology without having themselves to spend large amounts on research and development. 'Reinventing the wheel' is an expression used in English to denote a situation where an individual or group laboriously sets out, starting from scratch, to perform some task or design some device which has previously been successfully perfected by others. Trade enables countries to avoid reinventing the wheel – the car, and the microprocessor. Countries are said to benefit from the **transfer of technology** from one (usually advanced) country to another.

Moreover, many of the products and services that we now take for granted can only be produced on a large scale if they are to be produced at all. That is, if they are to be brought within the price range of the average citizen, the huge fixed costs associated with their production must be spread over a large number of sales units. Thus microchips can be produced for a few pence each, provided millions of them are sold. Hollywood films, such as *Jurassic Park*, which cost many millions of dollars to produce can make a profit because many millions of people buy tickets to see them. Thus companies must be able to sell to a large market – in many cases, a global market – if they are to reap the full benefits of **economies of scale**. This is even more important for small countries whose domestic market is not large enough to enable them to exploit the full benefits of scale economies. Thus, as we would expect, small countries such as Holland are more *open* than large ones such as the United States in the sense that the ratio of exports to GDP is much higher in Holland than in the USA.

CASE
ILLUSTRATION
• • • • • • • • • • • • • • •

Waterworld

Kevin Costner's film *Waterworld*, which opened in 1995, cost $225 million. It was at the time the most expensive film ever made. For the film to make a profit, how many people would need to go and see it? (Assume that a cinema ticket costs $10.) What proportion of the population of the United States does this represent? (The population of the USA is about 260 million.)

In fact it would require about $22\frac{1}{2}$ million people to go and see it for it to cover its costs – less than 10 per cent of the population of the USA. Only a small fraction of the population actually goes to the cinema – possibly less than 10 per cent – but the film will also be shown in Europe (population around 300 million) and elsewhere.

ACTIVITY **1**
• • • • • • • • • • • •

Over time, which do you expect to grow faster – world output or world trade? Is this confirmed by the figures in Table 7.1?

Check with answers/suggestions at the back of the book.

table 7.1

World output and world trade (index 1987 = 100)

	GDP (OECD)	World trade
1984	91.0	85
1985	94.0	88
1986	96.8	94
1987	100.0	100
1988	104.2	109
1989	107.9	116
1990	110.7	120
1991	112.2	125
1992	114.2	132
1993	115.2	137
1994	118.3	148
1995	120.6	162

Source: *National Institute Economic Review*, Statistical Appendix, derived from OECD, *Quarterly National Accounts* and UN, *Monthly Bulletin of Statistics*. The two series are not strictly comparable, since the OECD countries account for only about three-quarters of world output. Moreover, the data given for trade relate to goods only.

7.2 Specialisation and comparative advantage

However, trade brings with it additional benefits which are unrelated to the transfer of technology or economies of scale. A concomitant of trade is **specialisation**, and this specialisation itself brings benefits as the following hypothetical example will show.

Suppose we have two countries which, since this is a hypothetical example, we shall call Norway and Belgium. Both produce furniture and chocolate, and the **unit labour requirements** (ULRs) needed to produce one unit of furniture and one unit of chocolate in each country are shown in Table 7.2. Note that the ULRs are the *inputs* required to produce a certain *output*.

To avoid difficulties associated with exchange rates, we shall assume in this example that the ULRs are measured in a common currency, the ECU, and that the exchange rate between the ECU and the national currencies cannot change. For simplicity we also assume that labour is the only factor input to be considered.

We note first that Norway is better at producing both furniture and chocolate than Belgium, since it takes 84 man-hours to produce a unit of furniture in Belgium and only 60 in Norway. Similarly, it takes 7 man-hours to produce a unit of chocolate in Belgium and only 6 in Norway. We say that Norway is *absolutely more efficient* than Belgium in both furniture and chocolate production – it has an *absolute advantage* in both products.

table 7.2

ULRs in the production of furniture and chocolate

	Norway	Belgium
Furniture	60	84
Chocolate	6	7

Why then should Norway bother to trade? To answer this question we need to look at the **comparative advantage** of each country. In Norway to produce one unit of furniture requires resources which could have produced 10 units of chocolate. We say the **opportunity cost** of one unit of furniture is 10 units of chocolate. In contrast, in Belgium to produce one unit of furniture requires 12 units of chocolate to be given up. The opportunity cost of one unit of furniture is 12 units of chocolate.

To repeat:

➤ in Norway, the *opportunity cost* of one unit of furniture = 10 units of chocolate
➤ in Belgium, the *opportunity cost* of one unit of furniture = 12 units of chocolate.

Thus the opportunity cost of furniture is higher in Belgium than it is in Norway – Belgium has to give up more per unit of furniture produced than Norway. It would appear, therefore, that Norway has a comparative advantage in furniture production. The (opportunity) cost of furniture production is lower in Norway than it is in Belgium.

We can also look at chocolate production to see which country has a comparative advantage. In Norway, the opportunity cost of one unit of chocolate is one-tenth of a unit of furniture. In Belgium the opportunity cost of one unit of chocolate is one-twelfth of a unit of furniture. Since one-tenth is more than one-twelfth, this confirms that Norway is comparatively disadvantaged in the production of chocolate.

To repeat:

➤ in Norway, the *opportunity cost* of one unit of chocolate = $\frac{1}{10}$ unit of furniture
➤ in Belgium, the *opportunity cost* of one unit of chocolate = $\frac{1}{12}$ unit of furniture.

Thus, Belgium has a comparative advantage in chocolate production and Norway has a comparative advantage in furniture production. What would happen if each country decided to specialise in producing the thing that it is best at? Suppose Norway reduced chocolate production by 10 units. The resources thus freed could be used to produce one unit of furniture. Belgium for its part reduces furniture output by one unit and uses the resources to produce 12 units of chocolate. Thus we have:

Norway gives up 10 chocolate	−10 chocolate
and gets 1 furniture	+1 furniture
Belgium gives up 1 furniture	−1 furniture
and gets 12 extra chocolate	+12 chocolate
Therefore net increase in output equals	+2 chocolate

By specialising in this way, a net addition of 2 extra units of chocolate have been produced. These are the **gains from trade**. They have been achieved by each country specialising in the product in which it has a comparative advantage, even though one country has an absolute advantage in both products. Of course this analysis does not tell which country will benefit most from this specialisation – who gets the two extra chocolates!

7.3 Exchange rates
....

The example above assumed away the very obvious fact that – for the moment at least – Norway and Belgium use different national currencies, and that therefore the *exchange rate* between those two currencies will influence the amount and the direction of trade between the two countries.

Anyone who has travelled abroad will be familiar with the notion of converting one currency into another. Travellers to France in 1995 will have found that they could convert their pounds to francs at a rate of approximately £1 = 7.5 francs. Some of those travellers will remember that a few years previously (say in 1991) the exchange rate had been much more favourable to British visitors to France, who could then have got an exchange rate of approximately 10 francs to the pound (that is, £1 = 10 francs). What forces have been responsible for this decline in the value of the pound *vis-à-vis* the franc? Is the fall in the value of the pound bad for everyone in Britain, or do some people benefit from it? How are these exchange rates determined?

7.4 The determination of the exchange rate
....

The exchange rate is the price of one currency in terms of another. Unless special considerations apply (to be discussed later), this price will be determined by market forces. That is, the exchange rate will be determined by the forces of demand and supply.

Consider the foreign exchange market for pounds shown in *Figure 7.1*. The vertical axis shows the value of the pound measured in terms of French francs. A movement *up* the vertical axis represents an **appreciation** in the value of the pound – you get more francs per pound than previously. And a movement *down* the vertical axis means that the pound is falling in value *vis-à-vis* the franc (the pound is **depreciating** and the franc is appreciating). The foreign exchange market can be described as a **perfectly competitive market**, a technical term which means that there are so many private buyers and sellers that no one of them can have a significant effect on the price.

Every day on the foreign exchange market thousands of people will want to buy pounds. This is the demand side of the market. This demand – the actual and potential purchases of sterling – is represented by a **demand curve** (sometimes called a **demand schedule**). The demand curve is shown to be downward sloping, indicating that, as with any commodity, the higher the price, the less will be demanded, and the lower the price, the more will be demanded. This axiom – that demand is inversely related to price – is obviously true for commodities such as cabbages and carrots. Other things being equal, the lower the price, the more will people want to buy. And the higher the price, the less will people want to buy. However, *ceteris paribus* (other things being equal) what is true for cabbages and carrots will be true for any good or service – demand will be inversely related to price.

The supply side of the market – illustrated by the **supply curve** – shows the actual and potential sales of sterling. The supply curve is shown to be upward sloping, indicating that – as with cabbages and carrots – supply will be positively related to price. The higher the price, the more will be supplied.

Figure 7.1

The foreign exchange market for sterling

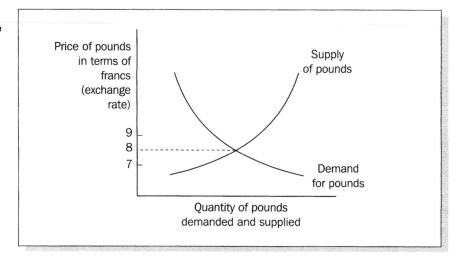

Of course, transactions in the foreign exchange market are carried out by foreign exchange dealers whose function is to adjust prices until the number of pounds that people wish to sell is exactly equal to the number of pounds that (other) people wish to buy. Foreign exchange dealers adjust the prices they quote to buyers and sellers until the number of pounds they have to sell is exactly equal to the number of pounds they have to buy. This is achieved in Figure 7.1 at a price of £1 = 8 francs.

Where does the demand for pounds and the supply of pounds come from? Well, people wishing to buy British exports will have to pay for those exports in sterling. French buyers of Scotch whisky (a British export), for example, will have to convert francs into pounds – they will have to sell francs to acquire pounds. Thus the *demand for pounds comes principally from the demand for British exports*. Other things being equal, the higher the demand for British exports, the higher will be the demand for pounds on foreign exchange markets.

The supply of pounds comes principally from people living in Britain who wish to buy foreign imports. They will have to sell pounds (supply pounds) in order to acquire francs, dollars, Deutschmarks or whatever. Thus if you go into Safeways or your local off-licence and buy a bottle of French wine, in so doing you increase the demand for francs on foreign exchange markets and you increase the supply of pounds to foreign exchange markets. At some stage, pounds will have to be converted into francs to pay the French wine producer.

Thus the demand for imports into Britain and exports from Britain will affect the supply and demand for pounds. However, note that, in addition to trade in goods (called **visible trade**), of almost equal importance to many countries is **trade in services** (sometimes known as **invisible trade**). For example, American tourists visiting London will have to buy pounds for spending during their visit. This tourism is one of the UK's *invisible exports*.

PAUSE FOR THOUGHT *Imagine the following news item:*

Dateline: Paris – January 1996
France has defied public opinion around the world by continuing to conduct underground nuclear tests at Muraroa atoll in the South Pacific. In disgust at French action, consumer groups around the world have urged a boycott of all French goods. In the last few weeks and months, sales of a whole range of French goods – from wine to cars and clothing – have declined disastrously. The French balance of trade has fallen so far into the red that the franc has been forced into a humiliating exit from the exchange rate mechanism of the EMS, a move which has led to the resignation of French Premier Jacques Chirac.

Why didn't it happen?

Well, there *was* widespread revulsion at the French tests, and consumer groups *did* urge a boycott of French goods. With the exception of a very few goods which were obviously of Gallic origin, however, it was rather difficult for consumers to identify which goods were in fact French exports. Consumers vented their wrath on the French Golden Delicious. Sales of these slumped, and to get rid of their surpluses French apple producers were forced to slash prices. This led to complaints from English apple producers that Golden Delicious were being dumped on the market at below the cost of production, threatening their livelihood.

ACTIVITY **2**

Using supply and demand analysis, illustrate the effect on the foreign exchange market *for francs* if there is indeed a decline in demand for French goods (sketch the foreign exchange market for francs). Which of the two curves will shift, and in which direction? What will happen to the value of the franc?

Check with answers/suggestions at the back of the book.

UK or GB?

In this part of the text, the terms 'UK' and 'Britain' tend to be used interchangeably. Strictly speaking, however, they should not be, since 'UK' refers to the *United Kingdom of Great Britain and Northern Ireland* and 'Britain' refers to England, Scotland and Wales only – that is, it excludes Northern Ireland.

You will find that most published statistics – such as trade statistics and figures for GDP and GNP – relate to the UK, although curiously, statistics for employment and unemployment normally relate to Great Britain. The difference in coverage is not very significant. The population of Northern Ireland in 1996 was about 2 million out of a total population for the UK of about 58 million.

Why do statistics for trade and GNP normally relate to the UK as a whole, whereas employment statistics are often reported for Great Britain only.

7.5 The current and capital account

Trade in goods and services makes up the **current account** of the balance of payments. In addition to this, there are **capital account** transactions which will also affect the demand for pounds and the supply of pounds. The essence of a capital account transaction is that it involves the *change of ownership of an asset,* which often then gives rise to current account transactions in future years.

For example, suppose a French utility company acquires a majority shareholding in one of the water and sewerage companies of England and Wales. It will have to pay for these shares in pounds – it will have to sell francs to buy pounds, in order to buy the shares. The ownership of these British assets, formerly British owned, thus passes to a French company. In future years, if dividends are paid on the shares, this will give rise to a current account transaction when the dividends paid in sterling are converted into francs.

The composition of the current and capital accounts is explained more fully in Chapter 8.

ACTIVITY **3**

State what effect the following will have on the *demand for pounds* or the *supply of pounds* on foreign exchange markets. State in each case whether the transaction will be recorded on the *current* account or the *capital* account of the balance of payments. Assume *ceteris paribus* throughout.

(a) More British people decide to take up motorcycling. (The Japanese have an 80 per cent share of the market for motorcycles.)
(b) An exceptionally cold and dreary winter encourages many British people to take a winter break in Spain.
(c) A famous British novelist receives a Nobel Prize for literature (which is worth several million Swedish kronor).
(d) BMW purchases a majority shareholding in the Rover car company.
(e) A government report reveals that eating British beef may involve risk to health.

Check with answers/suggestions at the back of the book.

In London in the summer, everywhere you look there are foreign tourists. They are an example of invisible trade – true or false?

7.6 Flexible and fixed exchange rates

Suppose that British people develop a penchant for holidays in France. Since this is an import of an invisible service, it will lead to an increase in the supply of pounds on foreign exchange markets – shown in **Figure 7.2** as a rightward *shift* in the supply of pounds as British people convert their pounds into francs for spending on their French holiday. At the pre-existing exchange rate of £1 = 8 francs, this will cause an excess supply of pounds.

The consequences of this will depend upon the type of exchange rate regime in operation. In a **flexible exchange rate** regime (otherwise known as a **floating** exchange rate), the excess supply of pounds will cause the value of the pound to float down, as foreign exchange dealers mark down the pound to encourage dealers to buy and discourage them from selling. In the same way as an excess supply of strawberries causes the price of strawberries to fall, so an excess supply of sterling causes the price of sterling to fall. The price adjusts so as to re-establish equilibrium in the market.

In contrast, in a **fixed exchange rate** regime, the authorities commit themselves to the maintenance of a particular exchange rate – known as a **par value** or **parity**. Suppose in this example that the authorities are committed to maintaining a parity of £1 = 8 francs. As can be seen from Figure 7.2, there is an excess supply of pounds at this rate. The authorities themselves will have to buy up this excess supply in order to preserve the parity. This they will do by buying pounds, paying for them with francs and other foreign currencies from their stock of foreign exchange reserves, which they keep for this express purpose. This **intervention** in the foreign exchange market will take place continuously – on some days, when there is an excess supply of pounds, the authorities will buy pounds, and on other days, when there is an excess demand for pounds, they will sell pounds (and acquire foreign currencies to replenish their reserves). Intervention buying to preserve a fixed parity of £1 = 8 francs is illustrated in *Figure 7.3.*

The best-known example of a fixed exchange rate regime is the **exchange rate mechanism** of the **European Monetary System** (the ERM of the EMS). In the late 1980s and early 1990s, sterling was a *de facto* member of this fixed exchange rate club (though Britain was never formally committed to membership), but since September 1992 the value of the pound has been allowed to float.

Figure 7.2
An increase in the supply of pounds on the foreign exchange market

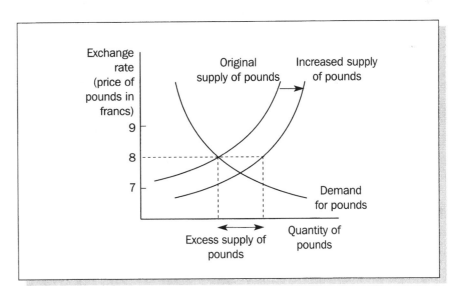

Figure 7.3

**Intervention buying
mops up excess
supply of pounds**

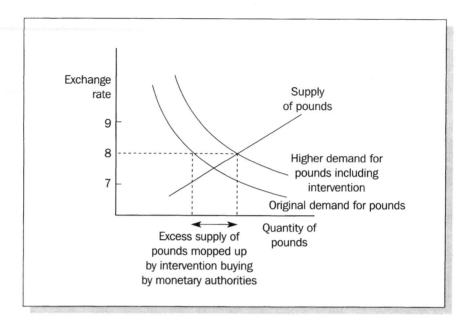

Note that the value of the pound can be expressed *vis-à-vis* the Deutschmark, the dollar, the yen or any other single currency, or it can be expressed against a *basket* of other currencies. The Mark is now the foreign currency against which the value of sterling is most often measured, since Germany is Britain's largest export market. Moreover, trade with the countries of the European Union (EU) dominates Britain's foreign trade, and the Mark is the most important currency in the EU. Several other EU countries – notably France – keep the value of their currency fixed to the Mark, and hence by expressing the value of the pound in terms of Deutschmarks, one in effect expresses its value *vis-à-vis* a basket of EU currencies.

In the light of the preceding paragraph, recall that we asked why the value of the pound had fallen *vis-à-vis* the franc from around 10 francs in 1992 to 7.5 francs in 1995. The answer to this is now apparent. Since 1992 the value of the pound in terms of Deutschmarks has fallen from a parity of DM2.95 = £1 to about DM2.25 = £1 in early 1996. Since the franc has been pegged to the Mark this has meant that the value of sterling in terms of francs has fallen by a similar amount. This does not, of course, explain why the sterling–Mark rate has depreciated by such a large amount. There is no simple monocausal explanation of this, though the following section provides some useful insights.

7.7 Internal and external purchasing power

The **external purchasing power** of the pound is the amount of other currencies – francs, dollars, marks, etc. – that can be bought with one pound at the bank or the *bureau de change*. In other words, it is the exchange rate.

The **internal purchasing power** of the pound is the amount of goods and services that can be bought with one pound in the shops in the UK. The faster the rate of domestic inflation, the faster is the fall in the internal purchasing power of the pound.

Clearly there must be some relationship between a currency's internal value and its external value. Countries with a high rate of domestic inflation will find inevitably that the external value – the exchange rate – will also fall.

CASE
ILLUSTRATION
......●......

Israel in the 1980s

The link between a currency's internal value and its external value can be seen most clearly in those countries which have experienced exceptionally high rates of domestic inflation. One such was Israel in the 1980s.

As can be seen from column 1 of Table 7.3, between 1980 and 1990 the price level in Israel increased 500-fold (an increase of 50,000 per cent). Column 4 shows that the change in the exchange rate also works out to be exactly the same – a 500-fold fall. Of course, in general we would not expect our calculations to reveal an *exact* correspondence between the fall in the internal value of a currency and the fall in its external value, but the general picture is clear from these figures.

table 7.3

The link between domestic inflation and the exchange rate

	Price index 1990 = 100 (1)	Inflation rate (approx., %) (2)	Exchange rate (3)	Exchange rate index 1990 = 100 (4)
1980	0.2	..	0.0051	0.2
1981	0.3	50	0.0114	0.6
1982	0.7	133	0.0243	1
1983	1.8	157	0.0562	3
1984	8.5	370	0.2932	14
1985	34.4	305	1.1788	58
1986	50.9	50	1.4878	74
1987	61.0	20	1.5946	79
1988	71.0	16	1.5989	79
1989	85.3	20	1.9164	95
1990	100.0	17	2.0162	100

Column (3) shows the exchange rate in New Sheqalim per US dollar. Column (4) expresses these data as an index with 1990 = 100, so that column (4) can be directly compared with column (1).
Source: *International Financial Statistics Yearbook*, 1995

Closer inspection of the data reveals how the very high inflation rates of 1982–85 result in an equally rapid depreciation of the New Sheqalim, the currency which was introduced because the old shekel was worth so little. After the mid-1980s, as the rate of inflation moderates, so does the fall in the external value of the New Sheqalim.

To see why there is a link between the internal and external purchasing power of a currency, consider the following hypothetical example involving two countries, Britain and France, which trade freely between themselves. Say that a typical good – say, a jar of coffee – costs £1 in the shops in Britain and 10 francs in the shops in Paris. Further suppose that the exchange rate between the two countries is a floating rate and that initially it is £1 = 10 francs. Thus for a coffee drinker in Britain, it makes no difference whether he buys his coffee in the supermarket in Britain, or converts his pounds into francs at the bank and then takes a trip to France to buy coffee in the supermarket there. Either way, he will be paying the same price.

Suppose, however, that Britain and France experience a different rate of domestic inflation. Suppose France has a 20 per cent rate of domestic inflation, whereas Britain has stable prices. The price of coffee in the shops in France rises in line with French prices generally, and therefore increases to 12 francs. If the exchange rate were to remain unchanged, it would pay French people to convert their francs into sterling at the bank (at the old exchange rate of £1 = 10F) and take a trip to Britain to buy coffee there at a price of only £1. In effect, therefore, they pay only 10F for the coffee in comparison to the 12F they would have paid in the shops in France.

Now suppose that this is true not just for coffee, but for goods and services generally. Entrepreneurs will buy goods in Britain for resale in France. There will be profits to be made as long as there is a discrepancy between the internal value of the franc and its external value. Thus imports into France (from Britain) increase. The supply of francs on foreign exchange markets increases and – given that we have assumed that the pound/franc rate is floating – the franc will float down to a rate of £1 = 12F.

At this new exchange rate, it will no longer be profitable to buy up coffee (or goods generally) in Britain for resale in France. The new external value reflects the internal purchasing power of the two currencies relative to one another. Thus we see how, if one country has a higher domestic rate of inflation than the other, this will be reflected in a change in the exchange rate, *provided* the exchange rate is free to vary.

This goes some way towards explaining movements in exchange rates in the longer term. The external value of a currency must reflect its internal value, and countries which experience higher than average rates of domestic inflation will see their currencies fall in value on foreign exchange markets. The notion that there must be a correspondence between the external and internal value of a currency is sometimes referred to as the **purchasing power parity theorem** of exchange rate determination. It is based on the so-called **Law of One Price** – the idea that a particular good, such as a jar of coffee, cannot be sold at different prices on different markets if trade is possible between those two markets. Only *one* price is possible in the long run.

However, it would be a mistake to believe that there is an exact correspondence between internal and external values – or even that the correspondence is particularly close. Some currencies, such as the Swiss franc, are expensive to buy on foreign exchange markets when one compares their value on foreign exchange markets with their internal value. For example, consider the data shown in ***Table 7.4***. These are estimates of comparative price levels calculated by converting pounds into the various national currencies *using market exchange rates*. If you converted your pounds into Swiss francs and took a trip to Switzerland, you would find that prices in the shops there were about 62 per cent higher on average than those in Britain. In other words, the external value of the Swiss franc is high in comparison to its internal value (its internal purchasing power).

ACTIVITY **4**
••••••••••••

(a) If you wanted a 'cheap' foreign holiday, which of the countries listed in Table 7.4 would you choose to visit?

(b) German and (particularly) Japanese tourists always seem to have lots of money to spend when they are visiting Britain. Explain why this appears to be the case, using the data in Table 7.4.

Check with answers/suggestions at the back of the book.

table 7.4

Comparative price levels, June 1996

Canada	88
United States	95
Japan	165
Australia	107
Austria	126
Belgium	119
Denmark	152
France	127
Germany[1]	128
Greece	97
Ireland	102
Italy	102
Netherlands	120
Norway	143
Portugal	82
Spain	98
Sweden	147
Switzerland	162
Turkey	49
UK	**100**

[1]Data refer to West Germany.
Source: OECD, *Main Economic Indicators*, September 1996.

Summary
• • • • • • • • • • •

The last half-century has seen an increasing globalisation of production. A concomitant of this is that economies have become more open, and as a result world trade has grown more rapidly than world output. The doctrine of comparative advantage illustrates the benefits to be derived from specialisation and exchange – the so-called gains from trade. Countries benefit from specialising in those goods and services in which they have a *comparative advantage*, even though they may have an *absolute advantage* (or disadvantage) in all goods.

Trade between nations involves the exchange of one currency for another. A market exchange rate is determined by the demand for a currency relative to the supply. Exchange rates can be freely floating (flexible rates) or fixed (such as the fixed exchange rates in the EMS).

Transactions which affect the demand for currencies (and the supply of them) relate to *visible trade* (trade in goods) and to *invisible trade* (trade in services, such as tourism). These appear on the current account of the balance of payments. In addition, items which appear on the capital account of the balance of payments relate to those transactions which involve the change of ownership of an asset, such as the sale of shares in a company.

The *external* purchasing power of the pound is the amount of foreign currency that can be bought with one pound (that is, the exchange rate). The *internal* purchasing power of the pound corresponds to the amount of goods and services that can be bought with one pound in the UK. In general, a currency's external value will not be exactly equal to its internal value. However, if they are not approximately equal then forces will arise which tend to make them move towards each other.

REVIEW QUESTIONS

1 An increase in foreign sales of British steel will *ceteris paribus* increase/reduce the demand for pounds on foreign exchange markets. If the value of the pound is market determined, it will therefore move up/down. This means that the value of the pound has appreciated/depreciated.

2 Suppose initially that the pound were to trade at a parity (that is, a fixed exchange rate) of £1 = DM2.5. Now suppose that holders of pounds decide to sell them. This results in:
   (a) an excess supply of pounds which can only be absorbed by intervention buying on the part of the Bank of England
   (b) an increase in demand for pounds, which means that the Central Bank has to sell them
   (c) a reduction in the demand for pounds, which means that the value of the pound goes down?

3 What effect will the following have on the demand for pounds and/or the supply. Indicate also whether the effect will appear on the *current account* or the *capital account* of the balance of payments (and assume *ceteris paribus*, of course):
   (a) A talented British footballer is signed by an Italian football club, who pay a £1 million transfer fee to the British club.

    (b) More Swedish students come to London to study.

    (c) An important international athletics event is held in Birmingham.

    (d) A talented French footballer (and poet) who plays for a British club is left some money in his grandmother's will. He uses the money to buy shares in ICI (a British company).

    (e) ICI pays a large dividend to shareholders. The talented French footballer mentioned above decides to use the money to take a holiday in America.

4 Suppose there is a fixed exchange rate between the pound and the Danish krone, but that the rate of inflation in Denmark is somewhat higher than that in the UK. Which of the following statements are true?

    (a) Over time and other things being equal, the external value of the krone will be worth more than its internal value.

    (b) Britain will become an increasingly attractive holiday destination for Danes.

    (c) The value of the pound (in terms of kroner) will stay the same in nominal terms but in real terms it will be worth less.

5 Suppose a UK resident travels to Germany in August 1992 and then takes a second trip in October 1992. Is he likely to find on his second trip that:

    (a) prices in the shops in Germany are lower than previously

    (b) prices in Germany seem to be higher than previously

    (c) there appears to have been no change in prices in Germany?
    (The pound left the ERM in September 1992.)

Key concepts
....

The following key concepts have been introduced in this chapter. Make sure you understand the meaning and significance of each of them. They are listed here in the order in which they first appear, and the page number where they appear is also given. You will find these key concepts in section headings or in **bold** in the text. Each chapter contains a list of key concepts and you may find these particularly useful for revision purposes.

internationalisation	(p. 95)
globalisation	(p. 95)
open economies	(p. 95)
autarky	(p. 95)
transfer of technology	(p. 96)
economies of scale	(p. 96)
specialisation	(p. 97)
unit labour requirements	(p. 97)
comparative advantage	(p. 97)
opportunity cost	(p. 98)
gains from trade	(p. 98)
appreciation (of exchange rate)	(p. 99)
depreciation (of exchange rate)	(p. 99)
perfectly competitive market	(p. 99)

demand curve/demand schedule   (p. 99)
supply curve   (p. 99)
visible trade   (p. 100)
invisible trade (trade in services)   (p. 100)
current account   (p. 102)
capital account   (p. 102)
flexible (floating) exchange rate   (p. 103)
fixed exchange rate   (p. 103)
par value (parity)   (p. 103)
intervention (in foreign exchange market)   (p. 103)
exchange rate mechanism   (p. 103)
European Monetary System   (p. 103)
external purchasing power   (p. 105)
internal purchasing power   (p. 105)
purchasing power parity theorem   (p. 106)
Law of One Price   (p. 106)

Sources of information

The basic source of information for balance of payments data for the UK is the so-called Pink Book, *UK Balance of Payments*. Like its counterpart the Blue Book, it is published annually in the autumn. *Economic Trends* also contains data relating to current account transactions and indices of competitiveness. Data for other countries are to be found in *OECD Main Economic Indicators* and in *International Financial Statistics*.

More information on these and other sources is to be found in the **Guide to Statistical Sources** at the back of this book.

CHAPTER **8**
•••••••••••••••

Policies to correct balance of payments deficits

Objectives:
•••••••••••••••

This chapter will enable you to:

➤ distinguish between the various parts of the current and capital accounts

➤ appreciate why a balance for official financing arises

➤ evaluate the consequences of chronic balance of trade deficits

➤ evaluate the merits of the policies that can be used to tackle a balance of trade deficit

➤ understand the effect that the exchange rate has on competitiveness.

8.1 Debits and credits
8.2 The current account
8.3 The capital account
8.4 The balance for official financing (change in reserves)
8.5 Autonomous and accommodating transactions
8.6 Interim summary
8.7 Current and capital account balances
8.8 Is a current account deficit 'a bad thing'?
8.9 Interest rates
8.10 Deflation (by fiscal means)
8.11 Tariffs and quotas
8.12 Devaluation
8.13 The elasticities approach
8.14 The relative profitability approach
8.15 Competitiveness

8.1 Debits and credits
••••••••••••••••••••••••••••

The UK balance of payments is a record of all transactions which give rise to the exchange of pounds for some other currency on foreign exchange markets. One can think of the balance of payments in terms of an *account* involving debits and credits.

A **credit** is a transaction which adds to the demand for pounds on foreign exchange markets. Thus a British export – such as the sale of Scotch whisky to Japan – is a credit on the UK balance of payments account.

A **debit** is the opposite to a credit, so as you would expect, any transaction which adds to the supply of pounds on foreign exchange markets is recorded as a debit on the UK balance of payments account. The purchase by a London resident of a new BMW motor car (a foreign import) will be recorded as a debit on the UK balance of payments account.

By convention, credits have plus signs and debits have minus signs.

The term 'balance of payments deficit' is used loosely to describe a situation in which debits exceed credits – that is, where the total supply of pounds exceeds the total demand for them. However, the system of double entry bookkeeping requires accounts to be drawn up in such a way that they always balance – total debits always equals total credits. So it is with the balance of payments accounts. Indeed, if you think about the currency transactions which have taken place, it is obvious that the number of pounds bought must equal the number of pounds sold. So what exactly is meant by a 'balance of payments deficit'?

To understand this we must look in more detail at how the balance of payments accounts are constructed. As we know, the balance of payments consists of current and capital accounts. We shall start by examining the current account.

8.2 The current account

The current account is made up of three parts, the first two relating to trade and the third relating to financial flows. Specifically, these three parts are concerned with:

➤ visible trade
➤ 'invisible' trade (services)
➤ interest, profits and dividends.

Each of these is explained in more detail below.

Visible trade

This is the most familiar and the easiest to understand. It relates to tangible goods such as coal, cabbages, cars and computers – and computer software, even though you cannot actually see it.

'Invisible' trade

This is often referred to as trade in *services*. It relates to things such as tourism, shipping and civil aviation, and financial services such as insurance and banking.

The balance of trade

The visible trade balance – that is, the difference between exports and imports of goods – and the invisible trade balance together make up what is correctly called the **trade balance**. However, the term 'trade balance' and related ones such as 'trade gap' are often used incorrectly to refer to visible trade only. In fact, the monthly 'trade figures', which are published and usually reported on the television news, relate only to visible trade, although the word 'visible' is often omitted in reporting. At other times the word 'trade' is used to relate to both goods *and services* – that is, it relates to both visible and invisible trade – and it is in this sense that we shall use it.

Interest, profits and dividends

The trade balance, even if it includes both visible and invisible items, is not the same thing as the current account balance, since the latter includes an item called **interest, profits and dividends** – IPD for short. This is not related in any way to trade. Trade is all about selling somebody some good or service. In contrast, the flow of IPD results by virtue of the ownership of some foreign asset (if the flow is inward) or by virtue of the foreign ownership of some British asset (if the flow is outward).

For example, suppose a British resident owns shares in Nestlé – a Swiss company. The dividends on these shares will be paid in Swiss francs, which the British resident will convert into pounds. This transaction adds to the demand for pounds on foreign exchange markets, and is shown in the current account under the heading 'interest, profits and dividends'.

In Chapter 4 we explained that the difference between gross domestic product and gross *national* product was an item called *net property income from abroad*. This is, in fact, the net flow of interest, profits and dividends.

DID YOU KNOW?
*The term **invisibles** is not synonymous with 'invisible trade'. The word 'invisibles' is used to refer to all current account transactions other than those involving trade in goods. That is, it refers to invisible trade, flows of IPD and any other current account transaction which does not fit neatly anywhere else. For example, the UK's net contribution to the EU, which is known as a **transfer**, would be included under the heading of 'invisibles', but would not be included in 'invisible trade'.*

8.3 The capital account

The other part of the balance of payments account is known as the capital account. This records transactions involving the change of ownership of physical and financial assets. For example, when Harrods department store in London was purchased by Egyptian businessmen the Al Fayed brothers, the purchase would have been recorded as a credit on the capital account of the UK balance of payments, since it added to the demand for pounds. Note that what was being transferred was the *ownership* of an asset – the asset itself stayed in Knightsbridge.

Normally a capital account transaction involving the acquisition of an asset will give rise to future flows of interest, profits and dividends, which, as we have just seen, will themselves be shown on the current account.

8.4 The balance for official financing (change in reserves)

The capital account includes one other item which is the key to understanding why the balance of payments always balances – that is, why the number of pounds bought equals the number of pounds sold. This item can be called the **balance for official financing** or, more simply, the **change in official reserves**. The change in official reserves results from the intervention undertaken by the Bank of England, the purpose of which is to preserve a fixed exchange rate parity or in some way *manage* the parity.

In theory, under a floating exchange rate regime there is no declared parity and no intervention, and therefore the change in reserves (the balance for official financing) is zero. In practice, however, this is not so. Even under an exchange rate regime in which there is no declared parity, the central bank does intervene to nudge the exchange rate up or down, or sometimes just to replenish its reserves of foreign currency when it sees an opportunity to buy them cheaply.

8.5 Autonomous and accommodating transactions

The transactions undertaken by the central bank to ensure that the official parity is maintained can be called **accommodating transactions**. The change in the stock of reserves is what results from these official transactions. All other transactions, which of course take place at the behest of private individuals and companies, can be called **autonomous transactions**. With this in mind, we are finally in a position to understand what is meant by the term 'balance of payments deficit'. It refers to the balance of autonomous transactions – in other words, the balance of all the foreign exchange market transactions with the exception of those transactions undertaken by the central bank.

8.6 Interim summary

It is worth pausing at this point just to make sure that the concepts that have been introduced are well understood. We can do this by recapping on the various types of 'deficit' that we have talked about.

➤ **visible trade deficit** – the excess of imports of goods over exports of goods
➤ **trade deficit** – the excess of imports of goods *and services* over exports of goods and services
➤ **current account deficit** – the excess of debits over credits on the current account. The current account is made up of trade in goods and services, interest, profits and dividends and transfers, such as the UK's contribution to the EU.
➤ **balance of payments deficit/surplus** – the balance on the current and the capital accounts added together.

ACTIVITY **1**

Suppose every single part of the balance of payments were to be in deficit. List the following in terms of ascending order of magnitude.

➤ a balance of payments deficit
➤ a visible trade deficit
➤ a trade deficit
➤ a current account deficit

Check with answers/suggestions at the back of the book.

DID YOU KNOW?
The balance of payments data for the UK economy are contained within a publication called The United Kingdom Balance of Payments. *It is normally referred to as the* **Pink Book** *because of the colour of its cover, and to distinguish it from the* **Blue Book** *(UK National Accounts).*

As with any other publication, the way in which the data are presented in the Pink Book tends to evolve over time, as does the terminology. Some of the terms we have used – such as autonomous and accommodating transactions, and the balance for official financing – tend to have fallen out of favour in recent years, reflecting the less deliberate pursuit of a fixed parity since the abandonment of the ERM parity in September 1992..

8.7 Current and capital account balances

••

We can now illustrate these concepts using the data in Table 8.1, which shows the current and capital account balances for the UK for the period 1983–93.

Note that there is a clear tendency for a deficit on one to be cancelled out by a surplus on the other. This is particularly evident in the period 1987–91, when large current account deficits were more or less offset by correspondingly large capital account surpluses. In fact, in an accounting sense, the current balance and the capital account balance must be equal and opposite in sign. The statistics would show this to be the case if there were no inaccuracies in recording the transactions.

The **balancing item**, shown in column (4), reflects the fact that some transactions are recorded inaccurately or at the wrong time, or are simply omitted. In our table, the balancing item is the sum which is necessary to make the sum of the current balance and the capital balance equal zero. That is, in **Table 8.1,** columns (1), (2) and (4) sum to zero. As can be seen, the balancing item is sometimes quite large – the data are in billions of pounds, and in one year a sum of £7 billion was required to make the accounts balance.

The capital account balance includes the change in reserves which is shown in column (3). What should be noted is that there is no correlation, either positive or negative, between the current balance on its own and the change in reserves. A current account deficit does not automatically lead to a run-down of foreign exchange reserves. This is because the autonomous transactions in assets and liabilities which make up the capital account will also affect the

table 8.1
Current and capital account balances, 1983–93 (£bn)

	Current balance (1)	Capital account balance (2)	Of which, change in reserves[1] (3)	Balancing item (4)
1983	3.5	−4.5	0.6	1.0
1984	1.5	−8.5	0.9	7.0
1985	2.2	−3.7	−1.7	1.5
1986	−0.9	−3.1	−2.9	4.0
1987	−5.0	6.7	−12.0	−1.7
1988	−16.6	11.0	−2.8	5.6
1989	−22.5	19.6	5.4	2.9
1990	−19.0	18.2	−0.1	0.8
1991	−8.0	8.6	−2.7	−0.4
1992	−9.8	3.4	1.4	6.5
1993	−10.3	8.3	−0.7	2.0

[1] Additions to reserves are indicated by a plus sign, drawings on are indicated by a minus.
Source: *UK Balance of Payments*, 1994.

demand for and supply of pounds. It is the *total* (autonomous) demand for and supply of pounds which determines the need for intervention on foreign exchange markets and therefore the change in reserves which results.

8.8 Is a current account deficit 'a bad thing'?

Economists like to pride themselves on their objectivity. They maintain that economics is a **positive** rather than a **normative** science – normative in this context meaning a science which contains value judgements about what is good or bad and about what *ought* to be. In contrast, a positive science confines itself to what *is* rather than what ought to be. It is somewhat heretical, therefore, to pose questions about whether such-and-such is a 'good thing' or a 'bad thing'.

However, we are now in a position to say what is, and we leave it to the reader to form his or her own judgement about what ought to be. Current account deficits, as we have seen, are normally accompanied by capital account surpluses. A capital account surplus means that on the capital account the demand for pounds exceeds the supply. The reason for this is that the demand by foreigners for British assets exceeds the demand by British residents for foreign assets. The implication of this is that the UK's ownership of net foreign assets declines.

It is this rundown of assets that enables UK households to *consume* goods and services in excess of those being *produced* by the UK economy. This is not sustainable in the long term, since – logically – there will come a time when there are no more assets left to sell. It is for this reason that current account deficits are regarded, if not as a 'bad thing', then certainly as something which cannot be maintained indefinitely.

Table 8.2 shows that the Lawson boom of the late 1980s in effect wiped out UK holdings of *net* overseas assets, which fell from 20 per cent of GDP to zero. One might conclude that this was 'not a good thing'. *You* might say this, but in a text on positive economics, I could not possibly comment.

The rest of this chapter is devoted to a consideration of policies which can be used to address the problem of current account deficits.

table 8.2

Current balance and net overseas assets, 1985–94

	Current balance		Net overseas assets	
	£bn	% of GDP	£bn	% of GDP
1985	+2.2	+0.6	72.7	20.4
1986	−0.9	−0.2	90.8	23.6
1987	−5.0	−1.1	78.3	18.6
1988	−16.6	−3.5	56.9	12.1
1989	−22.5	−4.4	47.1	9.1
1990	−19.0	−3.4	8.0	1.5
1991	−8.2	−1.4	4.8	0.8
1992	−9.8	−1.6	-6.4	-1.1
1993	−11.0	−1.7	27.0	4.2
1994	−1.7	−0.3	23.3	3.5

Source: *Economic Trends.*

8.9 Interest rates
....

Interest rates are the most powerful instrument in the hands of the policy-maker faced with a balance of payments deficit. An increase in interest rates in the UK will affect both the capital account and the current account of the balance of payments – each of them being affected in a way which will reduce the excess supply of pounds on foreign exchange markets.

On the capital account, an increase in interest rates in London in comparison to Paris, New York or Tokyo will make UK securities more attractive than those sold in France, the USA or Japan, since UK securities will now be offering a higher return than those available elsewhere. Even if foreign investors choose simply to put their money in the bank, British banks will now be offering a higher return, and therefore these investors will convert their francs, dollars or yen into pounds – that is, they will demand pounds – for deposit in a sterling interest-bearing account. Notice, however, that interest rates will have to be kept permanently higher than those in other countries for this policy to be effective. Capital is a very mobile factor of production and, as soon as interest rates in London are lowered, capital will flow out again, just as quickly as it flowed in.

An increase in interest rates will also affect the current account of the balance of payments, since an increase in interest rates is a deflationary policy – that is, it will reduce demand in the economy by making it more expensive for individuals and companies to borrow money to spend on consumption or investment. This will effectively reduce the demand for all goods and services, including imported goods and services. Unfortunately, it reduces the demand for domestically produced goods and services as well, which, other things being equal, will have an adverse effect on output and employment at home. That is, it will cause higher unemployment and reduced living standards within the UK economy.

8.10 Deflation (by fiscal means)
....

An increase in interest rates can be thought of as a deflationary monetary policy. In addition to this powerful monetary instrument, there are equally powerful fiscal instruments which are capable of reducing domestic demand and therefore the demand for imported goods and services. The fiscal instruments are taxation and government spending. As we saw in Chapter 3, an increase in taxation is a withdrawal of spending from the circular flow, which will reduce the overall size of the flow of spending. Similarly, a cut in government spending withdraws spending from the circular flow, leading to a fall in demand for both imported and domestically produced goods. As with an increase in interest rates, therefore, a policy of fiscal deflation has a beneficial effect on the trade deficit (in the sense that it reduces it), but a detrimental effect on domestic output and employment.

8.11 Tariffs and quotas

A **tariff** is a tax on imports. A **quota** is a limit on the physical number of imports of a particular type allowed into the country (such as a limit on the number of Japanese cars imported into Britain). However, the majority of the UK's trade is now with other members of the EU – about 57 per cent of the total in 1994 – and tariffs and quotas cannot legally be used against EU partners without breaking European law. For the remaining non-EU trade, the UK is committed formally to a policy of reducing barriers to trade. The UK is a member of the World Trade Organisation, the successor to GATT (the General Agreement on Tariffs and Trade), which was an international organisation set up to reduce trade barriers. As such, the imposition of tariffs and quotas cannot be seen as a policy which for practical purposes is available to the policy-maker in the UK.

8.12 Devaluation

The term **devaluation** is used here as a convenient shorthand. In terms of strict terminology, a currency is said to be *devalued* if the policy-maker decides to change the parity – that is, to bring about a step change (downwards) in a nominally fixed exchange rate. Devaluations therefore only occur – paradoxically – when countries are pursuing a fixed exchange rate policy. The term **depreciation**, on the other hand, is used to refer to the downward movement of a floating exchange rate. Thus, for example, in November 1967 there was a step *devaluation* of the pound from a fixed parity of $2.80 = £1 to a lower parity of $2.40 = £1. In contrast, in September 1992 the pound was allowed to float and it *depreciated* over the next few months and years from a starting point of DM2.95 to around DM2.3 by late 1995.

Whether we are considering a step change or a gradual decline, however, the central question is whether the fall in the exchange rate brings beneficial effects to the economy, and particularly to the balance of trade, or whether these effects are detrimental.

There are two ways of analysing the effect of devaluation on the trade balance, each based on a particular view of how the prices of exports and imports are set. We shall refer to these as the elasticities approach and the relative profitability approach, and we deal with each of them below.

8.13 The elasticities approach

Those readers who have completed a course in microeconomics will already have encountered – and hopefully mastered – the concept of elasticity. Those who have not should just take a deep breath and read on.

The word 'elasticity' when used in economics refers to the responsiveness of one variable to another – for example, the responsiveness of demand to changes in price. If a small change in price results in a large change in the amount demanded, demand is said to be **elastic** (that is, responsive). In contrast, demand is said to be **inelastic** (or unresponsive) if a large change in price results in only a small change in the quantity demanded. The **elasticity coefficient** is defined as follows:

$$\text{Elasticity} = \frac{\text{Percentage change in quantity demanded}}{\text{Percentage change in price}}$$

Note that the number will always be negative, since a fall in price leads to a rise in demand and vice versa. For simplicity, we shall often omit the minus sign.

The elasticity coefficient is a number which expresses the degree of responsiveness. It is helpful to distinguish three 'ranges' for this coefficient as shown in **Table 8.3**, which also summarises what has been said so far.

We shall use the concept of elasticity to analyse what happens to exports following a devaluation. Of course, similar considerations also apply to the demand for imports.

The price elasticity of demand for exports is defined as:

$$E_x = \frac{\text{Percentage change in quantity of exports demanded}}{\text{Percentage change in the foreign currency price of exports}}$$

Note two things. First, the numerator of this expression measures the *quantity* of exports (for example, the number of cars or the number of tonnes of wheat). This can be referred to as the *volume* of exports. The denominator of the expression is measured in foreign currency – we could choose dollars, Deutschmarks, francs or whatever.

Imagine a foreign consumer – a man living in Germany, say – who goes to the shop to buy a new television set. He is faced with a bewildering array of choice – products from Japan, Taiwan, Britain, Sweden and Germany itself. Each of these products has a different specification and a different price, but the choice that he eventually makes will still be based partly on price. Whether he is buying an expensive set or a cheap one, he will want to get value for money.

table 8.3
Elasticity of demand

Value of coefficient	Terminology	Meaning	Example
More than 1 (e.g. 1.3)	Elastic	A *small* change in price results in a *substantial* change in the amount demanded	A 10% change in price leads to a change in demand of 13%
1 (i.e. 1.0)	Unit elasticity	A price change leads to an equal proportionate change in quantity	A 10% change in price leads to a 10% change in the amount demanded
Less than 1 (e.g. 0.8)	Inelastic	A *large* change in price results in only a *small* change in the amount demanded	A 10% change in price leads to a change in demand of only 8%

Now suppose that the pound is devalued by, say, 10 per cent. Further suppose that this leads to a 10 per cent reduction in the DM price of the British product sold on the German market. Whatever its specification, the British product now represents better value for money than previously, and as a result some consumers who would otherwise have bought a Japanese or a German product will now buy the British one.

Suppose lots of German consumers are persuaded to switch to the British product – say that the number of British-made TV sets bought increases by 20 per cent as would be the case if demand were elastic (elasticity coefficient = 2.0). In this case, export revenue (in terms of Deutschmarks) will rise, since although the number of Deutschmarks received per TV will fall by 10 per cent this is more than offset by the 20 per cent increase in the number of units sold, giving UK exporters higher DM revenues than they previously received.

However, suppose that demand were rather inelastic – say the elasticity coefficient were only 0.8. In this case, export revenue would fall, since the increase in sales (8 per cent) is insufficient to offset the 10 per cent fall in revenue received from each unit. Hence UK exporters would end up with lower DM revenues than before.

Finally, consider the special case where the value of the elasticity coefficient is exactly 1. In this case, there will be no change in revenue following a devaluation, since the rise in the number of sets sold will offset exactly the drop in revenue for each unit sold.

To summarise: only if the demand for British exports is elastic (coefficient greater than 1) will the effect of devaluation be to increase export *revenues*. If demand is inelastic (coefficient less than 1), the devaluation will lead to a *drop* in export revenues.

Although this analysis has been conducted in terms of exports, similar considerations apply to imports as well. If the demand for imports is elastic, an increase in the price of imported goods relative to domestically produced ones will cause lots of UK consumers to switch from imports to British-made goods. As a result the UK import bill will be reduced. That is, total spending (in pounds) on imported goods will fall.

CASE
ILLUSTRATION
• • • • • • • • • • • • • •

The J-curve effect

Is the demand for exports sufficiently elastic to ensure that a devaluation will increase export revenues? And is the demand for imports sufficiently elastic to ensure that a devaluation will reduce our import bill? Taken together, are the elasticities sufficiently large to ensure the success of a devaluation – in other words, to guarantee that a devaluation will reduce and eventually eliminate a balance of trade deficit?

Economists have tended to argue that in the short run the answer to these questions is 'no', even though in the longer run it is probably 'yes'. In fact, the immediate effect of a devaluation may be to make matters worse rather than better. This is because it takes time for consumers at home and abroad to adjust to the changed set of relative prices. In the short run, they carry on buying more or less the same amount of goods irrespective of the change in prices. Gradually they do switch away from the goods that are now relatively more expensive, but only in the long run do volumes change sufficiently to ensure that the devaluation is successful.

Figure 8.1
The J curve

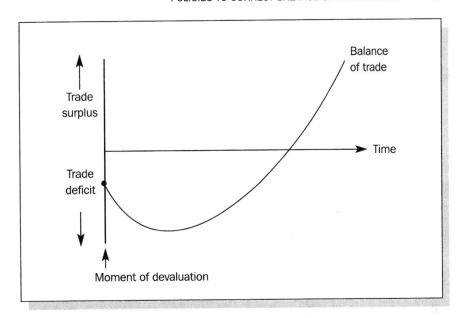

If this is true, it will give rise to what economists call a J-curve effect. The time path of the balance of trade following a devaluation will trace out the letter J as in ***Figure 8.1***. In the short run the curve is downward sloping because the elasticities are rather small. Only after a lag does the balance of trade start to improve, at which point the curve turns upwards.

8.14 The relative profitability approach

In the preceding section, we assumed that a devaluation led to an immediate change in the foreign currency price. That is, when the pound was devalued by 10 per cent the Deutschmark price of UK exports on the German market fell by 10 per cent. However, this will not always be the case. For example, the price of commodities such as oil is more or less determined by world market forces. Individual and rather small producers such as the UK cannot influence the world market price. Therefore, the price of North Sea crude – measured in dollars – will remain unchanged following a devaluation of the pound. What will change, however, is the profitability of North Sea oil exploration, since the value of the oil – measured in sterling – will increase by 10 per cent following a 10 per cent devaluation of the pound.

In the market for oil, the seller – the oil company – is what is known as a **price taker** rather than a **price maker**. Price takers have no discretion about the price that they will charge for their products. They have to accept the ruling market price. However, there are other markets in which sellers do have discretion about the price to charge, but nevertheless choose to respond to a devaluation by maintaining the pre-existing foreign currency price.

In the car market, for example, a 'UK producer' such as Jaguar or Rover will be selling cars on foreign markets which are in direct competition with products from rival manufacturers. Such companies are concerned about the image which their cars project. They wish them to be perceived as quality products (which can therefore be sold at a premium) rather than as products which are in direct competition with the volume producers such as Ford or Toyota. The consumer's perception of quality is *partly* influenced by price – expensive products tend to be perceived as being of high quality and cheap products as being of low quality. Therefore following a devaluation, Rover may decide not to cut its prices abroad, since it has pitched them at what it already considers to be an appropriate level relative to rival 'quality' manufacturers.

What does change, of course, is the profitability of selling abroad. For example, suppose that prior to a devaluation a Rover car sells for DM30,000 on the German market. At the pre-devaluation exchange rate of, say, £1 = DM3 this is equivalent to

$$\frac{30,000}{3} = £10,000$$

If the pound is devalued to £1 = DM2.50, but the foreign currency price is kept the same, the sterling revenue from each car sold on the German market now becomes

$$\frac{30,000}{2.5} = £12,000$$

This increase in the profitability of exporting will encourage firms such as Rover to concentrate their sales efforts on the export market rather than the home market, since exporting now becomes more profitable than was previously the case.

Which of these two models of the effect of a devaluation is the more appropriate? Well, it depends on the sort of products, being sold and the sort of markets they are sold on. For many types of product, however, the relative profitability approach is probably more realistic. At the time of the 1995 Budget (November 1995), the Red Book stated:

When sterling depreciated earlier this year, exporters maintained their prices in foreign currency terms, again taking the benefit in the form of higher profit margins. This pattern is consistent with the export price of standard products being determined on world markets, rather than being set by UK firms. High profit margins will increase the incentive to supply overseas markets. (p. 33)

8.15 Competitiveness

In the sense that it is used here, the word **competitiveness** refers to the ability of UK producers to sell their products on foreign markets (and to sell on home markets when in competition with foreign imports). There are various indices of competitiveness, but none of these measures competitiveness in absolute terms. Rather they measure *changes* in competitiveness relative to some arbitrarily chosen period in the past. There are a number of different approaches.

Relative export prices

Consider first the approach which looks at export prices. Foreign consumers face a choice when they buy products. Their decision to buy a British product in preference to one manufactured in Germany, Japan or the USA will depend on a whole host of factors – styling, quality and delivery dates. Most importantly, however, the *price* of the British product in comparison to one manufactured elsewhere will be a major consideration in their decision. The relative price which they face will, of course, be expressed in local currency. Hence, for example, for a German consumer we could define **relative export prices** as

$$\frac{\text{Price of UK exports measured in DM}}{\text{Price of other countries' exports measured in DM}}$$

Notice that both numerator and denominator are measured in a common currency – in this case Deutschmarks, although, of course, for a French consumer they would be measured in francs, for a Dutch consumer in guilder and so on.

An index of relative export prices is shown in **_Figure 8.2_** (which also shows a second index to be explained later). The index of relative export prices is an amalgam of the relative prices of UK exports on all foreign markets, using an appropriate weighting procedure. The index is constructed in such a way that a *fall* in the index represents an *improvement* in competitiveness. Thus the peak in 1980–81 represents a period when UK exports were very *uncompetitive*. More recently, notice the dramatic improvement in competitiveness in 1993 which followed the fall in sterling's value after September 1992. Notice also, however, that the improvement seems to have been completely reversed a few months later.

Figure 8.2
Two indices of UK export competitiveness: relative export prices and export profit margins, 1980–97 (1990 = 100)

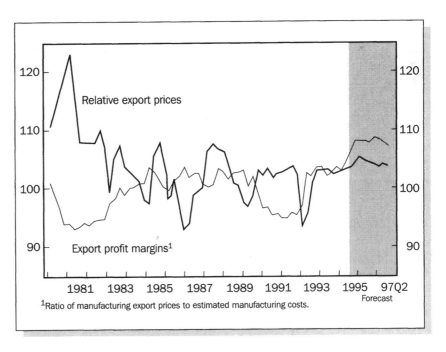

[1]Ratio of manufacturing export prices to estimated manufacturing costs.

Source: *Financial Statement and Budget Report 1996–97.*

Export profit margins

The recovery in export prices seems to confirm the view that, in response to a devaluation, exporters do not change their foreign currency prices. Rather they take the benefit in the form of higher profit margins.

What this implies is that any improvement in competitiveness occasioned by a depreciation of sterling will not show up at all if we look only at the index of relative export prices. It will, however, be manifest if we look at an index known as **export profit margins,** which is defined as

$$\frac{\text{Manufacturers' export prices}}{\text{Estimated manufacturing costs}}$$

This is the second of the two indices shown in ***Figure 8.2.*** Note that, unlike the index of relative export prices, the index of export profit margins is constructed in such a way that a *rise* in the index represents an *improvement* in competitiveness.

Whatever 'competitiveness' is, if it were possible to measure it perfectly, these two indices would be a mirror image of each other. By visual inspection of the two series, they do appear to be negatively correlated, but there are times when the message is unclear – particularly the period 1994–97, since here both curves seem to be moving in the *same* direction, rather than in opposite directions as we would expect.

Relative unit labour cost

A different approach to measuring competitiveness is provided by an index of unit labour costs in the UK relative to those of our major competitors. This is known as **relative unit labour costs** and can be defined as

$$\frac{\text{Unit labour costs in the UK measured in \$}}{\text{Unit labour costs abroad measured in \$}}$$

This is shown in ***Figure 8.3***. Notice that, as with relative export prices, a fall in the index represents an improvement. Notice also that, again as with relative export prices, both numerator and denominator are measured in the same currency (we have chosen dollars, but it could be yen or sterling or whatever).

The rationale for such an index can be thought of as follows. A company – particularly a multinational company – deciding where to locate its production will take into account the costs of various locations. The cost of labour will be a primary consideration. Thus anything which leads to a fall in UK labour costs relative to those abroad is likely to lead to an increase in the production of goods in the UK. The multinational will choose to locate production in the UK in preference to other countries because of the cost advantages of so doing.

Because of the way in which it is measured, there are three ways in which the index of relative unit labour costs can be made to show an improvement:

➤ Anything which raises the physical productivity of labour in the UK will *ceteris paribus* improve relative unit labour costs.
➤ If the employer is able to purchase that labour more cheaply by paying lower wages or offering less generous fringe benefits, this will also improve relative unit labour costs.

Figure 8.3

UK competitiveness: relative unit labour costs[1], 1980–97 (1990 = 100)

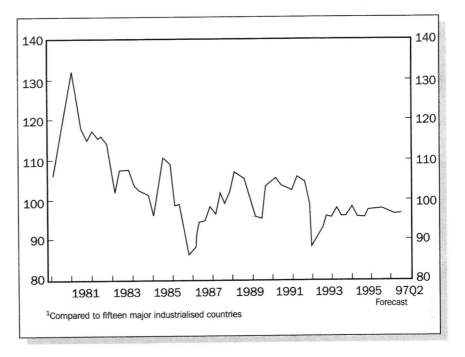

[1]Compared to fifteen major industrialised countries

Source: *Financial Statement and Budget Report 1996–97.*

➤ Devaluation of the currency will also improve competitiveness. Because of the way the index is constructed, a 10 per cent fall in the exchange rate will *ceteris paribus* mean a 10 per cent improvement in competitiveness as measured by this index.

ACTIVITY **2**

At the Maastricht talks in December 1991, the British Conservative government negotiated an agreement whereby Britain would 'opt out' of the proposed 'Social Chapter' of the Treaty of European Union. What is the rationale for this? To which of the strategies listed above does it relate?

Check with answers/suggestions at the back of the book.

Import price competitiveness

Finally, consider **import price competitiveness**, an index constructed in such a way that again a *fall* indicates an *improvement* in the ability of UK firms to compete on the home market against imports. This index, which is shown in Figure 8.4, can be thought of as

$$\frac{\text{Price of UK-produced goods in £s}}{\text{Price of imports in £s}}$$

Note again the common currency (this time, pounds). Notice from this index too the now familiar features of the peak of uncompetitiveness in 1980 and the improvement in competitiveness following sterling's slide after September 1992.

Figure 8.4

UK competitiveness: import price competitiveness, 1980–97 (1990 = 100)

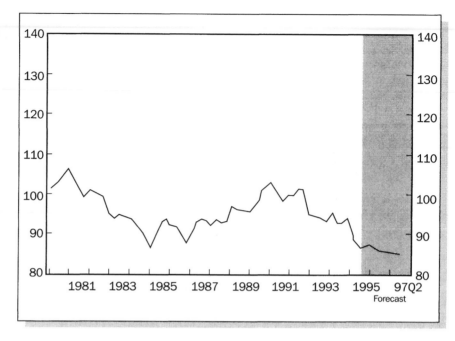

Source: *Financial Statement and Budget Report 1996–97.*

REVIEW QUESTIONS

1 The basic difference between a fixed exchange rate and a flexible exchange rate is:
   (a) there is no intervention with a fixed rate
   (b) there is no intervention with a floating rate
   (c) the need for reserves is greater under a fixed rate than under a floating one
   (d) only under a fixed rate are there declared par values.

2 Suppose initially the following exchange rates apply:

$$£1 = 10 \text{ francs} = \$2$$

and that the sterling/franc rate is fixed by the exchange rate mechanism (i.e. it is not free to vary).
   If the pound depreciated by 10 per cent *vis-à-vis* the dollar (to £1 = $1.80), what would you expect to happen to the dollar/franc rate?
   If the dollar/franc rate remained at 5F = $1, what would be the best way for a US resident to acquire francs to spend on his holiday in Paris?

3 Explain the mechanism whereby a reduction in German interest rates may cause the value of the pound to rise. For what reason might the German government wish to maintain interest rates at a high level?

4 Policies which can be used to tackle a balance of trade deficit are sometimes classified into one of two types – *expenditure switching* policies and *expenditure reducing* policies. How would you classify the following?

➤ raising interest rates
➤ deflation (by fiscal means)
➤ tariffs
➤ devaluation.

5 Suppose that in September 1992 the pound leaves the ERM and as a result its value against the DM drops by 13 per cent. Suppose the elasticity of demand for UK exports is known to be –1 in the short run. State whether the following are true or false.

(a) If UK exporters pass on the benefits of this to their customers, export revenues (in foreign currency) will rise.

(b) If UK exporters cut prices by the full extent of the devaluation, sales volume will increase, but export revenues will not.

(c) If UK exporters do not change their (foreign currency) prices, exporting becomes more profitable in comparison to selling on the home market.

(d) The elasticity of demand for UK exports is likely to be higher in the long run (than in the short run), and in the long run, therefore, export revenues are likely to rise *ceteris paribus*.

6 Which of the following result from a fall in the external value of the pound?

(a) *Ceteris paribus* British industry becomes more competitive.

(b) There will be a tendency for the domestic rate of inflation to be higher than it otherwise would have been.

(c) UK consumers will engage in expenditure switching and will therefore buy fewer Italian goods and more UK goods because of the change in relative prices.

(d) Italian consumers will do likewise and buy fewer British goods.

7 The Japanese and German economies tend to have trade surpluses and therefore their currencies tend to appreciate. So why do central banks not use these currencies as reserve assets?

8 The official reserves of the Bank of England fell by £15 billion in September 1992. Which of the following statements are true?

(a) This huge fall in reserves reflects the intervention buying which the Bank of England undertook to try to maintain the ERM parity of £1 = DM2.95.

(b) Speculators made a profit of £15 billion.

(c) Well, the money must have come from somewhere, but I'm not quite sure where.

(d) If it costs £50 million to build a hospital, this means we have lost resources which could have been used to build 300 hospitals.

Summary
••••••••••

In the UK balance of payments accounts, anything which adds to the demand for pounds on foreign exchange markets (such as the export of a British-made car) is recorded as a credit. Imports and other transactions which add to the supply of pounds on foreign exchange markets are debits.

The current account is a record of those transactions which relate to trade (both visible trade and trade in services). It also records currency transactions resulting from financial flows (interest, profits and dividends). The difference between inward and outward financial flows can be called net IPD or *net property income from abroad*.

Deficits on the current account tend to be associated with surpluses on the capital account, and vice versa. Any remaining imbalance must be made good by a change in official reserves – a balance of payments surplus leads to an inflow of foreign exchange reserves, and a balance of payments deficit leads to an outflow of reserves. A chronic outflow of reserves is unsustainable.

A variety of instruments are available for correcting balance of payments deficits. High interest rates reduce the demand for imports and more importantly lead to a capital inflow. But such a policy has adverse effects on the domestic economy. Domestic deflation by fiscal means can also be used to reduce the flow of imports, but has a similar adverse effect on the domestic economy. Tariffs and quotas are difficult to apply unilaterally, particularly to EU countries. Changing the exchange rate (devaluation) is a powerful weapon which is thought to improve price competitiveness (and hence trade volumes), but the mechanism whereby this is brought about is disputed. There are different measures of export competitiveness including relative export prices, export profit margins and relative unit labour costs.

Key concepts
••••••••••••••••••

The following key concepts have been introduced in this chapter. Make sure you understand the meaning and significance of each of them. They are listed here in the order in which they first appear, and the page number where they appear is also given. You will find these key concepts in section headings or in **bold** in the text. Each chapter contains a list of key concepts and you may find these particularly useful for revision purposes.

credit	(p. 111)
debit	(p. 111)
trade balance	(p. 112)
interest, profits and dividends	(p. 113)
invisibles	(p. 113)
transfers	(p. 113)
balance for official financing	(p. 113)
change in official reserves	(p. 113)
accommodating transactions	(p. 114)
autonomous transactions	(p. 114)
visible trade deficit	(p. 114)
trade deficit	(p. 114)
current account deficit	(p. 114)
balance of payments deficit/surplus	(p. 114)
Pink Book	(p. 115)
Blue Book	(p. 115)

balancing item (p. 115)
positive contrasted with normative science (p. 116)
tariff (p. 118)
quota (p. 118)
devaluation (p. 118)
depreciation (p. 118)
elasticities approach (to the effect of devaluation) (p. 118)
elastic/inelastic (p. 119)
elasticity coefficient (p. 119)
J-curve effect (p. 120)
relative profitability approach (p. 121)
price taker (p. 121)
price maker (p. 121)
price competitiveness (p. 122)
relative export prices (p. 123)
export profit margins (p. 124)
relative unit labour costs (p. 124)
import price competitiveness (p. 125)

CHAPTER **9**

Unemployment and the labour market

Objectives:

This chapter will enable you to:

➤ put current levels of unemployment into an appropriate historical perspective

➤ understand that some individuals in the population choose to be economically inactive and that this will influence the measure known as the participation rate

➤ distinguish between various 'types' of unemployment – frictional, structural, demand deficient and classical

➤ understand the Keynesian view that unemployment results from a deficiency of demand in the economy

➤ appreciate the classical view that unemployment is the result of a disequilibrium in the labour market and a failure of real wages to fall sufficiently to equate the demand for labour with the supply

➤ appraise the case for and against a national minimum wage

➤ understand the rationale for supply-side policies in the labour market

➤ appreciate that one way of understanding the world is through discovering statistical regularities and that the technique of correlation analysis can be used to do this.

9.1   Historical perspectives
9.2   Problems of definition
9.3   Types of unemployment
9.4   Frictional unemployment
9.5   Structural unemployment
9.6   Demand-deficient unemployment
9.7   'Classical' unemployment
9.8   The effect of a minimum wage
9.9   The emasculation of the trade unions
9.10 The labour market and inflation
9.11 Discovering statistical regularities – correlation

9.1 Historical perspectives

As we noted in Chapter 1, the control of unemployment is a key target of macroeconomic policy. Indeed, following the widespread mass unemployment of the inter-war period, the control of unemployment was at the top of the political agenda in the heyday of Keynesian economics in the post-war period. At this time and up until the mid-1970s, economists and politicians spoke glibly about 'full employment' as an objective of macroeconomic policy.

As **Figure 9.1** shows, unemployment remained below three-quarters of a million up until the mid-1970s (roughly equivalent to 3 per cent of the workforce). During the last 25 years, however, a sea-change in the labour market seems to have occurred. Although unemployment has continued to fluctuate in response to the fluctuations in economic activity, these short-term movements have been swamped

Figure 9.1
UK unemployment, 1972–96 (millions)

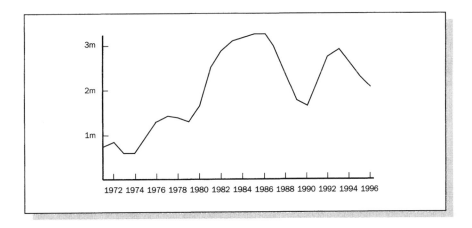

Source: *Economic Trends Annual Supplement*, 1995.

Note: The unemployment figures have been affected by several changes in coverage over the period shown. The data should be taken only as a broad indiction of trends.

by an inexorable upward trend. It appears as though some sort of ratchet effect is in operation. In the wake of a recession, the economy enters a period of rapid growth and at this time unemployment falls, but not to the same low level that existed before the recession. The overall trend is upwards.

This phenomenon is not, of course, restricted to the UK. As is shown in Table 9.1, similar trends have been experienced in most if not all advanced countries.

In addition, and in contrast to the upward trend in unemployment noted above, there is also some evidence that in the last decade there has been a further change in the labour market in the UK. This change has been characterised by what is euphemistically called increasing 'flexibility' in the labour market. More and more labour has tended to become a commodity to be hired and fired on a short-term basis, in response to the ups and down of the business cycle , rather than retained on a long-term basis providing security for the employee. Part-time and flexible working has become more commonplace, whereas full-time permanent employment has become more difficult to obtain.

table 9.1
Unemployment in selected years for selected OECD countries (% of labour force)

	USA	Japan	France	Germany	Italy	UK
1969	3.4	1.1	2.4	0.7	3.6	3.1
1973	4.7	1.3	2.6	0.9	3.7	2.8
1975	8.3	2.0	4.1	3.6	3.6	4.5
1977	6.9	2.0	4.9	3.6	7.0	6.1
1982	9.5	2.4	8.1	6.1	9.0	11.3
1985	7.1	2.6	10.1	8.6	10.5	11.3
1988	5.4	2.5	10.0	6.1	11.0	8.4
1992	7.3	2.1	10.3	4.7	9.8	9.9
1995	5.6	3.1	11.6	8.2	12.1	8.7

[1] OECD standardised definitions (which may differ from the national definitions).
Source: OECD, quoted in *National Institute Economic Review*, Statistical Appendix (various issues).

This seems to have made the labour market respond more rapidly to economic conditions – unemployment rises faster in a recession, but also falls faster when the economy recovers. The increasing prevalence of temporary and part-time working has also led government critics in the UK to claim that official statistics for unemployment underrecord the true extent of unemployment in the economy.

9.2 Problems of definition

The causes of these phenomena are, of course, the subject of considerable disagreement among economists. First of all, there are problems of definition which are by no means trivial. To begin with, unemployment cannot be equated with 'not working' since in our society there are many people who are not working – such as babies and young people, the elderly, housewives and so on. These individuals should not be regarded as unemployed. Economists use the term **economically inactive** to refer to those people who are neither in employment nor actively seeking work. The economically inactive will comprise:

➤ those *below* employment age (babies and school-age children)
➤ those *above* employment age (65 years old for men and 60 for women)
➤ those who for some other reason are unfit or unable to work (e.g. chronically sick and disabled people)
➤ those in prisons
➤ those in full-time further education or on government training schemes
➤ those who for reasons other than those above *choose* not to enter the labour market (e.g. the very wealthy or mothers who stay at home to look after children).

In contrast, the **economically active** part of the population consists of both those who are in employment *plus* those who indicate their willingness to work by registering as unemployed. The **activity rate** (also known as the **participation rate**) refers to that proportion of the population of working age who are economically active. This can also be expressed as:

$$\text{Activity rate} = \frac{\text{Total employed plus registered unemployed}}{\text{Total population of working age}}$$

To give some feeling for what this means, it is useful to distinguish **male activity rates** from **female activity rates**. Historically, male activity rates have been very high – not 100 per cent of course, but certainly well above 90 per cent, whereas female activity rates have been much lower. Ever since the Second World War, however, there has been a rising trend for women (both married and unmarried) to go out to work, and this has been reflected in an increase in the measured female activity rate.

A comparison of activity rates in different countries, among different ethnic groups or in different periods reveals a lot about social changes, and in particular about attitudes towards the role of women in society. **Table 9.2**, for example, compares activity rates for men and women in different countries in the EC in 1992. As can be seen, Britain had the second highest activity rate in the EC, for both men and women, second only to that of Denmark. Note that in Denmark the difference between male and female rates was less marked than elsewhere, and considerably less marked than in the Mediterranean countries and the Irish Republic.

ASK YOURSELF   *What social attitudes towards the role of women in society do you suppose is reflected in these measured activity rates?*

Table 9.3 shows that in Britain the economic activity rate varies among ethnic groups. As might be expected, the difference is most marked among women. Fewer than one in four women from Pakistan and Bangladesh were economically active, compared to three out of four white women (in the age range 25–44). For Black and for Indian women, however, the percentage was close to the average for the population as a whole.

table 9.2
Economic activity rates:[1] by gender, EC comparison, 1992 (%)

	Males	Females	All persons
Denmark	74.5	62.7	68.5
United Kingdom	74.0	52.8	63.0
Portugal	71.9	50.2	60.3
Germany[2]	71.5	48.4	59.4
Netherlands	71.1	46.5	58.6
France	65.7	48.0	56.4
Irish Republic	70.6	37.7	53.9
Luxembourg	69.7	39.5	54.2
Italy	65.4	34.9	49.5
Belgium	62.1	39.5	50.4
Spain	65.6	34.1	49.2
Greece	65.5	34.8	49.4
EC average	68.9	44.6	56.2

[1] The civilian labour force aged 16 years and over as a percentage of the population aged 16 and over.
[2] As constituted since 3 October 1990.

Source: Eurostat, as quoted in *Social Trends*, 1995.

table 9.3
**Economic activity
rates:[1] by ethnic
group, gender and
age, Great Britain,
spring 1994 (%)**

	Males			Females		
	16–24	25–44	45–64	16–24	25–44	45–59
White	77	95	79	67	75	70
Black[2]	62	86	77	51	71	72
Indian	55	93	76	51	69	53
Pakistani/ Bangladeshi	57	92	63	35	24	..
Other[3]	45	82	80	34	57	54
All ethnic groups[4]	75	94	79	65	74	70

[1] Percentage of the population of working age who are either in employment or registered as unemployed.
[2] Includes Caribbean, African and other Black people of non-mixed origin.
[3] Includes Chinese, other ethnic minority groups of non-mixed origin and people of mixed origin.
[4] Includes ethnic group not stated.

Source: Employment Department, quoted in *Social Trends,* 1995.

Tables 9.2 and 9.3 both illustrate an important fact about the labour market: namely, that the activity rate reflects a *choice* that people make, but that their choice is culturally and socially constrained.

9.3 Types of unemployment

In analysing the causes of trends in unemployment, it is helpful initially to distinguish different 'types' of unemployment. This classification of unemployment into different types is also, of course, in part an *explanation* of why unemployment occurs. The major types (or explanations) of unemployment are explained in sections 9.4 to 9.7. They are:

➤ frictional unemployment
➤ structural unemployment
➤ demand-deficient unemployment
➤ 'Classical' unemployment.

9.4 Frictional unemployment

Over time the pattern of consumer demand in the economy will change, both as a result of changes in incomes and tastes and in response to a changing set of relative prices. The change in the pattern of demand will in turn lead to a change in the amounts and the types of goods and services produced. This will then lead to a change in the type of labour required. Moreover, technical improvements will bring about changes in the way in which goods and services are produced, and this will alter the demand for the various types of labour. In short, all of these changes will lead to a change in the pattern of demand for labour.

Frictional unemployment results from this change in the pattern of demand for labour, as some workers will now find that their skills are no longer required. These workers will become unemployed for a period, until they eventually become re-employed either in a similar or in a different occupation. The use of the term 'frictional' to describe such unemployment suggests that it results from **imperfections** in the labour market. If there were perfect information – so that workers knew what jobs were on offer and employers knew what labour was available – and if labour were perfectly able and willing to move, there would be little or no unemployment of this type, since the unemployed workers would be *immediately* redeployed in a new occupation.

9.5 Structural unemployment

In contrast to frictional unemployment, which in theory at least is of short duration, **structural unemployment** is of a longer-term nature. However, it too results from the dynamic nature of an economy in which the changing pattern of consumer demand and changes in the way in which goods are produced lead to a decline in the demand for certain types of labour. For example, in the UK from the 1960s onwards there was a decline in the demand for British-built ships and hence a decline in the demand for shipbuilders. Equally noticeable in the last decade has been the decline in the demand for coal miners brought about, first by labour-saving technical progress, which has enabled coal to be mined using more capital-intensive (and hence labour-saving) techniques, but more importantly by the decline in the demand for UK-produced coal, as power stations have opted to buy cheaper imported coal or switch to gas.

By its very nature, structural unemployment tends to be concentrated in certain geographical areas. For example, shipbuilding was concentrated in the north east of England, so this area was severely affected by the decline in shipbuilding. This led to a further decline in the region because of a **regional multiplier effect**. Thus structural unemployment and **regional unemployment** tend to go hand in hand.

9.6 Demand-deficient unemployment

We expect the demand for labour – and therefore the level of unemployment – to be correlated with the business cycle. When the economy is in a recession the demand for goods and services falls. Consequently, there will also be a fall in the demand for the labour that produces those goods and services. Hence unemployment will rise. Because the level of such unemployment will vary with the business cycle, it is termed **cyclical unemployment**.

It is also sometimes referred to as **demand-deficient** or **Keynesian unemployment**. One of Keynes' great contributions was to argue that demand-deficient unemployment could be removed by bringing about an increase in the level of aggregate demand. For example, the government could bring about a *budget deficit*, thereby injecting spending power into the economy and raising the overall level of demand. This increase in the demand for goods and services would bring about an increase in demand for labour, and hence unemployment would fall.

9.7 'Classical' unemployment
....

In Chapter 7 we described the foreign exchange market as an example of a *perfectly competitive* market. In such a market, we argued, price would be determined by relative scarcity and the market would be in equilibrium when demand equalled supply. Some economists believe that this same analysis can be applied to the workings of the labour market. That is, they believe that the market for labour functions – or should function – in much the same way as the foreign exchange market, or the market for carrots and Brussels sprouts.

This view is variously known as the **classical view**, the **neo-classical view** and (sometimes) the **monetarist view**. It stands in contrast to a Keynesian analysis which suggests that, as a matter of observable fact, the market for labour does not function in the same way as the text book model of a perfectly competitive market.

In *Figure 9.2* we have drawn a demand curve for labour and a supply curve for labour. Note that the vertical axis measures the price of labour – that is, the wage rate. The demand curve for labour is shown to be downward sloping, indicating that the higher the wage, the less labour will be demanded; and the lower the wage, the more labour will be demanded. This is explained by the fact that labour is a *factor of production,* which is combined with other factors of production to make goods and services. The higher the price of labour, the more the incentive to economise on its use and to substitute other factors such as capital.

The supply curve of labour is somewhat more problematic. In Figure 9.2 it is shown to be positively related to the wage, indicating that the higher the wage, the greater the supply of labour. In practice, what this may mean is that at higher wage rates more people will wish to become economically active and/or those already in the labour market will wish to work more hours.

At a wage rate of W_e in Figure 9.2, the market *clears* in the sense that the demand for labour and the supply of labour are equal. W_e is described as the **market-clearing wage**. At this wage, the market is in equilibrium and there is

Figure 9.2
**Equilibrium in the
labour market**

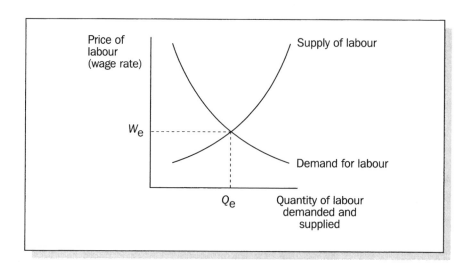

no unemployment. What this means is that all those wishing to be employed *at the going wage rate* will be able to find jobs. This is a rather surprising conclusion. It suggests that the existence of unemployment – a fact of life in the real world – can only be explained in the 'classical' model by labour market imperfections.

This is illustrated in Figure 9.3, where the wage rate is too high and as a result **involuntary unemployment** emerges. In **Figure 9.3** the wage rate W_H is above the equilibrium level. The amount of labour supplied at this wage rate (Q_s) exceeds the amount demanded (Q_d). The labour market is in disequilibrium and the amount of involuntary unemployment is $Q_s - Q_d$.

The analysis above may make more sense once we recognise that both the demand for labour and the supply of labour depend on the *real wage* as opposed to the *nominal wage* (or money wage). Thus we note that the vertical axis of Figure 9.3 is labelled *W/P* to indicate this. Recall from section 5.6 how real wages can be calculated by dividing the money wage index by the price index. Since the real wage depends upon both wages *and prices,* it is possible for the real wage to rise or to fall depending on how fast money wages rise or fall *relative* to prices.

Thus if real wages are above the market-clearing level, unemployment will emerge, because employers will only hire that labour whose contribution to output exceeds the real value of the wage paid. This was the explanation which the classical (or pre-Keyneian) economists gave for the existence of unemployment. In a variety of different guises, it is moreover an explanation which the monetarist school of economists has revived in the 1970s and 1980s.

The Keynesian response has been to argue that the analysis is unrealistic rather than to claim that it is logically flawed. It is overly simplistic and misleading, Keynesians would argue, to analyse the market for labour using the sort of demand and supply analysis we have used above, and hence to conclude that unemployment can be explained in terms of market 'imperfections' – features of the labour market in the real world which are not present in some text book ideal. These criticisms can be illustrated in the context of the debate about a minimum wage, which is discussed below.

Figure 9.3
Involuntary
unemployment

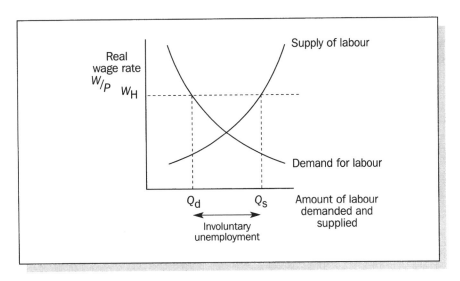

9.8 The effect of a minimum wage
······································

An area of political uncertainty for the Labour Party in the second half of the 1990s is the question of whether or not to support calls for a **statutory minimum wage**. Traditional Labour supporters argue that Labour's manifesto should contain a commitment to introducing a statutory minimum wage if and when they are elected. At the time of writing (mid-1996) the leadership of the party have side-stepped the issue, maintaining their commitment to such a policy in principle, but refusing to be drawn on how such a legal minimum should be specified.

To voters – and particularly to young voters who would have experienced nothing other than a decade and a half of free market economics in Britain – the debate must seem somewhat strange and anachronistic. Is it really feasible for the state to intervene to set a legal minimum wage? Will the result not be – as opponents claim – to produce higher levels of unemployment? Looked at in a slightly wider perspective, of course, the debate about a legal minimum wage is neither new nor confined to the UK. Most European countries have some form of minimum wage legislation and Britain too operated a system of **Wages Councils** which in effect protected the earnings of low-paid occupations. However, these Wages Councils were gradually abolished in the 1980s and 1990s as part of the Conservative government's 'structural reforms'.

The case against a minimum wage is in many ways similar to the classical analysis of involuntary unemployment, explained in the previous section. It is summarised in *Figure 9.4*. Suppose that in the absence of any intervention there is a market-clearing wage of £4 per hour. A blanket minimum of £4.50 per hour is then imposed by statute. It becomes an offence punishable by law to employ anyone at less than this rate. It can readily be seen that, in a simplistic analysis, the likely result would be to reduce the demand for labour and the level of employment from the equilibrium Q_e to the lower level of Q_d. At the same time, there is an expansion in the number of people who would like to take up jobs at the new rate of £4.50 per hour rather than the old equilibrium of £4, so the amount of labour supplied increases to Q_s. Involuntary unemployment of $(Q_s - Q_d)$ emerges (as in the previous Figure 9.3).

Figure 9.4

The case against the minimum wage

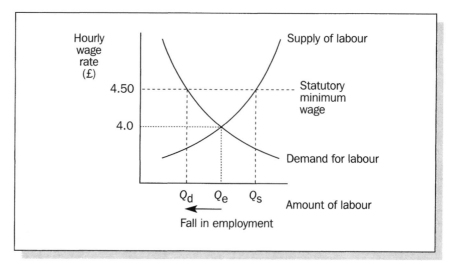

As we have noted, however, this analysis can be criticised for being overly simplistic and for ignoring certain key features of the labour market in the real world. In some ways the analysis exemplifies the maxim 'a little learning is a dangerous thing', since it may appear to lead us to a policy conclusion which is unjustified. To see why this is so we need to be aware of certain features of the labour market in contemporary society.

Which workers will be affected?

Labour is not a **homogeneous** factor of production. It is not all the same type. Skilled labour, because it is more productive and therefore more valuable to the employer, will command a higher price than unskilled labour. Minimum wage legislation will have no effect on the wage received by skilled labour because their equilibrium wage will already be above the legal minimum. The minimum wage will only affect those in unskilled occupations – those serving in McDonald's fast-food outlets, those stocking shelves at Tesco, office cleaners, hospital porters and the like.

Monopolies exploit people – and so do monopsonies

The formal proof of the argument that monopolies exploit people is complex and can be fully understood only by an appeal to the sort of microeconomic theory which lies outside the scope of this text. However, it is possible to give an intuitive understanding of the issues involved.

'Monopoly' means 'single seller'. A firm occupying such a position in the market will be in a strong bargaining position vis-à-vis other players. Indeed, the board game 'Monopoly' is based on this principle. Monopolists are said to enjoy **market power**. In general, the more market power a seller has, the more it is able to exploit buyers by charging a higher price than would otherwise be the case *ceteris paribus*. In the extreme case of market power – where one firm, a monopolist, has the whole market for a particular product to itself – buyers have no alternative source of supply. They are in a 'take it or leave it' situation where they have no choice and are in effect at the mercy of the monopolist.

Microeconomic theory can offer a formal proof of the proposition that prices will tend to be higher in monopolistic markets than in competitive ones, other things being equal. What is less intuitive, but which nevertheless can also be formally proved, is that *single buyers* – known technically as **monopsonists** – will also be in a strong bargaining position, and will *ceteris paribus* exploit the market by buying at a lower price than would be the case if there were more competition among buyers.

In the labour market there are lots of examples of firms who occupy monopsonistic or quasi-monopsonistic positions. The National Health Service, Local Education Authorities, and Railtrack are all more or less monopsonists – that is, monopoly buyers of the skills of health workers, teachers, train signalling staff and so on. Economic analysis can demonstrate that such buyers, if they exercise their monopoly powers, will be able to purchase labour at a price which is below the value that would be placed on such labour in a more competitive market. This is because those 'offering' their labour have no alternative opportunities and must take or leave the monopsonist's wage. This can quite reasonably be seen as exploitation.

ASK YOURSELF *Qualified nurses can often earn much more working in private medicine than they can working for the National Health Service. How do you explain this?*

Unskilled workers are in a weak bargaining position

By definition, unskilled workers have no skills to sell. The only thing that they can sell is their unskilled labour. There is a plentiful supply of unskilled labour – anyone can do the jobs they do – and these workers will therefore be in a very weak bargaining position *vis-à-vis* the employer. Moreover, the larger the employer – and therefore the more market power it is able to wield – the weaker the bargaining position of the individual employee. Even if employees form themselves into unions in an attempt to strengthen their position by acquiring market power for themselves, they will have little effective protection because the employer can easily hire non-union labour at lower wage rates. Indeed, recent trade union legislation encourages them to do just that.

This is the nature of the labour market

The nature of the labour market in contemporary society is such that individual sellers of labour face monopsonistic buyers – buyers with market power. If, in addition, those individual sellers of labour are unskilled, their bargaining position is very weak. In such a situation, the only protection such workers have is from the state in the form of minimum wage legislation. Of course, other things being equal, the higher the price that buyers of labour have to pay, the less they will demand. So minimum wage legislation *may* reduce the amount of labour demanded, other things being equal. But the state may have a moral obligation to ensure that the parties to a wage bargain are not too unequally matched.

Moreover, the demand for labour also depends on factors other than the price of labour – in other words, *other things are not equal*. In particular, the demand for labour depends on the level of aggregate demand in the economy, and it follows that the state therefore also has an obligation to ensure that aggregate demand is sufficiently high to ensure that the level of employment is kept high – in other words, that the level of unemployment is kept down.

DID YOU KNOW?
The term 'welfare state' was popularised by the then Archbishop of Canterbury in 1941, in a book in which he contrasted the idea of a welfare state with that of a 'power state', which had no moral or spiritual commitment to its people

(Source: David Brindle, *Guardian*, 8 May 1996).

Should minimum wage laws apply to young workers?

Many of the people performing unskilled work will be young people for whom the job is essentially short term as well as part time. The 'social justice' argument seems to be weaker here, when we recognise that most of the people in this group will be living at home and partially supported by their parents. Their 'needs' may therefore be less than those older people who support themselves and their families. If they are paid less, however, this violates the principle of equal pay for work of equal value.

Should the minimum wage be the same nation-wide?

The *equilibrium* wage will vary from one part of the country to another. Typically, for example, it will be higher in London and the south-east than in rural Wales. It is for this reason that the Conservative government elected in 1979 has tried to do away with **national pay bargaining** and replace it with **local pay bargaining**.

In many industries – particularly those in the public sector – there has been a tradition of national pay bargaining which has meant that all workers in a particular occupation on a particular grade will be paid the same nationally agreed rate. National pay bargaining does not recognise the fact that a particular type of labour may be relatively scarce in one part of the country and relatively abundant in another. Clearly a national minimum wage – because it is nation-wide – suffers from the same objection as national pay bargaining.

Trade unions have tended to favour national as opposed to local pay bargaining because they believe – probably correctly – that it places them in a stronger position *vis-à-vis* the employer. In contrast, advocates of the free market have argued that rewards should be higher in those geographical areas where a particular skill is scarce. Hence, they argue, wages should be determined locally.

A flexible national minimum wage?

The two previous sections serve to illustrate the difficulty in formulating minimum wage legislation in such a way that the law is able to take account of local market conditions. A single figure – whether it be £4 an hour or £5.20 an hour or whatever – would obviously be unable to do so. Therefore, although the Labour Party may indeed be genuinely committed to minimum wage legislation in principle, the practical application of any interventionist policy is fraught with difficulties.

9.9 The emasculation of the trade unions

A feature of labour relations in the 1970s in the UK was a widespread confrontational attitude between the employer and those employees organised into trade unions. Often the situation was one of **bilateral monopoly**, with a monopoly buyer of labour such as the National Coal Board facing a monopoly seller of labour such as the National Union of Mineworkers. The result was frequent and often prolonged industrial disputes, sometimes over issues of working practices, but normally over the key issue of pay. Economic theory predicts that there will be *no equilibrium* wage in a situation of bilateral monopoly. The outcome – the wage that is actually paid – will depend on the bargaining strength of the two parties involved.

The Conservative government which was elected in 1979 in Britain set about systematically weakening the position of the trade unions. This was achieved partly by the government's anti-inflation policy, which necessitated that the labour market was kept in a permanently depressed state (thus reducing the demand for labour and hence weakening the position of the sellers of labour *vis-à-vis* the buyers). More important, however, was a series of amendments to labour market legislation which had the effect of weakening the power of the trade unions.

For example, legislation was introduced which made it illegal for trade unions to call a strike unless a full postal ballot of its members had been carried out. Picketing – the physical presence of striking workers outside the employer's premises – was controlled, and 'secondary picketing' – the involvement of workers not themselves employed by the firm in dispute – was made illegal. Unions became legally liable for any losses the firm might sustain as a result of industrial action, unless that action was preceded by a lengthy process of formal consultation. Unions therefore became reluctant to sanction any form of industrial action, for fear that they could be sued by firms for losses allegedly sustained.

Collective action – whether sanctioned by the official union or not – thus became more difficult to organise and orchestrate. It became more difficult for workers to organise themselves into coherent and effective groupings capable of exerting any influence on employers over pay and conditions of work. Employees became increasingly individualised. In short, the combined effect of these and similar measures was to weaken the position of the trade unions, strengthening the power of the buyer and reducing the power of the seller of labour.

ACTIVITY 1

The way in which we express something is seldom value-neutral. We express either approval or disapproval by the choice of the words we use. Consider the following five statements and then place them in rank order. The ranking should begin with statements displaying the *most approval* of the legislative changes and end with those showing the *most disapproval*.

'The effect of the trade union legislation enacted by the Conservative government since 1979 has been ... '

(a) to emasculate the unions
(b) to reduce the market power of the unions
(c) to reduce the monopoly power of the unions
(d) to improve trade union democracy
(e) to make trade unions more accountable to their members.

Check with answers/suggestions at the back of the book.

9.10 The labour market and inflation

The 1970s was the heyday of union militancy in Britain, when those unions that enjoyed an element of monopoly power were able to exert an upward influence on wages. This increase in wages, unless accompanied by a genuine increase in productivity, was synonymous with an increase in *wage costs* per unit of output. This led to the sort of wage cost-push inflation we described in Chapter 5.

In the 1960s and 1970s, governments had tried to keep inflation in check by *demand management*. In effect by reducing demand in the goods market, they also reduced demand in the labour market and hence dampened down inflationary pressure there. However, such **demand-side policies** proved only moderately effective. Hence it was in the late 1970s, with the growing importance of free market and monetarist thinking, that a new phrase emerged – **supply-side economics**. The sort of labour market legislation alluded to above can be thought of as a classic example of supply-side policies. They were designed to introduce more 'competitive' elements into the labour market, and to render it more like the textbook model of a competitive market illustrated earlier in Figure 9.2. Supply-side policies are discussed more fully in Chapter 11.

9.11 Discovering statistical regularities – correlation

We end this chapter on unemployment with a detailed look at a particular statistical technique known as **correlation** analysis. This is used to discover **statistical regularities**. These are *patterns* in the data, which reflect **causal mechanisms** at work in the real world – mechanisms which may not be immediately apparent because the causal link is not very strong. In the social sciences, we are often faced with the idea that one thing *tends* to cause another thing to happen. It does not always cause it to happen, but it normally does. The relationship between these two things is a *statistical* one, not a *deterministic* one. So tall parents *tend* to have tall children, but sometimes they do not.

Earlier in this chapter we stated that unemployment is *correlated* with the business cycle. What this means is that there is a tendency for unemployment to rise as demand in the economy falls, and a tendency for unemployment to fall when demand in the economy rises. The two variables are said to be negatively correlated – they tend to move in opposite directions. Note, however, that the relationship between them is not *deterministic* – they will not always behave in exactly the way we expect them to.

As an example of correlation, we are going to illustrate the statistical relationship between household income and the ownership of certain consumer durable goods. Suppose that we have estimates of GDP per capita in the various regions of the UK, as shown in Table 9.4. Suppose that we also have data on the percentage of homes owning telephones. The figures for 1985–86 are presented in Table 9.5.

table 9.4

GDP per capita, by region, 1988 (index, UK average = 100)

South East	122
East Anglia	98
South West	95
East Midlands	93
Scotland	93
North West	92
West Midlands	91
Yorks. and Humberside	91
North	87
Wales	83
N. Ireland	75

Source: *Regional Trends.*

table 9.5		
Percentage of UK homes with telephones, 1985–86	North	74
	Yorks. & Humberside	79
	East Midlands	82
	East Anglia	85
	South East	88
	South West	84
	West Midlands	76
	North West	81
	Wales	75
	Scotland	80
	N. Ireland	72

We wish to investigate whether households in 'richer' regions are more likely to have a telephone than those in 'poorer' regions. It seems likely that these two things are related.

Initially, we could simply put the two sets of figures side by side in a way that makes comparison possible. In Table 9.4 the regions are *ranked* by income per capita. We could also rank the regions in Table 9.5 and see if the ranking was the same.

Income ranking		*Phone ranking*	
South East	122	South East	88
East Anglia	98	East Anglia	85
South West	95	South West	84
East Midlands	93	East Midlands	82
Scotland	93	North West	81
North West	92	Scotland	80
West Midlands	91	Yorks. and Humberside	79
Yorks. and Humberside	91	West Midlands	76
North	87	Wales	75
Wales	83	North	74
N. Ireland	75	N. Ireland	72

The ranking is not identical, but it is very similar. Quite clearly the two 'attributes' are related – we say they are *correlated* – richer regions *tend* to have a higher proportion of households with phones.

Implicit in our analysis of the association between these two variables is the hypothesis that a **causal relationship** exists. The direction of causation is important and we have to use our common sense to work out which way the causation runs. Clearly in this example it is the income level which influences whether or not a household has a phone.

Ownership of phone ← Income level

The ownership of phones *depends* on the income level. Phone ownership is said to be the **dependent variable**, which by convention is labelled Y and is plotted on the vertical axis. Income is the **independent variable**, which is labelled X and is plotted on the horizontal axis.

The information on Y and X can be plotted on a graph called a **scatter diagram**. This is shown in *Figure 9.5*.

Figure 9.5

A scatter diagram

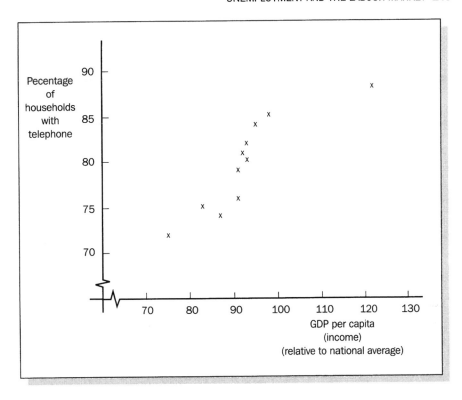

The scatter of points rises from the bottom left to the top right, suggesting a positive correlation between the variables. We can sometimes get a clearer picture of the extent to which these variables are related if we divide the *X–Y* space into four quadrants. To do this we must calculate the **mean** of each variable. We do this for each variable by summing all of the observations and dividing by the number of observations. Thus:

	Y *variable* (phones)	X *variable* (income)
South East	88	122
East Anglia	85	98
South West	84	95
East Midlands	82	93
Scotland	80	93
North West	81	92
West Midlands	76	91
Yorks. and Humberside	79	91
North	74	87
Wales	75	83
N. Ireland	72	75
	sum = 876	**sum = 1020**
Number of observations = 11		= 11

Therefore the mean of $Y = \dfrac{876}{11} = 79.6$

and the mean of $X = \dfrac{1020}{11} = 92.7$.

Thus we draw a horizontal line at $Y = 79.6$ and a vertical line at $X = 92.7$ (see Figure 9.6). This creates four quadrants. As can be seen, most of the observations fall into quadrants II and III, strongly suggesting a *positive* relationship between the variables.

ACTIVITY **2**
••••••••••••

In the worked example we investigated the relationship between income per capita in the various regions of the UK and the proportion of households with telephones. As might have been expected, regions with higher income per capita tended to have a higher proportion of households with telephones. There was a strong positive correlation.

In the following exercise you are asked to investigate whether there is any correlation (either positive or negative) between income and two other indices, both of which are sometimes regarded as reflecting the 'quality of life'. These variables are infant mortality and unemployment rates. The data in Table 9.6 are taken from *Regional Trends*, 1994. Column (1) shows income per capita expressed as an index. Column (2) shows infant mortality (deaths of infants aged under 1 year per 1,000 live births). Column (3) shows the unemployment rate for the region.

Figure 9.6
Four quadrants

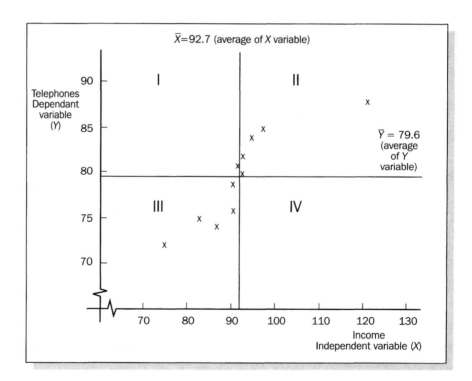

table 9.6 **Income per head,** **infant mortality and** **unemployment rates** **by region**	Income per head	Infant mortality	Unemployment rate (%)
Greater London	122.0	7.1	10.7
Rest of South East	110.4	5.3	7.8
East Anglia	100.4	4.6	9.7
South West	95.2	5.7	8.3
East Midlands	94.3	6.9	8.7
North West	93.3	7.0	9.9
Yorks. and Humberside	93.2	6.7	9.6
West Midlands	93.1	8.2	9.7
North	90.6	7.1	9.9

Sources: *Regional Trends*, 1994; *Economic Trends Annual Supplement*, 1995.

(a) Consider the relationship between income and infant mortality. What is your prior expectation about the relationship between these variables? That is, *without* looking at the figures, what do you expect the relationship to be?

(b) Does *casual inspection* of the data tend to confirm your prior expectation?

(c) Why does Greater London not fit the general pattern?

(d) Produce a scattergraph of the relationship between infant mortality (dependent variable) and income (independent variable). Note: exclude Greater London, since we have already seen that it will not fit into any general pattern. Divide the space on the scattergraph into four quadrants by calculating the mean of each variable. What do you expect to find? Do most of the observations fall into the top-left and bottom-right quadrants as expected, indicating a negative correlation?

(e) Now consider the relationship between income per head and the unemployment rate for the various regions. What is your prior expectation about the relationship between these variables?

(f) Does casual inspection of the data tend to confirm your prior expectation?

(g) Which regions appear not to fit the general pattern?

(h) Produce a scattergraph of the relationship between unemployment and income per capita (unemployment, the dependent variable, will be on the vertical axis). Note: exclude Greater London, as before. Divide the space on the scattergraph into four quadrants by calculating the mean of each variable. What do you expect to find? Do most of the observations fall into the top-left and bottom-right quadrants as expected, indicating a negative correlation.

Check with answers/suggestions at the back of the book.

Summary
. . . .

The post-war period has not seen a return to the mass unemployment of the 1920s and 1930s. Unemployment remained well below 1 million (roughly 5 per cent of the workforce) until the late 1970s, after which time it increased sharply, exceeding 3 million in the recession of the early 1980s.

Not all people who could work choose to do so. Some – such as married women – may be *economically inactive* in the sense that they have no paid employment. However, female activity rates have risen markedly in the last generation.

Various explanations for the existence of unemployment can be offered. These are sometimes described as different 'types' of unemployment. They consist of frictional unemployment, structural unemployment, demand-deficient unemployment and classical unemployment. Frictional and structural unemployment result from a mismatch between the type of labour being offered and that being demanded. Demand-deficient (or Keynesian) unemployment is correlated with the business cycle, rising in recessions and falling in booms. The classical explanation for the existence of unemployment is based on an analysis which views labour as a commodity to be bought and sold in a market. In this analysis, unemployment can only be understood as a disequilibrium situation brought about because the price of labour (the real wage) is too high to allow the market to clear.

In a naive analysis, the effect of the imposition of a minimum wage would be to cause higher levels of unemployment, but this ignores certain important structural features of the labour market. Supply-side policies can and have been used to change the terms under which labour is bought and sold on the labour market.

Social scientists often offer explanations which are based on the notion of statistical regularities, such as the idea that unemployment *tends* to fall when aggregate demand increases. Correlation analysis can be used to uncover these statistical regularities.

REVIEW QUESTIONS

1 What is meant by the activity rate (or participation rate)? Suggest why the activity rate is higher for women in Britain than in Italy.

2 Are you economically active or inactive?

3 Which region of the UK would you guess has the highest unemployment rate and which the lowest?

4 Consider the information in Table 9.7 on unemployment in the UK in the first quarter of 1996. What proportion of the UK's 2.2 million registered unemployed could be regarded as frictional?

table 9.7
Unemployment, 1996 Q1 (000s)

Total	2201.9
of which:	
under 26 weeks	1072.9
26–52 weeks	421.6
over 52 weeks	816.1

Source: *Employment Gazette.*

5 Would you expect the following pairs of variables to be:
  (i)   positively correlated
  (ii) negatively correlated
  (iii) uncorrelated?

  If they are correlated, how close do you expect the correlation to be?
  Give an *economic* as well as a *statistical* explanation of the link between them.
  (a) inflation rates and unemployment rates
  (b) money wage increases and price increases
  (c) growth rates (of GDP) and unemployment
  (d) personal disposable income and consumer spending.

Key concepts
....

The following key concepts have been introduced in this chapter. Make sure
you understand the meaning and significance of each of them. They are listed
here in the order in which they first appear, and the page number where they
appear is also given. You will find these key concepts in section headings or in
bold in the text. Each chapter contains a list of key concepts and you may find
these particularly useful for revision purposes.

economically inactive	(p. 132)
economically active	(p. 132)
activity rate	(p. 132)
participation rate	(p. 132)
male/female activity rates	(p. 132)
frictional unemployment	(p. 134)
imperfections in the labour market	(p. 135)
structural unemployment	(p. 135)
regional multiplier effect	(p. 135)
regional unemployment	(p. 135)
cyclical unemployment	(p. 135)
demand-deficient (Keynesian) unemployment	(p. 135)
classical view (of determinants of unemployment)	(p. 136)
neo-classical view	(p. 136)
monetarist view	(p. 136)
market-clearing wage	(p. 136)
involuntary unemployment	(p. 137)
statutory minimum wage	(p. 138)
Wages Councils	(p. 138)
homogeneous factor of production	(p. 139)
market power	(p. 139)
monopsonists	(p. 139)
national pay bargaining	(p. 141)
local pay bargaining	(p. 141)
bilateral monopoly	(p. 141)
demand-side policies	(p. 143)

supply-side economics (p. 143)
correlation (p. 143)
statistical regularities (p. 143)
causal mechanisms (p. 143)
causal relationships (p. 144)
dependent variable (p. 144)
independent variable (p. 144)
scatter diagram (p. 144)
mean (p. 145)

Sources of information

The *Employment Gazette*, published monthly by the Department of Employment, contains articles and a statistical appendix relating to all aspects of employment and unemployment in the UK, together with a few international comparisons. The annual publication *Social Trends* discusses activity rates and other features of the labour market.

More information on these and other sources is to be found in the **Guide to Statistical Sources** at the back of this book.

CHAPTER 10

Public spending . . . and taxing

Objectives:
....

This chapter will enable you to:

➤ appreciate the importance of the debate
  about the size of the public sector
➤ distinguish between the various ways of
  measuring the size of the public sector
➤ identify the major areas of public spending
➤ distinguish between spending on goods
  and services, spending on transfer
  payments, and the payment of debt
  interest
➤ understand the link between the budget
  deficit, the PSBR and the national debt
➤ make both international and
  intertemporal comparisons of the
  size of the public sector
➤ be aware of how public spending is
  financed
➤ distinguish direct from indirect taxes;
  and progressive from regressive taxes
➤ appreciate the rationales for the public
  provision of certain goods and services.

10.1 Public spending
10.2 Transfer payments
10.3 Spending on goods and services
10.4 Analysis by department
10.5 Debt interest
10.6 The budget deficit and the PSBR
10.7 The PSBR and the national debt
10.8 How big is the public sector?
10.9 The denominator of the expression
10.10 Historical trends
10.11 An international comparison – taxes
10.12 The financing of government spending
10.13 Direct and indirect taxes
10.14 Progressive, regressive and neutral taxes
10.15 Who pays the tax?
10.16 The structure of the tax system: an international
  comparison
10.17 The rationale for public spending
10.18 Public goods
10.19 The redistributive argument

One of the most important political issues of our generation – not just in the UK, but throughout Europe and worldwide – is that concerning the role of the state in the economy. In Britain, when Margaret Hilda Thatcher entered Number 10 Downing Street for the first time as Prime Minister in May 1979, she set about the task of 'rolling back the frontiers of the state'. Seventeen years later, in 1996, Kenneth Clarke, the then Chancellor of the Exchequer and thought by many to be a moderate man, was talking about cutting back 'the share *taken* by the state' (Interview on BBC Radio 4, 6 February 1996). Note carefully the use of words. Language is seldom neutral and in this instance the word 'taken' is a clear indication that public sector activity is seen as in some way detracting from the performance of the economy. The public sector in this view *takes away* from individuals what is rightfully theirs.

This view ignores the fact that most public sector activity is to do with the provision of goods and services from which individuals derive benefit – goods and services such as health care, education, street lighting, refuse collection, parks and museums. Thus one could talk about the share of national output *provided* by the public sector rather than that taken by the public sector. But here is the rub – this public sector output, no matter how desirable it may be, is not generally packaged up and sold to consumers like hamburgers or washing powder. Rather it is mostly provided free of charge to consumers and is paid for out of taxation – taxation to which all individuals in society contribute. Thus attention focuses on public spending *because of the implications that this has for the tax burden* imposed on you and me.

This chapter will consider some of the issues involved. First, however, we need to review some key definitions and to introduce some new ones.

DID YOU KNOW?

Milton Friedman, who we have encountered several times before in this book, is full of quotable quotes. One such is 'There is no such thing as a free lunch'. What this means is that, even though certain goods and services may appear to be provided 'free', there is always a resource cost involved in providing them. Free school meals are not really free, even though the person eating them may not pay for them. Free health care, similarly, is only free in the sense that the patient does not pay for it directly. Somewhere someone is paying for it. There is no such thing as a free lunch.

10.1 Public spending

Total public spending in the UK in 1996–97 is estimated at a little over £300 billion, which represents just over 40 per cent of GDP. **Figure 10.1** shows how this was made up.

It is useful to distinguish three main types of public spending. These are:

➤ transfer payments (social security spending)
➤ spending on goods and services
➤ debt interest.

Each of these is discussed separately below.

10.2 Transfer payments

As the pie chart shows, the largest *single* slice of public spending is devoted to **social security spending**: £97 billion in 1996, roughly one-third of total public spending. This refers to cash grants such as retirement pensions, unemployment benefit, invalidity benefit and maternity benefit. Collectively, these are officially known as spending on social security (which may seem a somewhat strange euphemism). Economists also refer to them as **transfer payments**. The rationale for these payments is based on the consensus that the state should provide a safety net for those individuals whose incomes would otherwise fall below what is regarded as an acceptable minimum level. These cash payments therefore redistribute income towards the lower paid in

Figure 10.1
**UK general
government
expenditure (X) by
function, 1996–97**

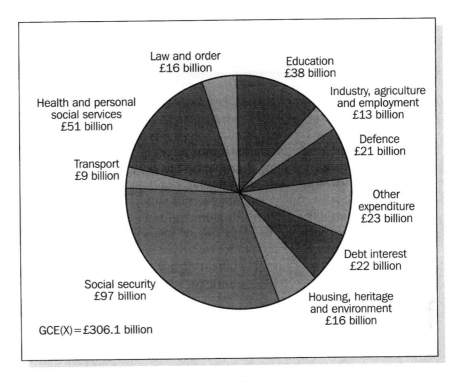

Source: *Financial Statement and Budget Report 1996–97.*

society, and more specifically towards those who are not in employment at all and who therefore have no employment income.

These transfer payments correspond to what is often referred to as spending on the welfare state. The foundations of our modern welfare state were laid in 1942 with the publication of the Beveridge Report. This led to our present system of National Insurance and later, in 1948, to the establishment of the National Health Service.

Beveridge envisaged the establishment of a fund (the National Insurance Fund) into which working people would make contributions (National Insurance Contributions). In times of sickness and in old age, people would be entitled to receive an income from this fund, thus ensuring security against poverty and hardship if they were to fall ill, and in their retirement.

Today everyone in employment pays National Insurance Contributions (NICs) in addition to income tax. Most people believe that this money is in some sense being set aside to pay for their pensions in the future. But NICs are not earmarked for specific purposes, any more than taxes paid by motorists (the road fund licence and duty on fuel) are earmarked for spending on road building. There are no earmarked taxes, only general taxes.

There never was a National Insurance 'Fund'. Pensions and other social security benefits are simply paid for out of current tax receipts.

10.3 Spending on goods and services
••

Spending on goods and services accounts for roughly two-thirds of total public spending. The public sector is responsible for providing a range of goods and services. The most important of these (in terms of spending) are health care, education and defence, which account for about 17, 12 and 7 per cent of total public spending respectively. In addition, spending on the police, prisons and the legal system accounts for a further 5 per cent, transport (which sadly, in our non-green and pleasant land, means roads) a further 3 per cent, and environmental services, such as housing, parks and museums, 5 per cent, with the remainder being made up of numerous other goods and services.

Some of these goods and services are funded directly by central government (universities, for example, receive their funding in this way). However, many services are delivered locally, but are financed by central government – for example, sea defences are commissioned and paid for by the local authority in whose area the defences are built, but the plans have to be approved by MAFF (the Ministry of Agriculture, Fisheries and Food), a department of central government which reimburses the local authority for almost the full cost of the scheme. Similarly, teachers' salaries in local authority schools are paid by the Local Education Authority, but some of the finance for this comes from central government funds. Roughly half of local authority spending is financed in this way.

10.4 Analysis by department
••

It follows from this that there are two ways of analysing total government spending. We can either analyse it by *function* or by *department*. The pie chart in Figure 10.1 which we looked at earlier is an analysis by function. An alternative analysis is provided in Table 10.1, where total spending is broken down by the various government departments responsible for spending it. Note that, as we would expect, total spending is the same in both Figure 10.1 and Table 10.1 – namely, £306.1 billion.

ACTIVITY **1**
••••••••••••

In Table 10.1, what do you think is meant by 'cyclical social security'? Why is this figure of £13.9 billion distinguished from the other figure for social security of £76.8 billion?

What do you think is the significance of the sub-heading called 'Control Total'?

Hint: these figures are derived from the November 1995 *Financial Statement and Budget Report* (the Red Book). They are *projections* of spending in 1996–97.

Check with answers/suggestions at the back of the book.

10.5 Debt interest
••••••••••••••••••••••••••

Figure 10.1 and Table 10.1 show that in 1996 debt interest accounted for some £22 billion, approximately 7 per cent of total government spending. This debt interest is the interest on outstanding public sector debt, sometimes known as

table 10.1		£bn	% of GGE
General government	Social security	76.8	25.1
expenditure by	Health	33.8	11.0
department,	DOE – local government	31.3	10.2
1996–97 (forecasts	DOE – other	8.2	3.2
given in 1995	Scotland, Wales and N. Ireland	29.4	9.6
budget, £bn)	Defence	21.4	7.0
	Education and Employment	14.0	4.6
	Home Office	6.5	2.1
	Transport	4.2	1.4
	Other departments	19.5	6.4
	Local authority self-financed expenditure	12.5	4.1
	Reserve	2.5	0.8
	Control total	**260.2**	**85.0**
	Cyclical social security	13.9	4.5
	Central government debt interest	22.3	7.3
	Accounting adjustments	9.7	3.1
	GGE(X)[1]	**306.1**	**100.0**

[1]GGE(X) is general government expenditure excluding privatisation proceeds and lottery-financed spending, and net of interest and dividend receipts.

Source: *Financial Statement and Budget Report 1996–97.*

the **National Debt**. As is explained more fully in the next section, the National Debt is the accumulated public sector borrowing requirement (PSBR). That is, it represents borrowing by governments in previous years.

10.6 The budget deficit and the PSBR

In Chapter 3 we defined the government's budget deficit as the difference between its receipts and its expenditure. Other things being equal, a budget deficit will give rise to a borrowing requirement of a similar amount. In other words, a budget deficit of £10 billion will mean that the **public sector borrowing requirement** is also £10 billion.

However, the Conservative government's policy of selling off state assets has provided the Chancellor with an additional source of funds – the proceeds of privatisations. The funds raised in this way are not, however, treated as income – the sale represents a once-and-for-all disposal of assets which cannot be repeated. But privatisation proceeds do help to reduce the requirement for loanable funds. In 1994–95, for example, the budget deficit was £40.5 billion, but because of privatisation proceeds, which netted £4.6 billion, the PSBR was only £35.9 billion (that is, 40.5 minus 4.6).

Figure 10.2 shows general government expenditure, general government receipts and the PSBR for the period 1972–2001 (the shaded area from 1996 onwards represents forecast values rather than actual values). The information on expenditure and receipts is presented in such a way that the gap between the two

Figure 10.2

UK expenditure, receipts and the PSBR, 1972–2001 (% of money GDP)

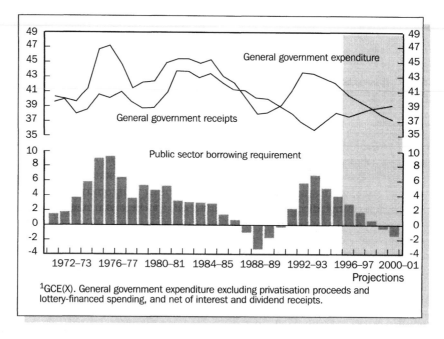

Source: *Financial Statement and Budget Report 1996–97.*

shows the budget deficit or surplus. As can be seen, spending exceeded revenue apart from a brief period between 1987 and 1990, at which time there was a budget surplus. The budget is also projected to go into surplus by the year 2000.

Although, as we explained, the PSBR is not exactly equal to the budget deficit, there will be a close association between the two. Thus a large budget deficit in the period 1993–95 is associated with a large PSBR.

On those occasions in which the budget is in surplus, however, the PSBR will be negative. One such period was 1987–90, at which time we could speak of a **public sector debt repayment,** since this will have resulted in part of the accumulated public sector debt being repaid.

10.7 The PSBR and the national debt

The national debt (otherwise known as *public sector debt*) is the accumulated PSBR – the sum total of the PSBR this year, last year, the year before that and so on. To use the Red Book definition: *net public sector debt is the stock analogue of the PSBR* (which is itself a flow, of course). In 1994–95 net public sector debt (the national debt) measured some £291 billion, about 42 per cent of GDP in that year. This percentage is of more than passing interest as we shall see in Chapter 11, since this ratio is one of the 'convergence criteria' established by the EU at Maastricht.

The term 'public sector debt' may be used in preference to the older expression 'National Debt,' since this latter term is sometimes erroneously taken to mean what the UK owes to other countries. This is incorrect since most of the UK national debt is held *internally* by financial institutions, companies and households *within the UK* in the form of Treasury Bills (held by companies) and National Savings Certificates and Premium Bonds (held by households). Only about 10 per cent of the National Debt is held by foreign firms and households.

10.8 How big is the public sector?

We have emphasised repeatedly throughout this book that one can only get a feel for the data by linking it to something to which one can personally relate, or by calculating ratios or rates of change. Thus to be told that in 1996–97 public spending amounted to a little over £300 billion would not mean much to the average reader.

It would become more meaningful, however, if we were also told that in the same period the total output of the economy measured just over £700 billion. We could then calculate what *proportion* of total output this public spending represented, and in this way get a feel for how large it was. In effect, we could assess the size of the public sector by measuring the G/Y ratio. Unfortunately, the calculation of this seemingly simple ratio is beset with difficulties about how G should be defined and what to use as our measure of Y.

Consider first the numerator of the expression, G. As we know, there are three main types of spending undertaken by the government – spending on goods and services, spending on transfer payments, and the payment of debt interest.

The reason why it is important to distinguish spending on goods and services from spending on transfer payments is as follows. When we measure the output of the economy (gross product) we wish to include not only the output of the private sector, but also the output of the public sector – the output of health care, education, roads, policing services and so on. As explained in Chapter 4, when calculating output by the expenditure method (and for simplicity assuming a closed economy) we use the following national accounts identity.

$$Y = C + I + G$$

The output of the consumer goods industry (C) will be exactly equal to the money spent by consumers purchasing consumer goods, and the output of the investment goods industry (I) will be exactly equal to the money spent by firms in purchasing investment goods.

But what can be said about G – the output of the government sector? This output is not purchased by consumers, but it is purchased by the state: the government pays doctors' salaries, it pays the salaries of policemen and high court judges, it pays for building roads and so on. Thus G represents expenditure on – and therefore the output of – goods and services produced by the public sector. It *excludes transfer payments* because there is no output that corresponds to these cash payments. Unlike doctors, teachers, lawyers and policemen who produce output – of health care, education and so on – pensioners produce no output. Nor do the unemployed (in return for unemployed benefit) or the bereaved (in return for death grant). Thus in calculating output (GDP) we *include* in G all of the spending on goods and services, but we *exclude* spending on transfer payments.

An important and contentious point follows from this. In measuring the size of the public sector – in effect, when calculating the G/Y ratio – should we include or *exclude* transfer payments from G? The answer is a moot point, but it seems more correct to *exclude* transfers from G (the numerator of the expression), since they are excluded from Y (the denominator of the expression). These cash transfers are precisely what their names imply – they transfer income and the ability to spend from one section of society to another. More precisely, they transfer income from taxpayers in general to the recipients of the grants. They do not directly affect the measured output of the economy, or the government's command over the economy's resources, or the size of the public sector. However, they do constitute part of public spending, and are thus part of the total financing requirement.

> **DID YOU KNOW?**
> The expression 'a moot point' refers to an undecided or disputed point. In measuring the size of the public sector, it is a moot point as to whether one should include or exclude transfer payments. But the answer may be important to whoever is using it: critics of the public sector are likely to include it and thus exaggerate the size of the government's role in the economy.

A further illustration may help to clarify the contentious and disputed issue of whether to include or exclude transfer payments when measuring the size of the public sector. Until 1977 parents were able to claim income tax relief for dependent children. These **child tax allowances** had the effect of reducing the income tax paid by the head of the household – normally the father. The government of the day wished to ensure that the money went directly to the mother for the benefit of the child, rather than to the father. Therefore it was decided to scrap child tax allowances and to replace them with **child benefit**, a cash grant paid directly to mothers. This involved no extra cost to the Exchequer, since the result was to collect an extra sum in tax from the fathers in order to pay the same sum in increased grants to mothers.

Consider the implications of this when measuring the size of the public sector. If G in the G/Y ratio is defined to include transfer payments, the move from tax allowance to cash grant will have the effect of increasing the measured G/Y ratio and hence, seemingly, increasing the size of state involvement in the economy. This seems to be incorrect because the extent of state involvement has not really been increased by the switch from tax allowance to cash grant. The switch has, however, increased public spending. We therefore conclude that in measuring the extent of state involvement in the economy:

➤ transfer payments should be *excluded* when calculating the size of the public sector

➤ but transfer payments must be *included* when calculating public spending.

Thus our assessment of state involvement in the economy – the calculation of the G/Y ratio – will crucially depend on what exactly one is trying to gauge from this ratio. Hence when this issue is being discussed in the media, one should always be alert to the ambiguity involved.

The decision as to whether or not to include or exclude debt interest when measuring the size of the public sector rests on similar considerations to those concerning transfer payments. If the question being asked relates to *public spending,* debt interest should be included. If it relates to the size of the public sector, it should not.

10.9 The denominator of the expression

Finally, when measuring the G/Y ratio, what should we use for Y? The short-listed candidates are:

➤ GDP at market prices
➤ GDP at factor cost
➤ GNP at either market prices or factor cost.

A sensible general rule is that both numerator and denominator of the expression should be measured on the same basis. Therefore since the public spending which forms the bulk of G in the numerator will be at market prices, it follows that the Y in the denominator should also be at market prices.

If we are interested in *domestic* activity – what goes on *within* the UK economy – then GDP is to be preferred to GNP.

In fact, it probably does not matter too much which of these measures is chosen, *provided* of course that, in making comparisons through time or with other countries, you compare like with like. That is, the estimates calculated must be constructed on a consistent basis.

10.10 Historical trends

No matter how we measure the G/Y ratio it is quite clear that it has risen over the last 100 years in the UK and elsewhere. *Figure 10.3* shows what has happened to the ratio in the UK.

The figure shows general government spending as a proportion of GDP. A number of features are apparent.

Figure 10.3

UK general government expenditure, 1901–96 (% of GDP)

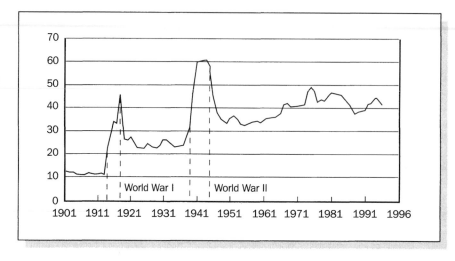

Source: Central Statistical Office.

➤ In each of the two world wars, government spending as a proportion of GDP rose above its trend value. This is to be expected, since at such times the government will wish to direct a greater proportion of the economy's resources towards the war effort.

➤ There is a rising *trend* – government spending is assuming a larger and larger proportion of GDP. The ratio rose from about 14 per cent at the turn of the century to around 45 per cent in the 1980s.

➤ We can see from the more recent experience of the economy that the ratio is *cyclical*. This can be seen from Figure 10.3, but more clearly from ***Figure 10.2*** (on page 156), which you should now have another look at. During the recession of the early 1980s, the ratio increased to 47 per cent (largely due to increased social security and unemployment expenditures). Following that, however, the boom conditions of the middle to late 1980s saw the ratio fall to 38 per cent in 1988 as expenditure on these transfer payments fell. More recently still, the ratio has risen again as a result of the recession of the early 1990s, before falling back to just over 40 per cent by 1996 as economic recovery gained momentum.

10.11 An international comparison – taxes

So far in this chapter, we have looked at the *G/Y* ratio – interpreted to mean total government spending as a proportion of GDP. As we argued at the beginning of the chapter, the reason why we focus on this ratio (rather than public sector *output* as a proportion of GDP) is that this spending in its totality has to be financed. It has to be paid for. Remember Friedman's maxim that there is no such thing as a free lunch.

If the budget is balanced – although there is no particular reason why it should be – then the *G/Y* ratio will be the same as the *T/Y* ratio, since

$$T = G \text{ (Total tax receipts = Total government expenditures)}$$

is how we define a balanced budget. We could therefore look at the T/Y ratio: total tax receipts as a proportion of GDP. There are no major advantages in looking at the T/Y ratio rather than the G/Y ratio. Both suffer from the sort of detailed technical problems we have discussed. Both ratios have, of course, been on a rising trend in the twentieth century and both are cyclical – they rise in a recession and fall back when the economy is more buoyant.

Here we are going to use the T/Y ratio rather than the G/Y ratio to make an international comparison of the size of the public sector. The reason for this choice is simply that we can then proceed to a more detailed investigation of how taxes are raised.

Figure 10.4 shows total tax receipts as a percentage of GDP. The information is displayed for the seven major industrial countries – the so-called Group of Seven. The data relate to 1982 and 1992, so one can use these data both to make an international comparison and also to assess changes over this ten-year period. As can be seen, there was less state involvement in the economy – as measured by this ratio – in the UK in 1992 than in France, Germany, Italy or Canada but somewhat more than in Japan or the USA. The ratio appears to have fallen somewhat in the UK and to have risen in Italy, Canada and Japan.

Table 10.2 gives a more detailed account. This shows the same ratio for a fuller list of European countries for 1992 and 1993. The picture here is clear. Within Europe the UK is a low-tax country, which may surprise you. Only Switzerland had a lower ratio.

Figure 10.4

Taxes and social security contributions in selected countries, 1982–92 (% of GDP at market prices)

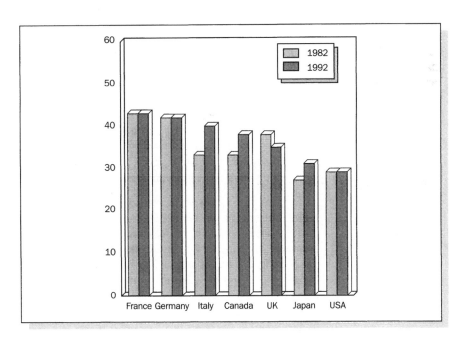

Source: 'Taxes and social security contributions: an international comparison 1982–92', *Economic Trends*, 1995.

table 10.2

Total receipts from taxes and social security contributions, 1992, and estimates for 1993 (% of GDP at market prices)

	1992	1993
Austria	43.6	43.4
Belgium	45.4	45.7
Denmark	48.9	50.0
Finland	37.7	46.8
France	43.7	44.0
Germany	40.0	39.7
Ireland	38.0	37.1
Italy	42.4	43.2
Netherlands	46.7	48.2
Norway	46.7	45.8
Spain	35.9	34.7
Sweden	50.4	49.5
Switzerland	32.2	32.5
United Kingdom	35.8	34.4

Source: 'Taxes and social security contributions: an international comparison 1982–92', *Economic Trends*, 1995.

10.12 The financing of government spending

We now turn to a more detailed analysis of how public spending is financed. *Figure 10.5* shows the financing of total government spending for 1996–97. This diagram is the counterpart of Figure 10.1, which we looked at earlier. Figure 10.1 showed that total government spending (GGE(X)) in 1995–96 was £306.1 billion, and Figure 10.5 shows how the finance for this was raised. As you can work out from the diagram, total receipts from all forms of tax in 1995–96 are expected to be £283.6 billion, leaving a borrowing requirement of £22.5 billion.

We now turn to an analysis of the major forms of taxation. There are two basic ways of classifying the various forms of taxation – either according to the *type* of tax or according to *who pays* the tax.

10.13 Direct and indirect taxes

It is helpful to distinguish two main types of tax – **direct tax** and **indirect tax** – though not all taxes fit neatly into one or other category.

➤ Direct taxes are **taxes on income**. They can be levied on households (such as income tax) or on companies (such as corporation tax).
➤ Indirect taxes are **taxes on expenditure**. The main forms of indirect tax are value added tax (VAT) and excise duties levied on petrol, alcohol and tobacco. Excise duties are paid by households and companies. VAT is also paid by both households and companies but companies can claim back most of the tax paid so that in fact the bulk of VAT receipts come from the spending of households.

There are a number of reasons for drawing a basic distinction between direct and indirect taxes. Direct taxes are more 'visible' than indirect taxes, which to

Figure 10.5
The financing of UK general government spending, 1996–97

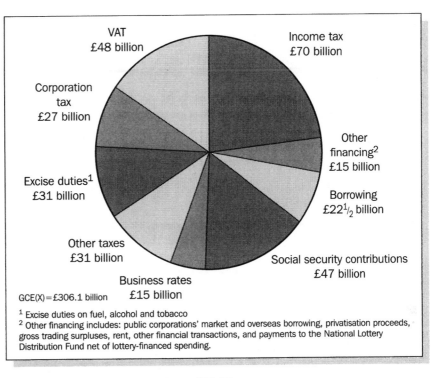

VAT
£48 billion

Income tax
£70 billion

Corporation
tax
£27 billion

Other
financing[2]
£15 billion

Borrowing
£22¹/₂ billion

Excise duties[1]
£31 billion

Social security contributions
£47 billion

Other taxes
£31 billion

Business rates
£15 billion

GCE(X) = £306.1 billion

[1] Excise duties on fuel, alcohol and tobacco
[2] Other financing includes: public corporations' market and overseas borrowing, privatisation proceeds, gross trading surpluses, rent, other financial transactions, and payments to the National Lottery Distribution Fund net of lottery-financed spending.

Source: *Financial Statement and Budget Report 1996–97.*

some extent may be hidden in product prices. It is sometimes argued that direct taxes may therefore cause greater resentment among those who pay them. Moreover, it is argued that indirect taxes give the taxpayer an element of choice about how much tax to pay – the more goods and services you buy, the more tax you pay – whereas direct tax allows no such choice.

Perhaps the most important reason for distinguishing direct from indirect taxes, however, is because of the impact that each type of tax has on the **distribution of income** after tax, which we discuss below.

10.14 Progressive, regressive and neutral taxes

We define a **progressive tax** as one that takes a larger proportion of high incomes than it does of low incomes. By this we mean not just that the rich pay more, but that they pay *proportionately* more – that is, they pay a larger fraction of their income in tax than the poor do. Income tax is a progressive tax. This results from two main features:

➤ The system of **initial allowances** means that the first tranche of income is free of all tax (in 1995–96 this was £3,525).

➤ There are **higher marginal rates** of tax for the higher paid. In 1995–96 the rates were:

　➤ 20 per cent on the first £3,200 of 'taxable income' (that is, income after deduction of initial allowances)

> ➤ 25 per cent on the next £21,100. This is known as the 'basic rate'.
> ➤ 40 per cent on taxable income over £24,300. This is known as the 'higher rate'.

ACTIVITY **2**

In 1995–96 two individuals receive the normal initial allowances. One has an income of £20,000 and the other an income of £40,000. What is the *average tax rate* for each individual (that is, what proportion of income is paid in income tax)?

Check with answers/suggestions at the back of the book.

Regressive taxes

The opposite to a progressive tax is a **regressive tax**. If a tax takes a larger proportion of small incomes than it does of large incomes, it is said to be regressive. Surprisingly, there are a number of regressive taxes in the UK tax system. One such is the employees' National Insurance Contribution. Although this tax is structured in such a way that there are higher bands for higher incomes, there is also a ceiling above which no further NIC is payable. The effect of this ceiling is that the proportion of higher incomes paid in tax is *smaller* not larger than that of lower incomes.

Lump-sum taxes such as the infamous and now discontinued poll tax (officially known as the *community charge*) are regressive. Rich and poor pay the same amount so that the *proportion* of income paid in tax is higher for low incomes.

More importantly – and perhaps unexpectedly – indirect taxes, particularly excise duties, are by and large regressive in their impact (as we shall see later). The main reason for this is that low-income families tend to spend a larger proportion of their income on heavily taxed items such as alcohol and tobacco than high-income families do.

Proportionate taxes

Finally, as one might expect, a **proportionate tax** (or **neutral tax**) is one that takes the same proportion of large incomes as it does of small. As we saw above, even taxes which are ostensibly neutral may not be neutral in their impact because of differences in spending patterns.

ACTIVITY **3**

The imposition of VAT on fuel caused a political furore. Why was this?

Check with answers/suggestions at the back of the book

10.15 Who pays the tax?

An alternative way of classifying taxes is to ask: who pays the tax? (to which the answer is either households or companies).

Taxes paid by households

➤ Direct taxes levied on households include income tax and the employees' NIC (which should really be treated as part of the income tax system).
➤ Indirect taxes paid by households include VAT, excise duties, council tax, vehicle excise duties, and betting and gaming duties.

Taxes paid by companies

➤ Direct taxes levied on companies include corporation tax and taxes such as petroleum revenue tax.
➤ Indirect taxes paid by companies include business rates, customs and excise duties and some VAT. The employers' NIC can be classified as an indirect tax.

10.16 The structure of the tax system: an international comparison

Given the complexity of the tax system in the UK and elsewhere, it is danger-ous to make simplistic comparisons between countries. However, it is revealing to compare the split between direct and indirect taxes in various countries. Figure 10.6 shows that in the UK, the burden of taxation falls comparatively heavily on indirect taxes. In fact, the UK raised a larger proportion of its total tax revenue from indirect taxes than any of the other G7 countries. Hence the UK's tax system is largely regressive rather than progressive. This has added to the increasing inequality of incomes experienced since 1979.

Figure 10.6
Indirect taxes in selected countries, 1982–92 (% of total taxes and social security contributions)

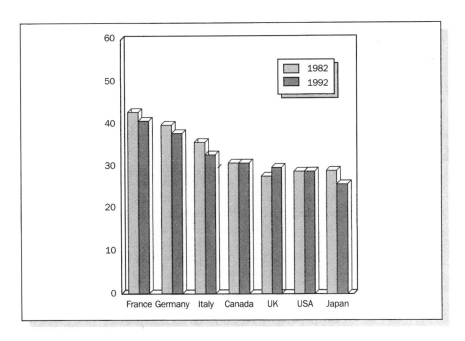

Source: 'Taxes and social contributions: an international comparison 1982–92', *Economic Trends*, 1995.

10.17 The rationale for public spending
....

We began this chapter by noting that total public spending in the UK, at around £300 billion in 1996, represents around 40 per cent of GDP. We also noted that the question of whether this share is too large – or too small – is one of the most important contemporary political issues. Our discussion so far has centred on how this share could most appropriately be measured. We also noted the growth of public spending in the twentieth century and compared the share in the UK with that in other countries.

Additional insights into these issues can be gained by considering the question of why we need public spending. What is the rationale for the public provision of certain goods and services, and what is the rationale for spending on transfer payments?

Note at the outset that the rationale for spending on goods and services is quite separate and quite different from the rationale for spending on transfer payments – hence an additional reason for considering them separately, as we do below.

10.18 Public goods
....

The term **public goods** when used in economics means something very specific (and indeed something rather different from what one might imagine). 'Public goods' stand in contrast to 'private goods'. Public goods, when used in this context, are not necessarily produced by the public sector, nor are they necessarily 'good' – that is, beneficial. Rather public goods are defined as those goods and services which possess two very specific attributes – *non-excludability* and *non-rivalness*.

If a good is **non-excludable,** those who do not pay for its provision cannot be *excluded* from enjoying the benefits which it provides. A classic example of such a good is a lighthouse, the purpose of which is to keep ships from running aground. Those mariners or ship-owners who do not pay for the building and maintenance of the lighthouse cannot be deprived of the benefits that it provides. Its light serves as a warning to all, keeping them away from sandbanks and other hazards.

ASK YOURSELF

As is well known, mermaids beckoned sailors on to the rocks to their deaths. In contrast, lighthouses were built to prevent ships from running on to the rocks by helping them to establish their position at sea. They were paid for publicly or by groups of ship-owners who banded together to provide the finance.

They are now largely redundant – at least for commercial shipping. Why is this? Have these public goods been replaced by private goods?

The lighthouse is also a **non-rival** public good, in the sense that the benefit which one individual derives from it does not detract from the benefit which others derive. The strength of the beam of light is not diminished simply because one individual sees it. It follows from this property of non-rivalness that, if the light is provided for one person, it might as well be provided for all, since one person's consumption does not reduce the supply of this public good available to all.

ACTIVITY **4**

Consider the extent to which the following possess one or other or both of the characteristics of non-excludability and non-rivalness.

(a) defence of the realm
(b) street lighting
(c) television broadcasts
(d) pornography on the Internet
(e) public parks
(f) sea defences along the coast
(g) cedar fences in gardens

Check with answers/suggestions at the back of the book.

Roads in Britain are an example of public goods which are non-excludable, in the sense that anyone can use them without paying for the cost of building them or maintaining them. In a strictly legal sense, of course, to use a car on a public road in Britain one must pay a road fund licence (purchase a 'tax disc'), but in fact the car runs just as well whether you have one or not, so that evasion is possible and indeed widespread. The road fund licence is an attempt to render excludable that which is intrinsically non-excludable.

Roads are also non-rival, but only until congestion reaches a level at which the presence of other road users detracts from the benefits which you derive. Roads then become increasingly rival. As **Table 10.3** shows, as a result of congestion average vehicle speeds in London are now lower than they were 25 years ago.

table 10.3

Average traffic speeds in London, 1968–94

(miles per hour)

	Central area	Inner area	Outer area	All areas
Morning peak[1]				
1968–70	12.7	15.1	20.5	18.1
1983–86	11.8	13.5	18.8	16.9
1990–94	10.2	13.3	17.5	15.8
Daytime off-peak[2]				
1968–70	12.1	18.3	26.5	21.3
1983–86	11.9	16.3	25.3	20.9
1990–94	10.5	15.8	22.8	19.3
Evening peak[3]				
1968–70	11.8	15.2	21.9	18.6
1983–86	11.5	13.1	20.1	17.2
1990–94	10.3	13.2	19.7	17.0

[1] 7 a.m. to 10 a.m.
[2] 10 a.m. to 4 p.m.
[3] 4 p.m. to 7 p.m.

Source: *London Traffic Monitoring Report.*

A concept related to rivalness is that of **externalities**, otherwise known as *external diseconomies* or *external costs*. When the level of congestion on a road reaches a certain point, each car driver imposes costs on every other car driver and everyone's average speed drops. Externalities in car usage relate not only to congestion, but also crucially to air and noise pollution. Each car driver imposes costs on his or her fellow citizens by forcing them to suffer the disutility associated with breathing exhaust fumes and being exposed to noise.

These costs are *external* to the motorist him or herself. In deciding whether or not to use the car, he or she takes into account the **private cost** – the cost of petrol, oil, wear and tear and depreciation of the vehicle – but does not take account of the costs imposed on others. The **social cost** of car usage exceeds the private cost by the amount of these negative externalities. Hence if decisions about car usage are based on purely private cost (which they are), too many people will choose to use their cars because they do not pay the full social cost of so doing.

This is an important point. But we should note that not all externalities are *negative externalities*. Some activities provide positive spillovers for our neighbours. These are *positive externalities*. If I grow roses in my front garden, passers-by will derive enjoyment from them, even though they do not help to grow them. And, of course, I cannot charge them for the benefits they derive from my horticultural efforts.

Some aspects of education and health care produce positive external benefits (positive externalities). Preventive medicine, such as screening for infectious diseases like tuberculosis, is a classic case. So is immunisation against whooping cough. If I have my child immunised against whooping cough, I confer benefits not just on my own child, but also on all those others with whom my child comes into contact. It follows from the existence of these positive externalities that the state should subsidise those activities, such as immunisation against communicable diseases, which provide positive external benefits to society at large. In this way, more individuals will become immunised than would be the case if they were asked to pay the full cost of the treatment themselves.

Education also provides positive external benefits to society at large, in the sense that it raises the productivity not just of the recipients of the education, but of other members of society as well. Moreover, a liberal education (allegedly) produces a more enlightened, literate and cultured society. Educated people are healthier, so they may make fewer demands on health services, and they certainly make fewer demands on the police and the criminal justice and prison services. And these societal benefits are passed on to future generations, since educated parents are more likely to educate their children.

ASK YOURSELF

Which former British Prime Minister of recent times said, 'There is no such thing as "society". There are only individuals and families.'?

What is the significance of the remark, particularly in the light of the preceding paragraph about the benefits of education?

The public good argument and the related concept of externalities, then, provide a major rationale for the public provision of certain goods and services. However, some things provided publicly are really *private goods*, since they are excludable and rival and do not possess significant positive externalities. Some aspects of health care are like this. It is difficult to argue that cosmetic dentistry is anything other than a pure private good – unless, of course, it is seen as preventive medicine, reducing the need for treatment at some later stage of the patient's life.

The argument for the public provision of these goods and services then rests on a different proposition – the **merit good** argument. There is a consensus – it is argued – that some goods and services are so important that every citizen should have access to an adequate supply of them, regardless of income. Health care and education and defence against crime are such goods.

Moreover, free education and health care also provide **income in kind** for the recipients. By providing this income in kind rather than in cash, the state ensures that income is not 'squandered' on other goods and services deemed less worthy.

10.19 The redistributive argument

The provision of services such as health care and education thus redistributes income in society, making it more equal than it would otherwise be. This forms a powerful argument in its own right for public provision.

The discussion so far has centred on the rationale for the public provision of goods and services, but as we saw earlier, a large slice of public spending – roughly one-third – goes on transfer payments. The rationale for these cash transfers is, of course, the redistributive motive. These payments constitute a financial safety net. Often referred to as an **income maintenance programme,** they prevent money incomes falling below what is deemed to be an acceptable minimum level.

Beveridge saw such payments as temporary – apart from those payments to the chronically sick and aged. However, some commentators argue that some recipients of social welfare payments develop a long-term dependence on income from the state, and that this produces a disincentive effect on work effort. Such commentators – generally those on the right of the political spectrum – therefore advocate a reduction in the real value of state cash benefits. The immediate effect of such a cut in transfer payments would, of course, be to make the distribution of incomes more unequal. These issues are considered in greater detail in the following chapter.

Summary

The output of the economy includes the output of the public sector – things such as education and health care. Since this output cannot be measured directly, the value of inputs is taken as a measure of the value of output. Thus *public spending on goods and services* can be regarded as a measure of the size of the public sector. This, however, will exclude spending on transfer payments (which accounts for about one-third of total public spending). Therefore to arrive at a measure of *total public spending,* these expenditures on transfer payments should be included, as should spending on the payment of debt interest.

The budget deficit is the difference between total public spending (including transfers and debt interest) and tax receipts. This will be the same as the public sector borrowing requirement, unless privatisation proceeds produce an additional (and non-recurring) source of revenue for the government. The national debt is the accumulated PSBR.

The size of the public sector (and public spending as a percentage of total spending) has increased throughout the twentieth century, both in the UK and elsewhere. Contemporary estimates for the UK put total public spending at around 40 per cent of GDP, which is on a par with or somewhat lower than other comparable countries.

Public spending is financed by two main types of tax – direct taxes (such as income tax) and indirect taxes (such as VAT). Direct taxes tend to be progressive (the higher the income, the greater the proportion paid in tax), whereas indirect taxes are regressive in their impact. Indirect taxes account for a somewhat larger proportion of total tax revenue in the UK than in most other countries, which makes the UK tax system less progressive than elsewhere.

The rationale for public spending on goods and services is based partly on the *public good* argument. Pure public goods possess the twin characteristics of non-excludability and non-rivalness. Public spending also redistributes income – in cash and in kind – towards the less well-off, so that the distribution of final incomes becomes less unequal than it would otherwise be.

REVIEW QUESTIONS

1. For the benefit of those who have never come across him, Student Grant is a character in *Viz* magazine, which is a sort of comic for adolescent grown-ups. Grant is a rather spotty young man who goes to university and receives a maintenance grant from his local authority. How should Grant's student grant be treated? Is it a transfer payment or is it part of spending on education (that is, spending on goods and services)?

2. Motorway tolls seek to render excludable that which was previously non-excludable. Explain what this means.
   Which European countries of which you have knowledge use this device?

3. Britain is the only civilised (*sic*) country where you can be sent to prison for watching television without a licence. How do the concepts of non-excludability and non-rivalness shed light on this issue?

4. Should infertility treatment be provided 'on the National Health'?

5. 'Britain's nuclear defence policy is a public good.' Discuss.

6. 'Defence against crime is not a public good. Otherwise private security companies would not exist.' Discuss.

Key concepts
....

The following key concepts have been introduced in this chapter. Make sure you understand the meaning and significance of each of them. They are listed here in the order in which they first appear, and the page number where they appear is also given. You will find these key concepts in section headings or in **bold** in the text. Each chapter contains a list of key concepts and you may find these particularly useful for revision purposes.

public spending	(p.152)
social security spending	(p.152)
transfer payments	(p.152)
spending on goods and services	(p.154)
debt interest	(p.154)
national debt	(p.155)
public sector borrowing requirement	(p.155)
public sector debt repayment	(p.156)
child tax allowances	(p.158)
child benefit	(p.158)
direct tax	(p.162)
indirect tax	(p.162)
taxes on income	(p.162)
taxes on expenditure	(p.162)
distribution of income	(p.163)
progressive tax	(p.163)
initial allowances	(p.163)
higher marginal rates	(p.163)
regressive tax	(p.164)
proportionate (neutral) tax	(p.164)
public goods	(p.166)
non-excludable	(p.166)
non-rival	(p.166)
externalities	(p.168)
private cost/social cost	(p.168)
merit good	(p.169)
income in kind	(p.169)
income maintenance programme	(p.169)

Sources of information
....

Information on government spending and taxing is found in a variety of sources. The most up-to-date and comprehensive statement of planned expenditure and receipts is found in the Red Book, *Financial Statement and Budget*

Report, published annually in November to coincide with the Chancellor's Budget. However, you may find that your library does not stock this publication. Alternative sources are the Blue Book, *UK National Accounts,* and *Economic Trends,* which also contains articles about the tax system. The Institute for Fiscal Studies publishes a 'Green Budget' report in October each year in anticipation of the Budget. This valuable commentary is available from the IFS, 7 Ridgmount Street, London WC1E 7AE.

More information on these and other sources is to be found in the **Guide to Statistical Sources** at the back of this book.

CHAPTER 11

Changes in the structure of the UK economy

Objectives:

This chapter will enable you to:

➤ identify the forces which have led to structural changes in the UK economy
➤ appreciate that in an open economy the forces of globalisation may be beyond the ability of national governments to control
➤ understand that, in addition to the external forces of globalisation, the Conservative government in the UK has used supply-side policies to bring about structural change
➤ appreciate that supply-side policies have been directed towards the market for goods and services by attempting to promote competition; and towards the labour market by weakening the power of trade unions
➤ be aware of the political and industrial events in the 1980s which weakened the power of the trade unions
➤ understand the rationale for the changes in the system of taxation and social security and their impact
➤ be aware of the various definitions of income used in the measurement of the distribution of income
➤ understand the impact that the system of taxation and social security has on the distribution of income
➤ appreciate that in the goods market supply-side policies consisted of attempts to 'extend market forces' by privatisation and liberalisation
➤ be aware that not all privatisations were successful in introducing competition
➤ be aware of the view that the alleged productivity gap suffered by UK industry has been narrowed.

11.1 The dog that didn't bark
11.2 The causes of structural change
11.3 The rationale for supply-side policies
11.4 Supply-side policies
11.5 Labour market policies: weakening the power of trade unions
11.6 A flexible labour market?
11.7 Changes in the structure of taxation and social security
11.8 The impact on the distribution of income
11.9 Privatisation and liberalisation
11.10 Competition: a panacea?
11.11 Closing the productivity gap

11.1 The dog that didn't bark

'[but] the dog did nothing in the night-time.' (said Dr Watson)
'That was the curious incident,' remarked Sherlock Holmes.
Sir Arthur Conan Doyle, *Silver Blaze*

One of the most difficult things to observe – in economics as in life – is something which *does not* happen. In the Sherlock Holmes adventure, it is the *failure* of a watchdog to bark when disturbed by intruders in the night that the master detective describes as a 'curious incident'. If you expect certain events to occur and they fail to do so, that in itself is noteworthy.

In September 1992 sterling left the exchange rate mechanism of the EMS and its value *vis-à-vis* the Deutschmark fell by about 20 per cent over the next few months. One might have expected that the rise in import prices which this caused would have resulted in a rapid rise in the domestic rate of inflation – bearing in mind that spending on imports accounts for about 30 per cent of all spending in the UK. Inflation, however, did not increase markedly. It was a curious incident. It was the dog that didn't bark.

The science of macroeconomics consists of establishing statistical regularities. These regularities comprise observed relationships between variables – relationships which seem to remain constant over an extended period of time. We can then use our knowledge of these relationships to *predict* what is likely to happen in a given set of circumstances. If the predicted event does not in fact happen, we conclude that some sort of **structural change** must have occurred. If we experience a heatwave in December, we conclude that some radical change in Britain's weather pattern must have happened – or that we must have been mysteriously transplanted to the southern hemisphere without anyone noticing.

Of course, nothing in economics is clear cut. The rate of inflation did in fact increase slightly in the period following the 1992 depreciation. The dog did bark. But it didn't bark very much, and much less than might have been expected on the basis of the past behaviour of the UK economy. It would be a reasonable statement to say that – like many other economies – the UK economy in the post-war period was prone to inflation. Indeed, in exasperation at the failure of successive counter-inflation policies actually to stem the rate of inflation, some economists remarked that the price system only works in one direction – upwards. The relatively modest rate of inflation in the period since 1992 is therefore all the more remarkable, since it provides some evidence of the UK economy apparently becoming less prone to inflation than was previously the case.

Further evidence of structural change in the UK economy comes from the labour market. In particular, the labour market seems to have behaved differently in each of the last two economic recessions – that at the beginning of the 1980s and that at the beginning of the 1990s. In the wake of the first recession:

➤ Unemployment continued to rise for almost two years after the economy had 'bottomed out'. Only after a very long lag did unemployment eventually start to fall.
➤ As soon as unemployment started to level out, real wages started to increase rapidly.

In contrast, in the wake of the second recession:

➤ Unemployment started to fall sooner. There was only a short lag between the trough of the recession and the time that unemployment began to fall.
➤ When unemployment did start to fall, real wages remained fairly 'flat' – that is, they did not increase very much.

This is summarised in *Figure 11.1*.

Figure 11.1

A tale of two recessions

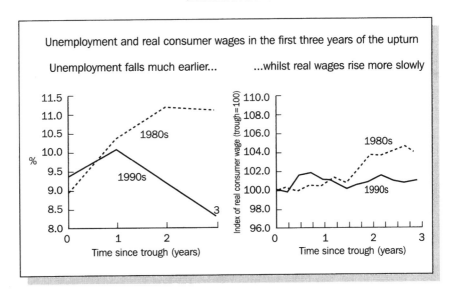

Source: Julian Morgan, 'What do comparisons of the last two economic recoveries tell us about the UK labour market?', *National Institute Economic Review*, May 1996.

11.2 The causes of structural change

If there has indeed been some structural change in the UK economy – and there is by no means a consensus on the issue – then we need to ask why the alleged change has taken place. At the risk of trivialising what is obviously an important and complex issue, we can identify a number of forces, all interlinked, which will be referred to as the eight Ts – trade, telecommunications, transport, transnational corporations, technology, tariffs, tastes and the Tories. The reader will appreciate that the labels are chosen so as to benefit from alliteration, but they do provide a useful mnemonic (and they make the four Ps used by marketing people look puny in comparison). Each of these factors can be seen as contributing to the structural change that is alleged to have taken place. We consider each of them below.

Trade

The word 'trade' is used here to refer to the growing **internationalisation** or **globalisation** of the world economy. The post-war period and the last quarter-century in particular has witnessed a trend for national economies to become more **open** – that is, for foreign trade to assume an ever increasing share of national income and output. We have moved from a scenario in which products are designed, built and sold within a national market to one where they are designed, built and sold on a global scale.

This has resulted in greater competition, not just in the market for final goods and services bought by consumers, but also in the market for those intermediate goods and services bought by companies. This growing competition has tended to lower prices and production costs as each firm increasingly has to match the performance of the least-cost rival producer in order to survive.

Telecommunications

The factors responsible for the growing globalisation of production are multifarious. One of the most important, however, is the revolution in telecommunications. As the reader will be aware, it is now possible to convert information – whether it be voice, text or video – into digital form and to transmit that digital information virtually instantaneously via cable or satellite to anywhere in the world. The associated computer technologies, particularly those linked to banking and money transfer services, have meant that doing business overseas is now no more difficult than doing it at home.

Transport

The communications revolution has been matched by almost equally revolutionary improvements in the transport of goods and people. The cost of carrying goods by sea has fallen dramatically as a result of the building of very large ships and especially as a result of containerisation (which has also made possible the more efficient delivery of goods by road). Scheduled air freight and passenger services have become cheap and reliable.

Transnational corporations

Companies which have production facilities in more than one country are known as multinational companies (MNCs) or transnational companies (TNCs). Such companies have been the major beneficiaries of the communications and transport revolutions mentioned above. Their share of world trade has increased so that the top few hundred TNCs now account for the majority of world trade.

Technology

The revolutions in the technologies associated with telecoms and transport have been a major force in enabling the TNCs to prosper. In addition, however, it is the cost savings to be derived from **economies of scale** which have been one of the driving forces responsible for the inexorable rise of the large multinational firm. To achieve lower unit costs, the fixed costs of production must be spread over as many units of output as possible. Most national markets are too small to allow the producer to spread the fixed costs sufficiently to reap the full benefit of the scale economies available. Often the most significant fixed costs are those associated with research and development (R & D) – cars, airliners and Windows 95 are all examples of this. The greater the sophistication of the technology, the higher the R & D costs and the greater the benefits to be derived from economies of scale.

Tariff reduction

International trading companies have benefited from tariff reductions in the post-war period, both via tariff reductions within trading blocs (such as the EU) and worldwide (GATT and the WTO).

Tastes

Consumer tastes have become increasingly similar – or have been made increasingly similar – by the power of advertising. Tastes too have become globalised. Thus households in Birmingham, Berlin and Brisbane all drink Coke and buy Nike trainers which they can pay for with their Visa credit card.

All of these factors – and so far we have mentioned only seven out of the eight Ts – have contributed to the structural change that has taken place in the UK economy. The UK market has become increasingly competitive as a result of becoming increasingly exposed to international competition and integrated into the world economy. This process has been actively promoted by the last of the eight Ts – the Tory government which was in power in Britain from 1979.

The policy was to encourage and to foster the increasing openness of the UK economy, rather than to protect domestic producers behind tariff walls. The rationale for this policy is that *in the long run, market forces will out*. It is pointless, it is argued, to try to stem the tide. The only sustainable policy is to accept the imperatives imposed by the forces of trade and technology (and all the other Ts). The policy has therefore been to remove all those restrictions which would have delayed or slowed down what is allegedly an inevitable historical process.

In addition, a series of policies have been specially designed to improve the competitive efficiency of the economy. These are *supply-side policies* designed to remove perceived obstacles to competition.

11.3 The rationale for supply-side policies

Supply-side policies stand in contradistinction to the demand-side policies which form the cornerstone of Keynesian economics. The essence of the Keynesian paradigm is the manipulation of the level of demand in order to achieve the desirable, though often conflicting, objectives of lower unemployment, a lower rate of inflation and a faster rate of economic growth. In contrast, the advocates of supply-side policies recognise that, in a price system, there are two sides to every market – a demand side certainly, but also a **supply-side**.

The factors which influence the supply-side of the market stem from the actions of individual economic agents – firms and consumers – all of whom are pursuing their own selfish ends. Consumers try to buy as cheaply as possible in order to maximise the satisfaction to be derived from their income. And firms try to reduce costs so that they can keep their prices as low as possible. They do this in order to persuade customers to buy from them rather than from some alternative supplier. By keeping costs down and increasing sales, they can increase their profits.

Note that firms are motivated by self-interest, not by the desire to do good. However, as Adam Smith, the founding father of neo-classical economics, argued in 1776, they *do good by doing well*. Although motivated by self-interest, they end up by acting in a socially useful way.

It is not from the benevolence of the butcher, the brewer or the baker that we expect our dinner but from their regard to their own interest. We address ourselves not to their humanity but to their self-love and never talk to them of our own necessity but of their advantage. (Adam Smith, *The Wealth of Nations*, 1776)

Supply-side policies attempt to harness this self-interest and to foster it in an attempt to 'make the market work better'. This is to be achieved by increasing the motivation and the ability of economic agents to pursue their selfish ends, by removing those obstacles which would prevent them so doing. Supply-side policies encourage private initiative, risk taking and competition by removing disincentives and by rewarding initiative.

Not surprisingly, supply-side policies are associated with the political right. The label 'monetarist' is often applied to them, even though they have almost nothing to do with the money supply. The term 'monetarist' is now used to refer to any right-wing, non-interventionist advocate of the free market.

11.4 Supply-side policies

Supply-side policies fall into two main types – those associated with the labour market and those associated with the goods market. Labour market policies have consisted, first, of those designed to weaken the power of trade unions and, second, of changes in the tax and benefit system. Policies associated with the goods market – which is economists' shorthand for the markets on which goods and services are supplied – have consisted of measures designed to introduce competition and to deregulate, and this has often been associated with privatisation. Each of these is considered in more detail below.

11.5 Labour market policies: weakening the power of trade unions

A major plank of labour market policy has been deliberately to weaken the power of the trade unions in Britain. The trade unions were seen by the Conservatives, particularly by Mrs Thatcher when she came to power in 1979, as inflexible, unrepresentative and undemocratic institutions that displayed intransigence in their bargaining behaviour. Often they exploited their monopoly position by resorting to the strike weapon as a means of forcing concessions out of employers, and the employer was often the government itself. Edward Heath's Conservative government had in effect been brought down by a miners' strike in the winter of 1973–74. Striking miners had posed a direct challenge to the government's incomes policy, and the government had been forced to back down in a humiliating 'U-turn'.

Five years later, striking public sector workers posed similar problems for the Labour government of James Callaghan in the 'Winter of Discontent' (1978–79). These events lead to the defeat of the Labour government and the election in May 1979 of a Conservative Prime Minister determined that such events would not be repeated.

In the years that followed, a number of detailed pieces of legislation were put on the statute book, aimed, it was said, at making unions more democratic. They also had the effect – probably not unintentional – of weakening the power of trade unions. Among the more important were the following:

➤ Restrictions were placed on the ability of unions to organise mass pickets.
➤ **Secondary picketing** became illegal. (Secondary picketing is the picketing by workers of firms which do not directly employ them.)
➤ All industrial action had to be preceded by a ballot of members.
➤ **Closed shops** were made illegal. (A closed shop exists where employment in a firm is conditional upon the employee being a member of a particular union. In a *pre-entry closed shop*, an individual must be a member of the union concerned before he or she can become employed in the firm.)

In addition to this legislation, Mrs Thatcher prepared for what she felt was an inevitable second confrontation with the miners. Coal was stockpiled and the dependence on coal was reduced by encouraging alternative energy sources, particularly nuclear energy. A protracted miners' strike began in 1984 and went on for almost a year. However, unlike the previous strike in 1973–74, which had led to severe disruptions in electricity supply, this time there were few power cuts. The National Union of Mineworkers was eventually defeated in what became one of the most bitter industrial disputes of the post-war era.

PAUSE FOR THOUGHT *'In a free society it is ironic that it is now illegal to organise mass demonstrations in support of one's fellow workers. Demonstrations in support of calves and sheep are, however, legal and widely supported.'*

The ending of the miners' strike was a high-profile victory for Mrs Thatcher. It marked a watershed in her plans to change the balance of power in the labour market. The defeat of the miners was made easier because the economic environment within which the dispute took place was changing in two specific ways:

➤ In the period after 1979, unemployment rose to levels which were unprecedented in the post-war period. The weakness of the demand for labour was thus a contributory factor in reducing union militancy. The government chose to allow unemployment to rise rather than taking action against it.
➤ The forces of trade and technology (and all the other Ts) were bringing changes in the structure of British industry, reducing the dependence on certain traditional technologies (for example, the skills of traditional newsprint workers) and opening up areas of the economy to foreign competition.

11.6 A flexible labour market?

In the last two decades, the labour market in the UK has undergone significant changes. These changes have been brought about partly as a result of government supply-side policies. But they are also partly the result of external forces acting on the UK economy (the eight Ts again). The more important changes have been as follows:

➤ There has been an increase in the proportion of employees who work *part time* as distinct from full time.

➤ There has been a marked increase in female *participation rates* (the participation rate is the proportion of the population of working age who choose to work).

➤ There has been a slight fall in male participation rates.

➤ The *decline in manufacturing employment* has continued. This has been going on since the 1960s, when roughly one person in three was employed in manufacturing. Now fewer than one in five is employed in manufacturing.

➤ The decline in manufacturing employment has been mirrored by an increase in employment elsewhere in the economy, which in effect means the service sector.

All of the above changes are related aspects of the same process of structural change. The increase in female participation has mostly been in the service sector (as one would expect, since this is where the growth in employment has been greater) and many of these jobs – roughly half – have been part time. In contrast, only about 10 per cent of male jobs are part time.

➤ In addition to the increase in part-time employment – and as distinct from it – there has also been an increase in the amount of *temporary* working. This is rather more difficult to define and measure accurately, since it could take in not only *casual working* (for example, bar staff hired on a daily basis), but also executives on fixed-term contracts.

These changes could justifiably be taken as an indication of increasing *flexibility* in the UK labour market. However, in the social sciences, language is seldom completely value-free. Consider the use of the word 'flexible'. Government speakers celebrate the advent of a more flexible labour market as if it were something which has a totally positive and benign impact on the economy and on society. Like motherhood and apple pie, flexibility has a very positive ring to it. It is something which we can all agree is 'a good thing'. However, other commentators decry the increased casualisation, job insecurity and fear of unemployment that are concomitants of this increased flexibility. These insecurities and fears may well be responsible for the lack of the 'feel good' factor, so conspicuously absent in the UK economy in the 1990s despite its apparent success.

ACTIVITY **1**

Consider the information on part-time and temporary working shown in Table 11.1. Calculate the percentage increase in part-time and temporary working. Does the evidence suggest that people are increasingly taking on part-time/temporary work because they choose to do so rather than having the choice forced upon them?

table 11.1		1984	1994
Reasons why people take part-time and temporary work, UK, spring 1984 and 1994 (%)	**All employees and self-employed working part time[a] (000s)**	4,913	6,121
	Reason for working part time:		
	Student	7	11
	Disabled/ill	1	1
	Could not find a full-time job	10	13
	Did not want a full-time job	68	74
	Other reasons	14	1
	All employees in temporary jobs[a] (000s)	1,236	1,396
	Reason for taking temporary work:		
	Job included contract of training	6	7
	Could not find a permanent job	35	43
	Did not want a permanent job	32	27
	Other reasons	28	24

[a] Part-time status is self defined, as is temporary status.

Source: 'Progress towards a flexible labour market', *Employment Gazette*, February 1995. Information derived from the Labour Force Surveys.

Check with answers/suggestions at the back of the book.

11.7 Changes in the structure of taxation and social security
● ●

Similar in purpose to the detailed changes in union legislation have been the large number of changes to the tax and social security system. These supply-side reforms – supply-side *measures* would perhaps be a more neutral term – have been aimed at:

ACTIVITY 2
● ● ● ● ● ● ● ● ● ● ●

➤ reducing the alleged 'disincentive effect' of taxation
➤ reducing the benefits available to unemployed workers.

When Mrs Thatcher came to power in 1979, state pensions were linked to an index of average earnings. This was discontinued and state pensions henceforth became linked not to average earnings, but to an index of prices (the RPI). What is the effect of this detailed change?

Hint: you may find the data in Table 5.7 on p.70 useful in answering this question.

Check with answers/suggestions at the back of the book.

Changes in the tax system

As we saw in section 10.13, the last fifteen years have seen a shift in the burden of taxation away from direct taxes and towards indirect taxes. This has resulted from deliberate policy decisions. The rationale for this is that direct taxes – that is, taxes on income – are alleged to have a disincentive effect on work effort. This applies particularly to high marginal rates of tax. Government policy has therefore been to reduce these high marginal rates, reducing the alleged disincentive effect.

However, some writers have argued that, far from producing a disincentive effect, income taxes actually have an incentive effect. This will be the case if the thing which workers seek to maximise is their *post-tax* income. The greater the deductions from their gross income, the more pre-tax income they will have to earn in order to secure a given amount of post-tax income. Thus taxation encourages greater work effort, not less.

The assertion that high marginal rates of tax produce a disincentive effect has been investigated in a number of academic studies. It is not, however, something which can be easily proved or disproved. Most studies seem to show that for some groups of workers there is a disincentive effect and for others there is an incentive effect, though the majority of writers conclude that the disincentive effect is slightly more significant.

We also noted (in section 10.14) that direct taxes tend to be *progressive* in their impact, whereas indirect taxes are *regressive*. The shift in the burden of taxation since 1979 has therefore meant that the tax system as a whole is less progressive than it was. In other words, the redistributive effect of the tax system is less marked than formerly, and the result of this is that the distribution of income in the UK has become more unequal. This is discussed more fully in section 11.8.

Changes in the benefits system

The structural (supply-side) reforms brought about by the changes in labour market legislation and in the tax system have been reinforced by numerous detailed changes in the entitlement to social security benefits. The objective of these changes to the social security system has been:

➤ to reduce the cost to the taxpayer of social security spending as part of an overall programme of reducing public spending, thus making possible reductions in the level of taxation needed to pay for it
➤ to focus benefits more narrowly on those in need
➤ to remove the 'benefits trap' (see below).

In addition to simply cutting spending on welfare provision, therefore, these reforms were intended to reduce the disincentive effect to work effort associated with the benefits system.

The **benefits trap** (or 'poverty trap') mentioned above is an unintended consequence of the income maintenance programme. If the low paid earn small increases in income (as a result of working more hours or getting a slightly better-paid job), this will lead to the removal of certain means-tested benefits for which they no longer qualify. An individual's income after the payment of tax and receipt of benefits may as a result be *lower* than before. Thus the **effective marginal rate of deduction** from income is more than 100 per cent, and this clearly produces a strong disincentive to work effort. It is, however, difficult to devise a benefits system which does not possess some such disincentive effect for certain people at certain times.

Britain's system of social security benefits appears to have become rather ungenerous in comparison to the benefits available in most European countries, particularly in those more affluent north European countries such as Germany and the countries of Scandinavia. Table 11.2 compares the level of benefits available in the UK with the *average* available in the EU in 1992. In this table, the level of benefits is expressed as a percentage of the average earnings of manual workers in manufacturing industry in the country concerned. As can be seen, the level of benefits available in other European countries is very much more generous than that now available in Britain.

Of particular interest is the extent to which state benefits for the unemployed 'replace' the income they would have earned had they been in employment. This is the so-called **replacement ratio**. As the table shows, the replacement ratio in the UK is less than a quarter, whereas the European average is significantly more than one-half.

11.8 The impact on the distribution of income

Almost all of the supply-side measures that we have talked about so far will have the effect of making the distribution of income more unequal, and this is in fact what has happened in the period since 1979. This is in very marked contrast to what had been going on for a hundred years previously: a tendency for the distribution of both income and wealth to become gently but definitely less unequal.

There are a number of different ways of defining the concept of household income. As can be seen in *Figure 11.2,* these are:

table 11.2

Welfare benefits in the UK in comparison to those in Europe, 1992 (% of average earnings of manual workers in manufacturing industry)

	UK	EU average
Sickness and invalidity benefit[1]	28	69
Unemployment benefit (general)[2]	23	61
Unemployment benefit (18-year-old)[3]	18	25
State retirement pension	44	75

[1]Short-term illness.
[2]First period, approximately 12 months.
[3]Not previously worked, living alone.

Source: Commission of the European Communities, *Social Protection in Europe, 1993*; quoted in A. Griffiths and S. Wall, *Applied Economics*, 6th edn, 1995, chapter 23.

Figure 11.2

Stages of redistribution

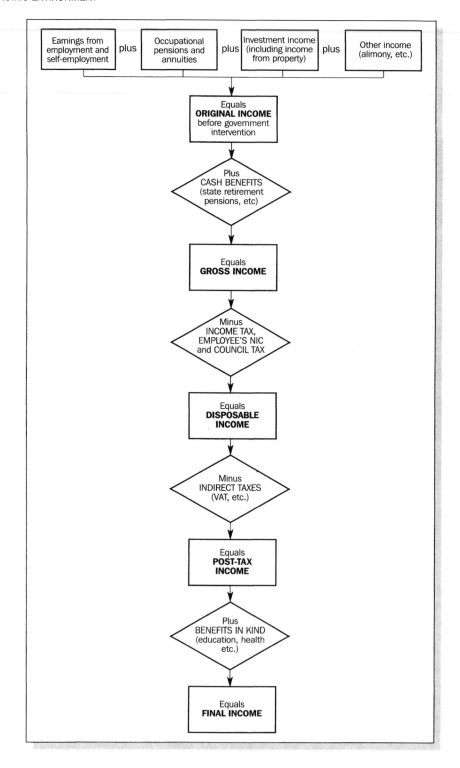

Source: 'The effects of taxes and benefits on household income 1990', *Economic Trends*, January 1993.

➤ original income
➤ gross income
➤ disposable income
➤ post-tax income
➤ final income.

Original income is the income received by the household before any government intervention. It is income from employment, from private pensions (but not state pensions) and investment income (such as interest on bank accounts or dividends on shareholdings). The distribution of original income is very unequal. The bottom 20 per cent of households have almost no original income because they have no income from employment.

Gross income is calculated by adding to original income those cash benefits known as *transfer payments* – things such as state pensions, unemployment benefit and invalidity benefit. These cash grants raise the incomes of all households but are much more important for low-income households than for those with high incomes. Thus the distribution of gross incomes is more equal than the distribution of original incomes.

This can be seen by looking at *Table 11.3,* which shows the percentage shares of total national income received by each *quintile group* (a quintile group is 20 per cent of the total number of households). As can be seen, the bottom quintile group (that is, the poorest 20 per cent of households) received only 2 per cent of original income, but once cash benefits are taken into account their share of income rises to 6.7 per cent. Similarly, the share of the top quintile falls from 51 per cent to 44 per cent.

ACTIVITY 3

Consider your own income in terms of the various definitions given above: namely,

➤ original income
➤ gross income
➤ disposable income

table 11.3
Percentage shares of total household income, 1990

	Original income	Gross income	Disposable income	Post-tax income
Quintile group				
Bottom	2.0	6.7	7.0	6.3
2nd	7	10	11	10
3rd	15	16	16	15
4th	25	23	23	23
Top	51	44	43	45
All households	100	100	100	100
Decile group				
Bottom	0.8	2.9	2.9	2.4
Top	33	28	28	30

Note: A decile represents one-tenth of the population.

Source: 'The effects of taxes and benefits on household income 1990', *Economic Trends*, January 1993.

➤ post-tax income
➤ final income.

How do the various stages of intervention affect your income? That is, do they increase it or reduce it?

Check with answers/suggestions at the back of the book.

Disposable income equals gross income minus direct taxes (that is, income tax and employees' National Insurance Contribution). As can be seen from **Table 11.3**, these have an equalising effect – albeit a rather small one. The share of the top quintile falls from 44 per cent to 43 percent, and the share of the bottom quintile rises from 6.7 to 7 per cent.

Post-tax income is estimated by subtracting from disposable income the amount the household pays in *indirect* taxes such as VAT and excise duties. Indirect taxes are *regressive* – they make the distribution of incomes more unequal. Consequently, the share of the top quintile rises again from 43 to 45 per cent and the share of the bottom quintile falls from 7.0 to 6.3 per cent.

Final income is estimated by adjusting post-tax income to take into account the value of **benefits in kind**, such as health care under the NHS and the provision of education by the state.

Figure 11.3 illustrates the impact which the various taxes and benefits have on the incomes of the quintile groups. Figure 11.3 is yet another of those pictures that presents a visual impression which can easily be misinterpreted. The impact of each form of government intervention on the distribution of

Figure 11.3
The effects of taxes and benefits on quintile groups of UK households, 1990

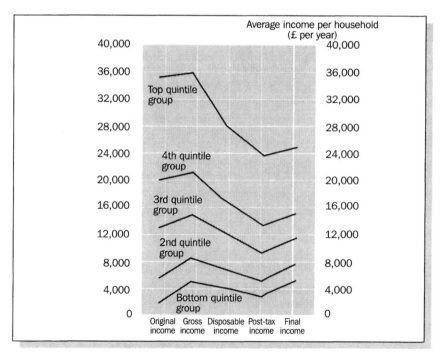

Source: 'The effects of taxes and benefits on household income 1990', *Economic Trends*, January 1993.

income is represented by the *distance between* the line for each quintile group, not the slope or steepness of the line. The steepness of the lines does, however, indicate the *relative importance* of each form of intervention – thus cash transfers are more significant for the bottom quintiles than they are for the top quintile, and direct taxes take a larger slice of top incomes than of low incomes.

Table 11.2 and Figure 11.3 present a snapshot of the economy at a particular point in time. If we wanted to know what had happened to the distribution of income over time, we would have to take a number of snapshots and compare them. This we could do, but it would result in a rather bewildering amount of figures. It would help to overcome this problem if we were to use a single statistic – a single number – to summarise all of the information on the distribution of income. The **Gini coefficient** is a summary statistic which does just this. It can be understood most easily by considering a **Lorenz curve** such as that shown in *Figure 11.4*.

Both axes on a Lorenz curve are scaled from zero to 100 per cent. The vertical axis shows the percentage of the population (measured from the highest-income households to the lowest). The horizontal axis shows the proportion of total income received by each group of households. If the distribution of incomes were perfectly equal, the top 1 per cent of households would receive 1 per cent of total income, the top 10 per cent of households would receive 10 per cent of total income, and so on. The Lorenz curve illustrating an equal distribution of incomes such as this would therefore be a diagonal line joining point *A* to point *B* in Figure 11.4.

However, as we know, the distribution of incomes is not equal. The top 10 per cent of households receive about 30 per cent of total income the top 20 per cent receive about 50 per cent of total income. The Lorenz curve therefore looks like the curved dotted line joining points *A* and *B*. The extent to which the Lorenz curve (the curved line) deviates from the straight-line diagonal therefore gives us an indication of the degree of inequality in the distribution of incomes – the more it deviates, the more unequal is the distribution of incomes.

Figure 11.4
A Lorenz curve

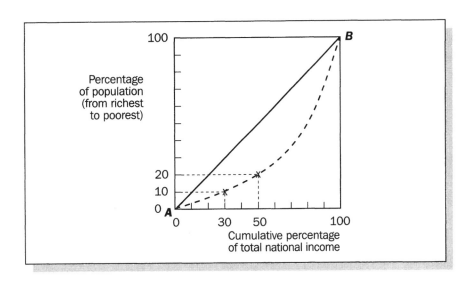

Now consider Figure 11.5 (a) and (b). The greater the shaded area, the more unequal the distribution of income. The Gini coefficient expresses this by measuring the proportion of the triangle *ABC* accounted for by the shaded area. A value of the Gini coefficient of zero (no shaded area) corresponds to a completely equal distribution of incomes. A value of 100 (shaded area occupies 100 per cent of the triangle *ABC*) represents a situation in which one household receives 100 per cent of national income!

Armed with this useful tool, we can now look at **Table 11.4**, which shows Gini coefficients for each of the various definitions of income for the period 1977 to 1990. As can be seen, *no matter how we choose to define income*, the distribution of income became steadily more unequal year by year over this period. For original income (that which is produced by the market mechanism before any government intervention), the value of the Gini coefficient rose from 43 to 52. For post-tax income, the value of the Gini coefficient rose from 29 to 40.

This growing inequality in society is the result of the supply-side measures we have outlined earlier. These have affected the **distribution of income** in the following ways:

➤ The tax system has become less progressive. That is, the redistributive effect of the system has become less marked.
➤ The benefits system has become somewhat less generous. Hence again the redistributive effect has been reduced.
➤ The combined effect of the changes in the tax and benefits system has meant that high-income households have been able to retain a higher proportion of their original income. In contrast, low-income households have experienced a relative decline in their post-tax incomes. These changes in the flow of income will in turn affect the *stock of wealth* which each household is able to accumulate. This will therefore affect their incomes in future years. High-income households become wealthier and therefore receive more investment income. Low-income households become poorer (that is, have even less wealth) and therefore receive even less investment income.

Figure 11.5
Relatively equal and unequal distributions of income

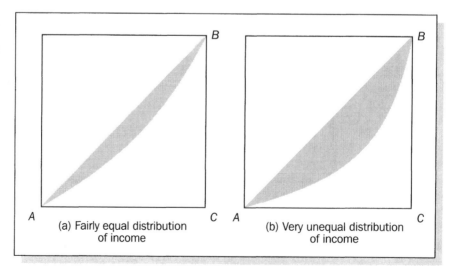

(a) Fairly equal distribution of income

(b) Very unequal distribution of income

table 11.4

Gini coefficients for the distribution of income at each stage of the tax–benefits system, 1977–90 (%)

	1977	1979	1981	1983	1985	1987	1989	1990
Original income	43	44	46	48	49	51	50	52
Gross income	29	30	31	32	32	36	36	38
Disposable income	27	27	28	28	29	33	34	36
Post-tax income	29	29	31	31	32	36	37	40

Note: Gini coefficients expressed as a percentage of equivalised income.

Source: 'The effects of taxes and benefits on household income 1990', *Economic Trends*, January 1993.

➤ In addition (and independently), there have also been changes in the **distribution of earnings** (as distinct from the distribution of income). The distribution of earnings has become more unequal as a result of decreasing trade union influence, and also as a result of changed perceptions of what constitutes appropriate rewards.

11.9 Privatisation and liberalisation

In addition to those policies designed to make the labour market 'work better', there was a second set of supply-side policies – those directed towards the goods market. The major thrust of these policies was to introduce competition into those industries where previously there had been none, the belief being that competition would *in itself* ensure that firms would become more efficient and more responsive to the wishes of consumers. In this regard there was, at least in the early days, some confused thinking and a failure to distinguish between the concepts of *privatisation* on the one hand and *liberalisation* on the other.

Privatisation is the term coined to describe the process by which assets owned by the state are sold back to the private sector. Most of these assets had been acquired in the post-war period by various acts of **nationalisation** – a term which means to take into public ownership assets which were previously in private hands. The reasons why certain industries had been nationalised were partly economic and partly political.

Clause Four of the Labour Party's constitution (now amended) had spoken of 'the common ownership of the means of production, distribution and exchange'. If taken literally, this would have implied state ownership of the whole economy, so for practical purposes it was assumed to refer to the 'commanding heights' of the economy. Thus the post-war Labour government took into public ownership the public utilities such as electricity and gas, the transport industries, and the coal and steel industries. Some smaller firms followed later, while others, such as the Post Office, had been in the public sector since the nineteenth century.

The macroeconomic argument for nationalisation rested on the belief that a strong public sector would have a stabilising effect on the economy, because publicly owned corporations, particularly in their investment activity, would not be subject to the ups and downs of the business cycle in the same way that private sector firms were.

The microeconomic argument for many of these nationalisations revolved around the concept of a **natural monopoly** – by their nature, firms such as the Post Office would operate most efficiently if they supplied the whole market. Competition would be wasteful of resources because it would involve unnecessary duplication of services – or replication of services if there were more than two firms. If such monopolies were privately owned, however, there was no guarantee that they would be operated in the best interest of society as a whole. More likely, they would be operated in the interest of shareholders. Firms would maximise profits by charging high prices to consumers who had no alternative source of supply for these basic services. To ensure that they operated in the public interest, therefore, these firms should be controlled by the state, and the best way of ensuring this was to take them into public ownership.

Because of the absence of competition, however, there was no incentive for these publicly held resources to be used efficiently. Moreover, it was difficult to judge just how efficient or inefficient these state-owned monopolies were because the normal yardstick of efficiency – the profitability of a company – could not be applied to monopolistic firms, which could always increase profits by raising prices rather than by cutting costs. The prices charged by nationalised industries were in fact controlled, but nevertheless there was a general view – held in particular by the incoming Conservative government in 1979 – that the nationalised industries were inefficient. It was the desire to raise the efficiency of this sector of the British economy which constituted the microeconomic rationale for privatisation.

There was, however, a naive and misguided belief that privatisation *per se* would increase competition. To quote Lord Cockfield, then Minister of State at HM Treasury: 'Privatisation represents by far the most effective means of extending market forces' (19 November 1981).

Some newly privatised industries did indeed find themselves in markets where they were forced to compete with other powerful players. Others, however, were converted from public sector monopolies into private sector monopolies where they still faced no competition, a situation which benefited shareholders at the expense of customers. The water companies, for example, were local monopolies as were the RECs (regional electricity companies). A household had no alternative but to buy these essential services from the local monopoly supplier. Thus **liberalisation** – the introduction of competition – did not follow automatically as a result of privatisation.

However, it came to be realised, albeit somewhat belatedly, that competition could sometimes be introduced, even into those industries such as the supply of electricity and gas which were apparently natural monopolies. For example, in the electricity and gas industries, a natural monopoly exists in the *distribution* of services to households. It would clearly be nonsensical to have more than one national network of gas pipes and one National Grid. However, in the *generation* of electricity and the *manufacture* of gas, it is possible to have competition. Thus the distribution systems – the pylons, cables and gas pipelines – are set to remain as natural privatised monopolies, but in future firms will be able to compete to supply electricity to the National Grid and to supply gas to the gas distribution network.

How gas competition will work

From April 1996, consumers in the south-west of England will be able to choose which firm to buy gas from. Up to six firms (in addition to British Gas) will compete for business. The prices being quoted are shown in Table 11.5.

table 11.5

Annual gas bill in the south-west (based on standard tariff for customer using 650 therms a year)

	Bill(£)	Extras
British Gas	327	–
Amerada Hess	278	Bills capped to 2001
Eastern	295	Free home accident insurance
SWEB Gas	268	–
Total	288	£10 shopping voucher[1]
British Fuels	276	£150 holiday voucher[2]
CalorTex	257	–

[1] up to £50 termination fee.
[2] £10 termination fee.

Source: *Observer*, 3 March 1996.

There will, however, be no new pipes. All that will happen is that a customer will sign a contract with one of the new suppliers, which will read the meter and charge the customer for the gas used. This supplier will buy gas from a North Sea producer – and at the moment there is plenty of gas available, so prices are low – and put that gas through Transco, the pipeline network owned and run by British Gas.

The gas that the customer uses will not, of course, be the same gas that the supplier puts into Transco's pipes in the North Sea. But all gas is identical – it is what economists call a *homogeneous* product, or as a student once so succinctly remarked, 'Gas is gas.' In the same way, the £10 that you withdraw from a cash-point in London is not the same £10 that your employer paid into your account in Birmingham a few days earlier.

What implications does this have for the introduction of competition into the supply of water? 'Gas is gas', but is water, water? What other features of the water distribution system make it difficult to introduce effective competition into the industry?

11.10 Competition: a panacea?
•••••••••••••••••••••••••••••••••••••

We saw earlier that it was naive to believe that privatisation would automatically ensure competition. We could also argue that there was an equally simplistic belief that competition, once established, would automatically increase efficiency. Lord Cockfield's dictum quoted earlier reads in full: 'Privatisation represents by far the most effective means of extending market forces, *and in turn of improving efficiency and the allocation of resources.*' (Lord Cockfield, my italics).

Competition in this view is seen almost as a panacea. Thus it was, for example, that measures were enacted to introduce competition into the National Health Service. These required the individual parts of the Health Service to compete against each other, competing for business in the same way that private firms do. Information – on prices, outputs and the availability of resources – is never costless, however, and the introduction of these market reforms introduced *transactions costs* which some critics argue effectively increased the administrative cost of the system as a whole.

In other areas of the public sector, local authorities were forced to **contract out** to private firms many of the services that had previously been provided by local authority employees – services such as refuse collection, street cleaning and the maintenance of parks and gardens. As with the marketisation of the NHS, the competition introduced by these reforms brought cheaper services, but it also brought with it an increase in those administrative costs necessary to oversee that the terms of the contract were being met.

There was, moreover, a change in the fundamental ethos of public sector work. Previously this could be characterised (most charitably) as 'Doing the best job possible with the funds available'. Contracting out changed this to: 'Doing the cheapest job possible, subject to the terms of the contract not being breached'.

The terms of the contracts specified the minimum quality standards which had to be met. 'Quality' is always rather subjective. For the purposes of the contracts, however, it had to be measured objectively, and to this end various **performance indicators** (PIs) were established. Quality thus became rather *narrowly* defined and measured (for example, by measuring the average length of waiting lists in hospitals, the number of patients treated, or the number of times per month that the grass in the local park is cut). As measured by these PIs, the market reforms did bring an improvement in measured quality (or reduced costs without a reduction in quality), but many critics argued that the improvement in efficiency was apparent rather than real, that quality was being defined too narrowly and that genuine quality was declining.

11.11 Closing the productivity gap

All of the supply-side policies introduced by the government since 1979 have been directed towards improving competitiveness – the ability of the UK economy to compete in world markets. When used in this sense, the word 'competitiveness' tends to be a rather vague concept and hence one which is difficult to measure. Nevertheless it goes to the very heart of the issue. An economy which is 'competitive' is one which performs well by all of the conventional yardsticks – there is a high growth of output and of exports, leading to balance of trade surpluses, low unemployment and low inflation. Thus competitiveness is often used as a synonym for performance. Poor competitiveness equals poor performance. Good competitiveness equals good performance.

We can make the concept somewhat less nebulous, however, by equating competitiveness with **productivity**. Productivity means *output per worker*, or output per unit of input. The concept itself is very precise, although as we shall see it is difficult to measure in a satisfactory way. Increases in productivity are far and away the most important source of growth in the economy. Growth – that is, an increase in GDP – can be achieved in only two ways: either by increasing the inputs to the production process or by increasing the efficiency with which those inputs are converted into output. This latter source of growth – productivity increases – is by far the more important, since in a mature economy with a stable population there will be little or no increase in inputs of labour, or of any other resource.

ASK YOURSELF

In the British economy – and in particular in the Scottish economy – in the 1980s there was a significant exception to this rule. There was in fact a substantial increase in natural resources. What was this?

Hint: Aberdeen on the Scottish coast became a boom town as a result.

Our attention therefore turns to productivity, and in particular to labour productivity. This is the ratio of two numbers – a numerator (output) and a denominator (labour input). For specific industries such as mining, this can be measured quite easily, since both numerator and denominator can be measured in physical units – tonnes of coal produced and the number of man-hours. However, for the economy as a whole – or even for a subset such as the manufacturing sector – there is an **aggregation problem**.

How do we add up lots of disparate outputs – tonnes of coal, millions of cars, thousands of CDs and millions of household insurance policies – to produce an aggregate figure? Clearly it cannot be done in physical units, so we have to add up the *value* of the coal produced, the value of cars produced, the value of the insurance policies and so on.

We have a similar aggregation problem with the denominator. Can we simply add together hours worked by miners, car workers and insurance sales people, even though these hours will all be valued differently? It may make more sense to use the *value* of labour input as the denominator.

Thus we define productivity as the value of output divided by the value of inputs:

$$\text{Productivity} = \frac{\text{Value of output}}{\text{Value of input}}$$

But the problem now is that this measure no longer reflects the physical realities of what is going on in the economy. If producers are able to charge higher prices, then by this measure productivity will be seen to have increased, since the value of output has increased. Similarly, if highly paid workers are replaced by cheaper part-time workers, productivity according to this measure will be seen to increase.

The problem of how to measure productivity is intractable. It can be made somewhat more manageable, however, if we confine our attention to the manufacturing sector (thus ignoring the insurance policies). In the manufacturing sector, it is just about possible to count the physical number of units of output and to aggregate into some suitable weighted average. Thus **manufacturing productivity** is a variable which is measured and which has received considerable attention. However, the reader is strongly advised to bear in mind the difficulties of measuring this concept.

Forewarned with this information, we are now in a position to look at *Figure 11.6* which is taken from the government's third Competitiveness

Figure 11.6

**Manufacturing
productivity in
selected countries,
1979–1994
(UK = 100)**

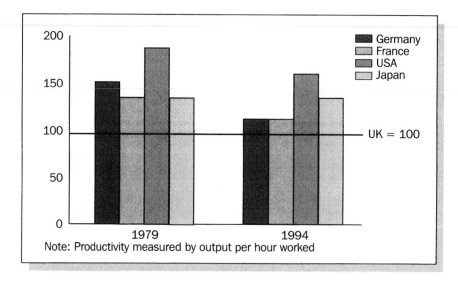

Note: Productivity measured by output per hour worked

Source: *Forging Ahead*, the Second Competitiveness White Paper, 22 May 1995.

White Paper, published in 1996. This compares productivity in the manufacturing sector in the UK with that in Germany, France, the USA and Japan. Productivity is measured by output per hour worked. The impression given is that in 1979 productivity in the UK was way below that in these other countries, whereas in 1994 it was still below that elsewhere, but the gap had been significantly narrowed. In particular, in 1979 French and German productivity levels were 35 per cent and 51 per cent respectively above those in the UK. By 1994 French and German productivity levels were only 10 per cent higher than those in the UK.

The result of this improvement in competitiveness will be an improvement in living standards, as measured by output per head. The White Paper also presents evidence on this, shown in **Figure 11.7**. The UK ranks 16th among the 25 countries listed in 1995, but the gap with twelve of the fifteen higher-ranked countries is 20 per cent or less. That is, only in Luxembourg, the USA and Switzerland does GDP per head exceed that in the UK by more than 20 per cent.

If the UK still lags behind its competitors – albeit seemingly by a somewhat smaller margin than previously – then this lack of 'competitiveness' can be attributed, according to the White Paper, to a variety of reasons. In particular it identifies:

➤ the education and technical ability of the labour force
➤ the quality of the infrastructure, particularly that relating to transport and communications
➤ the ability to innovate by applying scientific knowledge
➤ the cost and availability of finance, which reflects the efficiency of the financial system
➤ the quality of management
➤ the openness of the economy and its ability to attract international capital
➤ the 'efficiency' of the labour market

Figure 11.7
GDP per head at purchasing power parities, 1995 (UK = 100)

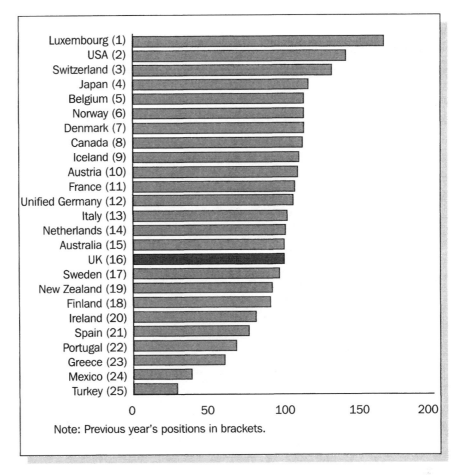

Note: Previous year's positions in brackets.

Source: *Forging Ahead*, the Second Competitiveness White Paper, 22 May 1995.

➤ public purchasing and supply policies
➤ the macroeconomic environment within which firms operate.

Some of these aspects of economic performance have been given detailed consideration in this chapter and elsewhere in this book. We conclude this chapter by looking at the data presented in the White Paper which relate to the first of these aspects of supply-side competitiveness – the education and technical ability of the labour force.

In 1979 participation in higher education in the UK was confined to about 12 per cent of the population of 18–21-year-olds. In the 1980s the government set about increasing the number of graduates, which it did in a spectacular fashion as can be seen from ***Figure 11.8***. By 1994 the number of graduates had increased from about one in eight of the population of 18–21-year-olds to about one in three.

However, funding for higher education was not increased commensurately – in fact, it was progressively cut and in 1995 'efficiency savings' were imposed on universities which represented a reduction in funding in real terms of about

Figure 11.8

UK participation in higher education (API), 1979–94

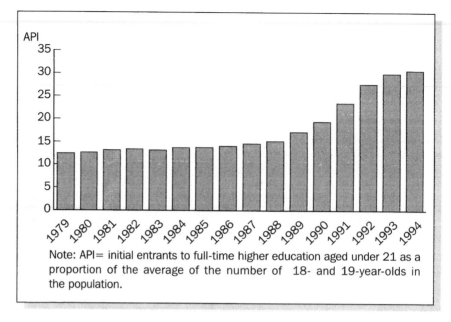

Note: API= initial entrants to full-time higher education aged under 21 as a proportion of the average of the number of 18- and 19-year-olds in the population.

Source: *Forging Ahead*, the Second Competitiveness White Paper, 22 May 1995.

7 per cent in one year. Thus it was that the resources per student became very much smaller than they had previously been, and universities were compelled to adopt more cost-effective methods of delivering the curriculum.

Thus, if you find yourself as a student in classes which are bewilderingly large, don't blame your teacher. Think about why it happens. You may also care to ponder on the extent to which the apparent efficiency gain is actually offset by a decline in quality.

Summary
....

Significant structural changes have taken place in the UK economy, partly as a result of the increasing globalisation of production and partly as a result of the supply-side policies introduced by the Conservative government. These supply-side policies, which stand in contrast to the policies of demand management advocated by Keynesians, aim to improve the efficiency of the economy by increasing incentives and removing obstacles to competition.

The policies were directed, first, towards the labour market with a series of measures aimed at reducing restrictive practices and weakening the bargaining power of trade unions. As a result, the labour market has become more 'flexible' – but there is less security of employment and an increased casualisation of the labour force. Changes in the structure of taxation and social security have reinforced these changes. Welfare benefits are now significantly less generous in the UK than in other European countries and the tax system has become less progressive. The distribution of income – however it is measured – has therefore become more unequal.

In the market for goods and services, supply-side policies have attempted to promote competition as a supposed spur to efficiency. Privatisation has been seen as the main vehicle by which this is to be achieved. But although some privatisations have introduced an element of competition, others have simply led to public monopolies being replaced with private ones. Moreover, in some markets, competition may be wasteful of resources. But according to some estimates, the productivity gap between the UK and its competitors has been narrowed.

REVIEW QUESTIONS

1 In the 1980s, bus services in the UK were deregulated. What was the rationale for this? In your opinion has deregulation brought benefits to the consumer?

2 Are railways a natural monopoly? Now that they are being privatised, how is the government trying to introduce competition into the railway system?

3 Unemployment has traditionally been thought of as a *lagging indicator*. It now appears to be more of a *coincident indicator*. Explain what you think this means. Look back at Figure 11.1 for a clue.

4 Consider the data on full-time and part-time employment shown in Table 11.5.
(a) Present the data in a way which brings out the trends more clearly.
(b) Identify the main trends.

5 Consider Figure 11.9, which relates to real household disposable income in the UK. What *changes* in the distribution of income are illustrated by this diagram?

table 11.5

Full- and part-time[1] employment[2]: by gender, UK, 1984–94 (000s)

	Males		Females	
	Full time	Part time	Full time	Part time
1984	13,240	570	5,422	4,343
1985	13,336	575	5,503	4,457
1986	13,430	647	5,662	4,566
1987	13,472	750	5,795	4,696
1988	13,881	801	6,069	4,808
1989	14,071	734	6,336	4,907
1990	14,109	789	6,479	4,928
1991	13,686	799	6,350	4,933
1992	13,141	885	6,244	5,081
1993	12,769	886	6,165	5,045
1994	12,875	998	6,131	5,257

[1] Full/part-time is based on respondents' self-assessment.
[2] At spring each year. Includes employees, self-employed, those on government training schemes and unpaid family workers.

Source: Employment Department, quoted in *Social Trends*, 1995.

Figure 11.9

UK real household disposable income,[1] 1971–92

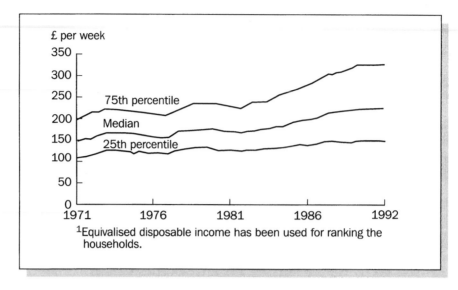

£ per week

[1]Equivalised disposable income has been used for ranking the households.

Source: Institute of Fiscal Studies, quoted in *Social Trends*, 1995.

Key concepts
••••••••••••••••••

The following key concepts have been introduced in this chapter. Make sure you understand the meaning and significance of each of them. They are listed here in the order in which they first appear, and the page number where they appear is also given. You will find these key concepts in section headings or in **bold** in the text. Each chapter contains a list of key concepts and you may find these particularly useful for revision purposes.

structural change	(p. 174)
internationalisation	(p. 175)
globalisation	(p. 175)
open economy	(p. 175)
telecommunications	(p. 176)
transnational corporations	(p. 176)
economies of scale	(p. 176)
tariff reduction	(p. 176)
tastes (globalisation of)	(p. 177)
supply-side policies	(p. 177)
secondary picketing	(p. 179)
closed shops	(p. 179)
'flexible' labour market	(p. 179)
benefits trap	(p. 183)
effective marginal rate of deduction	(p. 183)
replacement ratio	(p. 183)

definitions of household income

original   (p. 185)
gross   (p. 185)
disposable   (p. 186)
post-tax   (p. 186)
final   (p. 186)
benefits in kind   (p. 186)
Gini coefficient   (p. 187)
Lorenz curve   (p. 187)
distribution of income   (p. 188)
distribution of earnings   (p. 189)
privatisation   (p. 189)
nationalisation   (p. 189)
natural monopoly   (p. 190)
liberalisation   (p. 190)
contracting out   (p. 192)
performance indicators (PIs)   (p. 192)
productivity   (p. 192)
aggregation problem   (p. 193)
manufacturing productivity   (p. 193)

Sources of information
....

Structural changes in the labour market may be discernible by inspecting the labour market data in the *Employment Gazette*, which also contains relevant articles. *Economic Trends* has occasional articles about the tax/benefit system and its impact on the distribution of income. The Institute for Fiscal Studies (see 'Sources of information' for Chapter 10) publishes more detailed research findings.

More information on these and other sources is to be found in the **Guide to Statistical Sources** at the back of the book.

CHAPTER 12

The international monetary system

Objectives:

This chapter will enable you to:

➤ be aware of the major developments in the international monetary system since 1944

➤ understand the features of the Bretton Woods system and the reasons for its demise in 1972

➤ appreciate the advantages and disadvantages of fixed and floating exchange rates

➤ enquire into the nature of speculation on foreign exchange markets and appreciate the difficulties which it creates for stable exchange rates

➤ be aware of the significant developments in the process of European integration since 1957

➤ understand the key features of the European Monetary System

➤ understand the reasons for sterling's enforced exit from the exchange rate mechanism

➤ appreciate the rationale for the Maastricht convergence criteria

➤ put into context the debate about monetary union.

12.1 The Gold Standard
12.2 Bretton Woods
12.3 Problems of liquidity, confidence and adjustment
12.4 The Smithsonian Agreement
12.5 The pros and cons of fixed versus floating rates
12.6 European monetary integration
12.7 The Werner Report
12.8 The European Monetary System
12.9 Black Wednesday
12.10 Speculative selling on foreign exchange markets
12.11 Maastricht
12.12 Rationale for the convergence criteria
12.13 A two-speed Europe
12.14 Just do it

12.1 The Gold Standard

> 'We could learn a lot from history ... but we don't' (Danish proverb).

This chapter is concerned with the development of an international money. As we saw in Chapter 6, money has to fulfil three functions: namely, it has to be:

➤ a medium of exchange
➤ a unit of account
➤ a store of value.

Moreover, it should be *scarce* (to help retain its value), but above all it must be *acceptable*. When international trade first developed (as distinct from merely robbing, looting and pillaging one's neighbours), there was no acceptable medium of exchange, and hence the only trade possible was barter trade. During the course of time, however, precious metals, particularly silver and gold, came to be regarded as universally acceptable, and hence took on the status of an international money. By the early nineteenth century, the role of gold in the international payments system had been formalised into a regime that was called the **Gold Standard**. These arrangements persisted throughout the nineteenth and early twentieth centuries.

The essence of the Gold Standard was that the value of a currency was fixed in terms of gold. Since the price of gold in any one national currency never varied, this meant that there was also an immutably fixed exchange rate between each national currency and any other national currency. Gold, moreover, played an important role in determining the *domestic* money supply because the amount of paper money that could be created was limited by the amount of gold in the vaults of the central bank. This was because, under the Gold Standard, paper money was backed by gold.

The vestiges of this still survive today on British banknotes, all of which bear the words 'I promise to pay the bearer on demand the sum of ... five pounds' (or whatever the denomination is). In the Gold Standard era, it was at least theoretically possible to present such a note at the Bank and receive five pounds' worth of gold in exchange. Nowadays paper money is not backed by anything. It is purely **fiduciary** (based on faith).

In theory, these two characteristics – the fixed price of gold and the fact that paper money was backed by gold – ensured that there would be an automatic adjustment mechanism for countries experiencing balance of payments disequilibria. Countries with a balance of payments deficit would experience an outflow of gold to pay for those deficits. Such countries would be forced to reduce their domestic money supply, since they now had less gold with which to back the note issue. The reduction in the money supply would cause two things to happen. First, the amount of spending would fall, thus reducing spending on imports. Second, the price level would fall (a simple quantity theory of money), and this would restore the competitiveness of that country's goods on foreign markets, boosting its exports. Thus the rise in exports and the fall in imports would eliminate the balance of trade deficit.

Similarly, surplus countries would experience an inflow of gold. They would thus purchase more imports. Additionally, however, the price level would rise as a result of the expansion in the money supply made possible by the increase in the amount of gold in the vaults of the central bank. This increase in prices would reduce the competitiveness of the country's exports. The fall in exports coupled with the rise in imports would eliminate the balance of trade surplus.

It is doubtful whether the Gold Standard ever worked as smoothly as this brief account suggests. In particular, countries were reluctant to allow an outflow of gold. What is certain is that the Gold Standard compelled countries to attach greater priority to their balance of payments position and to the external value of their currency than to the state of their domestic economies, and in particular to income and employment levels therein. In any event, the Great Depression which started in 1929 brought an end to the Gold Standard as one by one countries went 'off gold,' preferring to devalue their currencies in an attempt to boost their domestic economies. In the 1930s a series of 'beggar-thy-neighbour' devaluations occurred, causing great uncertainties for traders, which led to a further decline in world trade. The Great Depression lasted throughout most of the 1930s, being brought to an end only by the boost to domestic demand occasioned by rearmament for the Second World War.

12.2 Bretton Woods

Thus it was that in 1944 a conference took place in which the Allies met to map out a blueprint for the post-war period. This was the **Bretton Woods** conference, named after a small town in New Hampshire. The objective of the new system was to prevent a return to the chaotic and counter-productive policies which had so bedevilled the 1930s. The Bretton Woods system is best described as an **adjustable peg system**. It was a system of fixed exchange rates, like the Gold Standard, but unlike the Gold Standard these exchange rates were not immutably fixed. It was called the 'Gold Exchange Standard,' since gold still played a key role, but this diminished over time. The key features of the system were as follows:

➤ There were to be fixed exchange rates (known as 'par values' or 'parities').
➤ Countries undertook to maintain these par values (plus or minus 1 per cent) and not to devalue (or revalue) unilaterally.
➤ Changes to par values were allowed in cases of 'fundamental disequilibrium': that is, situations which could not be corrected by a 'reasonable' amount of domestic deflation or reflation.
➤ Countries would hold reserves of **intervention currencies** necessary to buy up their own currency when it was in excess supply on foreign exchange markets. The **IMF** (the International Monetary Fund) was established to assist central banks in this process, by providing them with overdraft facilities (they could borrow from the IMF). These facilities were known as **IMF Drawing Rights**.
➤ Gold and dollars were the main intervention currencies. The value of the dollar was linked to gold (at $35 an ounce). All other currencies had their value linked to the dollar. (A few currencies were linked to the pound – the old 'sterling area').
➤ Protectionism was discouraged. Tariffs and quotas and other forms of import restrictions were to be reduced and gradually eliminated. **GATT** (the General Agreement on Tariffs and Trade) was established to promote this.

12.3 Problems of liquidity, confidence and adjustment

The Bretton Woods system proved to be extremely successful. Its introduction ushered in a post-war period of prosperity made possible by the rapid growth of world trade. However, over time it began to manifest three fundamental problems. These were the problems of liquidity, confidence and adjustment, which led to the eventual downfall of the system.

Because the price of gold was fixed under the Bretton Woods system, the supply of new gold, being mined and refined, increased only fairly slowly. The expansion in the gold supply was not fast enough to keep pace with growth of world trade. This gave rise to a **liquidity problem** – there was not enough internationally acceptable money to finance the growing volume of world trade. This problem was only partly resolved when central banks began holding larger stocks of dollars for intervention purposes as well as holding gold. There was no shortage of dollars; quite the reverse in fact. Because of America's persistent balance of payments deficits at the time, there was always an excess supply of dollars. However, these chronic US deficits led to fears that the dollar would be devalued, so central banks lost confidence in the dollar and became unwilling to hold stocks of dollars. This was the **confidence problem**.

The twin problems of liquidity and confidence were partly resolved by the negotiation of larger quotas from the IMF. These were known as **Special Drawing Rights** or **SDRs**. These were first introduced by the IMF in 1970 as a response to the liquidity problem mentioned earlier. They were held by central banks as an additional reserve asset, alongside gold and the dollar, to be used for intervention purposes when the occasion demanded.

The creation of SDRs was a significant step for the world community, since SDRs were in effect 'world paper money' which could be used as a means of settlement of international indebtedness. That is, balance of payments deficits could be paid for with this paper money. Since they could import goods and pay for them with paper, countries which were allocated SDRs by the IMF were thus given a claim to real resources, the size of the claim being equal to the number of SDRs that they were allocated. However, the member countries of the IMF found it difficult to reach agreement on the size of the allocation to be awarded to each country – each arguing for a larger quota for themselves – and it is for this reason that the number of SDRs created has been limited. No new SDRs have been created since 1981 and the sum total of extant SDRs (21 billion) represents only a small fraction of countries' reserves.

The third problem inherent in the Bretton Woods system was that of **adjustment**. Over time, currencies moved 'out of line' and there existed no mechanism for realignment. The dollar and sterling became increasingly overvalued, and in consequence America and the United Kingdom experienced persistent balance of payments deficits. In contrast, Germany and Japan had undervalued currencies and trade surpluses. These imbalances persisted to the discomfiture mostly of the deficit countries, on whom the **burden of adjustment** fell most heavily. This was because the requirement to monitor the exchange value of their currency in the face of balance of payments deficits forced urgent action.

Those countries with surpluses and a tendency to appreciate were in a strong position to force the deficit countries to act. The UK particularly was repeatedly compelled to engage in domestic deflation in order to protect the external value of the pound. The United States fared somewhat better, since the high status of the dollar and its role as a reserve asset allowed the United States to run balance of payments deficits and pay for these deficits in dollars. This gave the USA an advantage known as **seigniorage**.

Seigniorage is a term which refers to the privilege enjoyed in former times by those kings and princes who had the right to create money. They would often debase the coinage by reducing the amount of precious metal contained in the coins they minted, thus effectively producing more money from a given amount of gold. They kept the surplus coins for themselves to pay for raising armies, building castles and other kingly pursuits.

Imagine that you could pay for things with money that you yourself created at no cost. This in effect was the advantage enjoyed by the United States when other countries allowed it to run persistent balance of payments deficits and pay for those deficits in paper money which America herself created.

12.4 The Smithsonian Agreement

In 1967 Britain was forced to devalue (from \$2.80 to \$2.40). This led to a domino effect, exposing the currency which was next in line, the dollar. The United States was consequently forced to suspend gold convertibility, and since that time gold has been 'demonetised', effectively ceasing to have any monetary significance and becoming just like any other metal.

In December 1971 a last attempt to save the Bretton Woods system was worked out at a conference at the Smithsonian Institute in Washington. The **Smithsonian Agreement** consisted of:

➤ a realignment of parities. The dollar and sterling were devalued. The mark and the yen were revalued.
➤ a system of **wider margins** around these new parities. The permitted band of fluctuation was to be $2\frac{1}{4}$ per cent around these newly aligned parities (as opposed to 1 per cent under the original Bretton Woods system).

The new parities could not be sustained, however, and in June 1972 the British government abandoned the sterling parity entirely and announced that it would henceforth allow the pound to float freely. The rationale for this was that domestic objectives would no longer be sacrificed in favour of the external value of the pound.

The decision to float the pound in 1972 marks the end of the Bretton Woods era. Since that time, currencies have floated freely and there have been no declared parities (apart from those in the European Monetary System). Following the breakdown of the Bretton Woods system, there has been considerable instability in exchange rates. Notwithstanding this, however, world trade has continued to expand rapidly, and some authors have argued that the system of floating exchange rates has been able to absorb shocks more effectively than a fixed system could have done. The following section considers the arguments for and against fixed rates.

12.5 The pros and cons of fixed versus floating rates

This section is a summary of the various arguments that have been used in support of the two types of exchange rate regime – floating and fixed rates. Curiously, the same argument is sometimes used in support of *both* types of regime – for example, it has been claimed that speculation is reduced under a fixed exchange rate regime, but this is the same argument which is used by the supporters of floating rates. A brief assessment of the strength of each argument is also provided.

Floating rates – the supposed advantages

1. There is an *automatic adjustment mechanism* which ensures that currencies cannot get 'out of line'. Verdict: this is basically correct although somewhat simplistic. It calls into question what it means when one says that a currency is 'out of line'.

2. There is *no need for reserves*. Verdict: not quite true, but the need for reserves is *smaller* if the currency is floating than under a fixed rate.

3. There is *freedom to pursue domestic objectives* without having to worry about the balance of trade, since this will correct itself. Verdict: the policy-maker has more freedom with floating rates than under a fixed rate, but it would be unreasonable to expect payments imbalances to be completely self-correcting under any regime.

4. There is *less speculation* with floating rates. Verdict: it is difficult to decide which regime produces the more speculation.

5. *Changes to rates occur more smoothly* than the step changes to nominally fixed parities that are necessary under a fixed exchange rate. Verdict: more or less true by definition, but with floating rates it is possible for rates to 'overshoot' in a downward or upward direction.

Fixed rates – the supposed advantages

1. There is *greater stability* than under floating rates. The *reduced uncertainty* which results is beneficial to the growth of trade. Verdict: fixed rates are certainly stable – unless they are forced to change.

2. It *imposes greater discipline* on domestic economic policy. In particular, it forces the policy-maker to keep domestic inflation in check. Verdict: true. This is the opposite to point 3 above. It depends whether you like freedom or discipline.

3. There is *less speculation* with fixed rates. Verdict: the counter argument to 4 above and, as already noted, difficult to disprove or prove. Further insights into the nature of speculation are provided below and in section 12.10.

PAUSE FOR THOUGHT *Unlike motherhood and apple pie, which everyone agrees to be a good thing, **speculation** is by common consent 'a bad thing'. However, unlike apple pie, which is relatively easy to identify, speculation is not quite so easy to spot. How should we define speculation and measure the amount that takes place?*

Speculative transactions in currencies can be defined as those that are in no way related to trade. They are essentially a bet on future currency movements, similar in most respects to a bet on the outcome of a horse race or a football match. Speculators believe that they can correctly anticipate future movements in the exchange rate and that their forecast of the future is better than that of everyone else.

It is difficult to measure what proportion of currency transactions are related to trade and what proportion are not related (that is, are purely speculative). This is because buyers and sellers are no longer compelled to state why they wish to buy or sell a particular currency. One estimate suggests that out of the one trillion dollars' worth of foreign exchange market transactions which take place each day, only 5–10 per cent are involved in financing trade, the remainder being 'speculative'. However, this would appear to be a guesstimate rather than an estimate. (See Bernard Foley, 'Developments in the international financial system', *Quarterly Journal of the Economics and Business Education Association,* autumn 1994.)

ACTIVITY **1**
....

Suppose you are planning a trip to the United States in three months' time. You may decide to acquire your dollars now on the forward currency market rather than waiting and acquiring them on the spot market in three months' time. If you did so, would this constitute speculation?

Check with answers/suggestions at the back of the book.

12.6 European monetary integration
....

One of the most important and contentious issues facing the British economy in the period up to 1999 and beyond is the question of whether or not to join a single European currency, if and when it is established. Whatever the immediate outcome of moves towards a single currency, the history of European integration since the inception of the Common Market in 1957 suggests that the issue of a single currency will not simply go away. This part of the chapter provides a brief history of integration in Europe and the moves towards a common currency.

The key events in the process of European integration are as follows:

➤ 1951: **European Coal and Steel Community** established, the antecedent of the European Economic Community.
➤ 1957: the **Treaty of Rome** establishing the European Economic Community signed by Germany, France, Italy and the Benelux countries (Belgium, Luxembourg and Holland).
➤ 1970: publication of **Werner Report,** which set out the steps by which a common currency was to be achieved.
➤ 1979: establishment of **European Monetary System (EMS)**.
➤ 1990: sterling joins the **exchange rate mechanism** (ERM) of the EMS.
➤ 1992 (September): Sterling forced out of ERM.
➤ 1992: the **Single European Act** establishes a **single market** throughout Europe, effectively eliminating all tariff barriers.
➤ 1992 (7 February): the **Treaty on European Union** at **Maastricht** sets out a timescale by which a single European currency is to replace national currencies among all of the members of what is henceforth to be called the *European Union.*

➤ 1999: Ready or not, a **single European currency** is meant to be in place by this date at the latest; in 1996 EU members agreed that it would be called the 'euro'.

12.7 The Werner Report
....

Among supporters of a European union, the monetary question has always been seen as vital if further integration among the European economies is to be achieved. Jacques Rueff, one of the founders of the Community, had said 'L'Europe se fera par la monnaie ou ne se fera pas' – the monetary question is make-or-break for the Community. Thus it was that in 1970 the Werner Report was published. This report, with considerable *naïveté* in hindsight, set out the steps by which monetary union was to be achieved by 1980. These steps were:

➤ a progressive narrowing of exchange rate margins between the individual European currencies
➤ a pooling of reserves
➤ the establishment of a European Central Bank to manage these reserves and to assist countries in maintaining these exchange rates
➤ the eventual elimination of margins altogether and, once this became irrevocable, the replacement of national currencies by a single European currency.

In the short term, the monetary system envisaged by the Werner Report was thus a mini-Bretton Woods system of fixed exchange rates. However, as we saw in section 12.4, by the early 1970s the Bretton Woods system was itself starting to collapse. Although the Smithsonian Agreement provided a brief respite, the floating of the pound in June 1972 effectively marked the end of the adjustable peg system and began the move towards floating exchange rates worldwide.

The Werner Plan thus came into operation at a particularly inauspicious time; in consequence its success was very short lived. Arrangements for tying the European currencies together more closely when other currencies were floating further apart became rather complex. To explain how the system operated commentators used the analogy of a **Snake in a tunnel**, illustrated in Figure 12.1. The Snake represented the European currencies as a group wriggling around within a tunnel, the confines of which represented the wider margins permitted in the Smithsonian Agreement. Any one individual European currency would be contained within the skin of the Snake.

In the event, the Snake survived for only a few months. One by one the European currencies left the Snake until it contained little more than the Mark. In retrospect, the failure of the Snake can be seen to have been, if not inevitable, then at least predictable, since the Werner Plan concentrated almost exclusively on monetary convergence with scarcely a thought for the economic convergence which could be seen as a precondition for monetary union. In contrast, as we shall see later, the Maastricht proposals place great emphasis on the issue of economic convergence.

Figure 12.1

The Snake in a tunnel

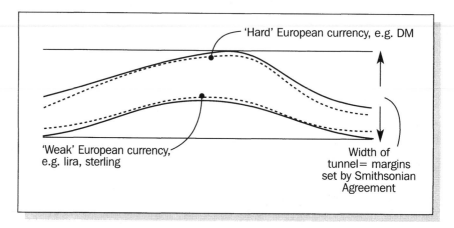

12.8 The European Monetary System

The arrangements which had collapsed with the demise of the Snake in 1972–74 were replaced in 1979 with a new set of arrangements known as the European Monetary System. Like the Snake before it, the EMS was seen by its designers as a set of transitional arrangements which would eventually lead to full monetary union. The most important part of the EMS was (and remains) the exchange rate mechanism (ERM). The main features of this are as follows:

➤ It is an adjustable peg system.
➤ Unlike the Bretton Woods system, which worked on the basis of bilateral exchange rates, the ERM considers multilateral exchange rates. This is achieved by a **parity grid** arrangement, which establishes a central rate for each currency against each of the other European currencies.
➤ The permitted margin of fluctuation is $2\frac{1}{4}$ per cent for those currencies in narrow band (and 6 per cent for those in wide band).
➤ A new unit of account, the **European currency unit** or ECU was established. The ECU is a basket of currencies, with the weights of the currencies in the basket depending on their importance in European trade.
➤ A divergence indicator is triggered when any of the European currencies exceeds its permitted margin of fluctuation against the ECU. The central bank of the country concerned is then obliged to act to bring the currency back within its permitted range. This it does by intervention buying (or selling).

Although sterling was nominally part of the European Monetary System from its inception in 1979, it did not become part of the exchange rate mechanism until 1990. At this time it adopted a central rate of £1 = DM2.95, but remained within the wide band, so that sterling was required to keep within the range DM2.95 plus or minus 6 per cent.

12.9 Black Wednesday
....

16 September 1992 is known as **Black Wednesday** (or for some politicians who never the liked the idea of monetary union very much in the first place, 'Bright Wednesday'). It was on this date that speculative selling forced sterling below its ERM floor, compelling the British government to abandon its membership of the ERM and to revert to a floating exchange rate once more.

Some special circumstances contributed to this débâcle.

High level of German interest rates

Since German reunification in 1990, interest rates in Germany had been high. This was thought necessary both to dampen down inflationary pressures and to attract the investment funds needed for reconstruction in the former East Germany. Because capital is a very mobile factor of production, it will tend *ceteris paribus* to flow to whichever country is offering the highest rate of interest. Thus funds flowed into the German economy and out of the UK economy, weakening the demand for sterling.

This was made worse by the fact that the mark and the pound were linked so closely together by a fixed exchange rate (since 1990 the pound had been 'shadowing' the Deutschmark). Had they not been linked in this way, investors would not have viewed investment opportunities in Germany to be such perfect substitutes for those in Britain, since future expected movements in exchange rates might have had the effect of offsetting interest rate differentials between the two countries.

Weight of speculative selling pressure

Whatever the longer-term structural reasons for the weakness of sterling, there is no doubt that the immediate cause of sterling's enforced exit from the ERM was the very large amount of speculative selling of sterling which built up in the days preceding 16 September. The sheer volume of this selling completely overwhelmed the ability of the Bank of England to maintain the parity. It simply had insufficient reserves to withstand the short-term assault, despite receiving some assistance from other European central banks (though arguably it could have received greater assistance from the German central bank, the Bundesbank).

During this period a number of other currencies both inside and outside the ERM came under unprecedented speculative attack, forcing many commentators to question whether any fixed exchange rate could in future withstand the forces of international liquidity. To understand the significance of this last comment, we need to examine more closely the nature of speculation on foreign exchange markets. This will also give us additional insight into the pros and cons of fixed and floating exchange rates.

12.10 Speculative selling on foreign exchange markets

Common sense would suggest that the speculative selling of a particular commodity must come to an end when everyone who wishes to sell has done so and has no more left to sell. However, this is not the case.

When one is selling a house, or a plot of land, or a second-hand car it is first necessary to own the item in question before you can sell it. However, on commodities markets, and other financial markets including markets for foreign exchange, you can enter into a contract to sell something which you do not in fact own. Of course, when such a contract becomes due for settlement, the person who has contracted to sell sterling will have to take out another contract to buy the quantity of sterling that he has contracted to sell. But the contract does not become due for settlement immediately – typically, it may be several days or even weeks before the contract is due for settlement, and in the interim the seller of sterling can sit back and hope to see its value fall. If it does go down then when the time comes for the seller to buy sterling, he or she will be paying a lower price for it. This is how speculators make their profit – or at least it is how successful speculators make their profit.

Three things follow from this. First, the greater the amount of international liquidity, the greater the ability of speculators to indulge in this sort of activity. Second, deregulation and globalisation of financial markets have increased the amount of liquidity which can be brought to bear at any one time on any one market (such as the market for sterling on 16 September 1992).

Third – and this may help to inform our views about the desirability or otherwise of fixed exchange rates as opposed to floating ones – in a fixed exchange rate system the odds are stacked in favour of the speculator. Say, for example, that speculators decide to attack a currency that is operating a fixed exchange rate. If they succeed in forcing a devaluation of the currency, they make a big profit (since they buy the currency back at a lower price than the price at which they sold). But if they do not succeed, they do *not* make a loss (since they buy the currency back at the *same* price as the price at which they sold). This is an example of 'Heads I win. Tails I don't lose.'

Under a floating exchange rate, in contrast, there is a more genuine two-way bet. 'Heads I win. Tails I lose.' This is because a floating rate can go up as well as down, and arguably is equally likely to move in one direction as in the other. In a fixed rate system, the bet is on a one-way currency movement.

Finally, we may wish to note the view of right-wing commentators regarding the activities of speculators: successful speculators are the instrument which causes to happen that which needs to happen anyway. In the summer of 1992, sterling was overvalued – as we can now see with the benefit of hindsight, since its value has fallen from the ERM parity of DM2.95 to about DM2.2 in 1996. Speculators pushed sterling down to a more realistic rate.

12.11 Maastricht

As we noted in section 12.7, the deficiency of the original Werner Plan for monetary union was that it concentrated too much on *monetary* convergence and ignored the question of *economic* convergence between the countries of Europe.

This deficiency was addressed at Maastricht, where a number of **convergence criteria** were established. According to the treaty, only those economies which satisfy the criteria will be eligible to participate in the moves towards a single European currency. The timescale for these moves begins in 1996–97. According to the treaty, these moves will culminate in the establishment of a single currency by 1999 at the latest. Countries which meet the criteria will be able to proceed along a 'fast track'. Those which do not meet the criteria will have to wait until 1999 to join. The convergence criteria are set out below.

➤ *Inflation.* To be eligible for membership, the country's inflation rate should be 'close' to the average rate of the three best-performing members. ('Close' is interpreted to mean within $1\frac{1}{2}$ per cent.)
➤ *Interest rates.* To be eligible for membership, interest rates should be close to the rates in the three best-performing countries. Here 'close' is defined explicitly to mean not more than 2 per cent higher. The interest rate in question is that on long-term government bonds.
➤ *Budget deficit.* The budget deficit should not exceed 3 per cent of GDP.
➤ *Outstanding government debt* (that is, the national debt). This should not exceed 60 per cent of GDP.
➤ *Exchange rate stability in the ERM.* For the previous two years, the normal margins of fluctuation should not have been exceeded.

By early 1996 it became apparent that few if any countries would be able to satisfy the convergence criteria within the timescale envisaged. These doubts applied even to the German economy, which was having the greatest difficulty keeping its budget deficit within the required limits. Ironically, the United Kingdom – always a reluctant European – was better placed to satisfy the criteria than most of its EU partners (with the nominal exception of exchange rate stability in the exchange rate mechanism, since Britain is not part of the mechanism).

12.12 Rationale for the convergence criteria
....

Does it really matter if countries do not meet these convergence criteria? Are they merely a set of regulations which are essentially arbitrary, or is there some sound economic rationale behind them?

To answer this question it is necessary to appreciate that monetary union is a bit like taking your car on holiday to the Western Isles of Scotland. All the benefits accrue when you arrive at the end of your journey, and all the costs accrue on the journey itself. Similarly, if there are benefits to be gained from monetary union, they will only be enjoyed once full and irrevocable union is in place. On the arduous journey towards this destination, economies may have to undergo somewhat painful readjustment of certain structural features. Moreover, their exchange rate may be attacked by bands of marauding speculators on the way.

Suppose, however, that you eventually reach your destination. Only now can the significance of the convergence criteria be fully appreciated. If two countries share a common currency, they must have price levels and inflation rates which are, if not the same, then 'close' to one another. Hence the relevance of the first convergence criterion.

Our experience bears out the validity of this point. Take the example of two countries which share a common currency – England and Scotland. It is clear that the price level and the rate of inflation in these two countries has to be the same. At least, this is true for the **tradables sector** – things which are capable of being traded from one country to another. It will not generally be true of **non-tradables**. Thus the price of baked beans and Ford Escorts will be the same in Edinburgh as in London, but it may be cheaper to get your Ford Escort serviced in Edinburgh (since services are generally non-tradable) and house prices will certainly be cheaper in Edinburgh.

ACTIVITY 2

Make a list of non-tradable goods (which will include services). Why is it possible for the price of non-tradables to be different in different parts of the country when the price of tradeables has to be similar in all parts of the country?

Check with answers/suggestions at the back of the book.

What has been said about inflation rates applies *a fortiori* to interest rates. Interest rates are not *approximately* the same in Scotland as they are in England – they are *exactly* the same. Households and companies will always seek out the lowest price – in this example, the lowest interest rate – and there are no transport costs involved in transferring capital (money) from Scotland to England. We would therefore expect to find that, if information about prices were perfect, interest rates would be identical in two countries which share a common currency.

The reason why two countries with separate currencies can have different interest rates is that the expected future change in the exchange rate will partially or totally offset the interest rate differential.

ACTIVITY 3

Suppose you wish to borrow £10,000. Banks in the UK offer you a loan with an interest rate of 10 per cent. German banks will lend at a rate of only 6 per cent. However, you fear that over the next twelve months the value of the pound will fall from its current rate of £1 = DM2.2 to £1 = DM2.0. From which bank should you borrow the money?

Check with answers/suggestions at the back of the book.

We have explained that, if two countries share a common currency, the rate of interest and the rate of inflation will be the same in those countries. This helps to explain the rationale for the first two convergence criteria listed above. Of course, there is a slight *non sequitur* here. We have established that *after* monetary union the rate of inflation and the level of interest rates will be the same, not that they *need to be* the same prior to monetary union in order that such a union can be formed. However, what we can conclude is that, if they were not the same prior to union, a rapid process of structural readjustment would take place as soon as the union was established, and this might be a painful experience.

But what of the other convergence criteria – those related to public sector deficits and public sector debt? What is the rationale for these?

This is based on the notion – which may be quite incorrect – that public sector borrowing influences and may determine interest rates. It is at this point that the Keynesian economist would part company with the monetarist. While both would agree that market forces will equalise inflation and interest rates within a monetary union, only monetarists would argue that the level of public sector borrowing is the thing which determines interest rates.

Keynesian economists would argue that this view is incorrect, being based on a particular piece of dogma known as the **crowding out hypothesis**. This states that high levels of public sector borrowing drive up interest rates, since public borrowing increases the demand for loanable funds, increasing the price of funds in the money market. Since the price of funds (the market interest rate) has to be the same in all countries in a monetary union, it follows, monetarists argue, that the amount of government borrowing also has to be the same in all countries of the union.

ASK YOURSELF   *In December 1995 there were riots in the streets of Paris. People were protesting against the French government's policy of draconian cuts in welfare state spending. It is all the fault of Maastricht, it was claimed. Why should this claim have been made?*

12.13 A two-speed Europe

As stated previously, it was beginning to look unlikely by early 1996 that any of the member countries would satisfy all of the convergence criteria within the agreed timescale. Table 12.1 shows the degree of success of each member country by early 1996.

The driving forces behind the move towards monetary union are the political leaders of France and, in particular, Germany. Their enthusiasm is such that it has always been assumed that they will want to go ahead with monetary union regardless of whether the conditions have been satisfied and regardless of the wishes of the 'reluctant Europeans'.

One scenario is that of a **two-speed Europe** – those countries which enthusiastically endorse the idea of monetary union and which satisfy or almost satisfy the convergence criteria will proceed at a faster pace than the rest. A similar idea is expressed in the notion of **concentric circles**. There could be an inner core of countries which would be the first to adopt a common currency. This core would probably comprise France, Germany and the Benelux countries. Around this inner core would be a ring comprising countries such as Italy, Spain, the Nordic countries and possibly the UK. Finally, there would be an outer ring of countries such as Greece and some of the aspiring members from eastern Europe.

12.4 Just do it

Finally note the view which is popular among some economists who favour a **Big Bang approach** to monetary union. This view is based on the experience of the German economy following the reunification in 1990. The former East

table 12.1

Convergence potential of EU countries (forecast for 1996 made in September 1995)[1]

	Inflation rate[2]	Ratio of budget deficit to GDP	Ratio of public debt to GDP	Interest rate	EMS bands
Germany	1.9	2.4	58.0	7.2	yes
France	2.5	4.0	55.0	7.9	yes
Italy	4.8	6.5	114.9	12.3	FF
UK	3.0	3.4	52.7	8.6	FF
Spain	4.5	4.8	65.0	11.5	yes
Netherlands	2.4	3.0	79.2	7.3	yes
Belgium	2.1	3.2	136.5	8.0	yes
Sweden	3.2	5.5	85.7	10.9	FF
Austria	2.4	4.3	65.9	7.4	yes
Denmark	2.4	1.2	76.8	8.7	yes
Finland	2.5	1.5	66.8	9.6	FF
Portugal	4.3	4.7	70.5	12.1	yes
Greece	7.2	7.7	111.1	17.4	FF
Ireland	3.0	2.0	83.4	8.7	yes
Luxembourg	2.6	1.5	7.8	8.0	yes

[1] The first three columns are forecasts for 1996 made in September 1995. The interest rate figure shown is the actual interest rate on long-term debt at August 1995. 'EMS bands' shows the position at September 1995 (FF = free floating).
[2] Average inflation rate of the 'best' EU countries (Germany, Belgium, Netherlands) in 1996 = 2.1 per cent.

Source: *Die Europäische Währungsunion (EWU) Konsequenzen für die Anlagestrategie*, Deutsche Bank Research, September 1995.

Germany adopted on unification an exchange rate for its Ost Mark against the Deutschmark of one to one. Before reunification the East German currency, the Ost Mark, had been worth only about 20 per cent of the West German currency, the Deutschmark. The choice of a 1:1 exchange rate was equivalent to a very substantial revaluation of the Ost Mark. This, of course, meant that East German industry became, overnight, hopelessly uncompetitive. Many firms went bankrupt and unemployment quickly reached unprecedented levels. However – so the argument runs – the process of transition has been relatively swift and five years later the structural readjustment which had to take place has been more or less completed.

A Big Bang approach to monetary union, it is argued, would similarly produce short-term traumas, but these would be relatively short lived. However, there now seems to be little support for such an approach.

Summary
....

The Gold Standard operated before 1914 and briefly in the inter-war period. The rigid nature of the Gold Standard system and its subsequent failure led countries to adopt a fixed-but-adjustable (adjustable peg) system known as the Bretton Woods system. This lasted until 1971 when it broke down and was replaced by floating rates. Floating rates have certain advantages over fixed rates – they provide automatic adjustment for balance of payments imbalances and allow countries to pursue their domestic objectives independently. But fixed rates may provide greater stability and impose greater discipline on the policy-maker to contain domestic inflation.

Moves towards European monetary integration began as early as 1970 with the publication of the Werner Report. Subsequent attempts at fixing EC currencies – known as 'the Snake' – broke down after a few months, because the Economies concerned diverged so much in their performance. It came to be realised that fixed exchange rates could be maintained only if Economies performed in a similar manner – in terms of inflation rates, interest rates and so on.

As a result of all this, the Treaty on European Union signed in 1992 at Maastricht established certain convergence criteria. Only those economies which satisfied the criteria would qualify for membership of an immutably (and irrevocably) fixed exchange rate club, which was to pave the way towards a single European currency. The start date for the single European currency is 1999. However, by 1996 few if any economies satisfied all the convergence criteria. Some commentators argue that countries which wish to do so should go ahead anyway. Other commentators are much less enthusiastic, fearing the loss of independence which would result from the adoption of a single European currency.

REVIEW QUESTIONS

1 List the convergence criteria established at Maastricht. State which of the fifteen EU countries listed in Table 12.1 satisfy all these criteria.

2 In Table 12.1 it can be seen that certain EU countries have comparatively high inflation rates – countries such as Greece, Italy, Spain and Portugal. What do you notice about interest rates in these countries? How do you explain this?

3 A few years ago British holiday makers to France got 10 francs to the pound sterling. Now they get less than eight. What explanations can you offer for this?

4 Would you expect the price of goods and services to be the same in London as in rural Wales? If not, which prices would be similar and which would be higher in London?

5 If Britain shared a common currency with France and Germany which of the following prices would be the same in all three countries (or more or less the same, having made due allowance for transport costs)?
(a) shoes
(b) houses
(c) mineral water
(d) computers
(e) hairdressing services
(f) motorway tolls

6 Nowadays, in many Latin American countries, dollars circulate alongside national currencies and in many cases dollars are the preferred currency for transactions. In Russia, dollars and Deutschmarks are often preferred to roubles.
(a) Explain the reasons for this.
(b) What does this tell you about the privileged position enjoyed by the United States and Germany?

Key concepts
....

The following key concepts have been introduced in this chapter. Make sure you understand the meaning and significance of each of them. They are listed here in the order in which they first appear, and the page number where they appear is also given. You will find these key concepts in section headings or in **bold** in the text. Each chapter contains a list of key concepts and you may find these particularly useful for revision purposes.

Gold Standard	(p.200)
fiduciary currency	(p.201)
Bretton Woods system	(p.202)
adjustable peg system	(p.202)
intervention currency	(p.202)
IMF	(p.202)
IMF Drawing Rights	(p.202)
GATT	(p.202)
liquidity problem	(p.203)
confidence problem	(p.203)
Special Drawing Rights (SDRs)	(p.203)
adjustment problem	(p.203)
burden of adjustment	(p.203)
seigniorage	(p.203)
Smithsonian Agreement	(p.204)
wider margins	(p.204)
speculation	(p.205)
European Coal and Steel Community	(p.206)
Treaty of Rome	(p.206)
Werner Report	(p.206)
European Monetary System	(p.206)
exchange rate mechanism	(p.206)
Single European Act (single market)	(p.206)
Treaty on European Union (Maastricht)	(p.206)
single European currency	(p.207)
'Snake in a tunnel'	(p.207)
parity grid	(p.208)
European currency unit (ecu)	(p.208)
Black Wednesday	(p.209)
Maastricht convergence criteria	(p.211)
tradable/non-tradable goods	(p.212)

crowding out hypothesis (p.213)
two-speed Europe (p.213)
concentric circles (p.213)
Big Bang approach (p.213)

CHAPTER **13**

The macroeconomic environment and business

Objectives:

This chapter will enable you to:

➤ understand the nature of business cycles and the reasons for the volatility of various categories of spending

➤ distinguish between exogenous and endogenous spending

➤ be aware of leading and coincident indicators of economic activity

➤ understand how interest rates affect the level of investment spending and how interest rates are determined

➤ understand the principles of investment appraisal and how to calculate the net present value and internal rate of return of a project

➤ appreciate the impact of inflation on business

➤ understand the importance of the real exchange rate in determining competitiveness.

13.1	Business cycles
13.2	The volatility of investment
13.3	The accelerator
13.4	Exogenous spending
13.5	Forecasts and indicators
13.6	Investment and the rate of interest
13.7	Net present value
13.8	The internal rate of return
13.9	What determines market interest rates?
13.10	The impact of inflation on business
13.11	The exchange rate and business
13.12	The single European currency

This book has been about the macroeconomic environment. However, certain macro variables have such an important impact on the behaviour and performance of firms that they deserve special emphasis – hence this chapter.

13.1 Business cycles

All economies are subject to fluctuations in economic activity – at times the level of spending, income and output grows rapidly, at other times it grows more slowly or may even decline. When output grows rapidly we speak of a **boom**, when it declines, of a **recession**. Figure 13.1 illustrates the fluctuations that have occurred in the UK economy in the last twenty years. As can be seen, there have been two major recessions in this period. The first of these was at the beginning of the 1980s, the second at the end of the 1980s. Note also the rapid expansion of demand which took place in the period 1987–89 – the so-called 'Lawson boom' (named after the then Chancellor of the Exchequer, Nigel Lawson).

218

Figure 13.1
**UK GDP at constant
1990 prices,
1977–96 (£bn)**

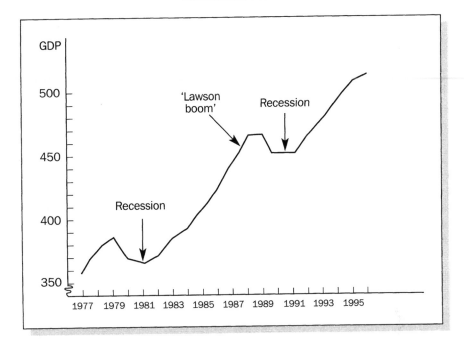

Source: *UK National Accounts*.

These fluctuations will affect households and firms. However, some firms will be affected more than others by cycles in economic activity. Firms which rely solely on the UK market will be hit harder by a recession in the UK than those which sell to foreign markets as well. This is because the timing and the severity of recessions varies from one country to another, even though cycles in economic activity tend to be propagated throughout the world economy. Therefore a firm which sells in more than one national market can compensate to some extent for the decline in home sales by increasing sales effort abroad. This provides firms with a powerful incentive to expand their activities beyond their national boundaries and to seek new markets overseas.

In a recession, the severity of the decline in sales which any one firm experiences will also depend to some extent on the *type* of product or service being sold. Those firms selling durable goods such as cars and furniture will experience a bigger fall in demand than those selling non-durables such as coffee, cakes, cough sweets and condoms.

Durable goods are by their nature long-lived assets. They do eventually wear out, but only after a period of years, and therefore the decision to replace them can be postponed. In contrast, non-durable goods are not assets at all. Non-durables can be thought of as being 'used up' as soon as they are purchased. Households wishing to reduce their spending are therefore more likely to delay the purchase of a consumer durable, such as a new dining room table, rather than to decide to cut down on their non-durable consumption. Similarly, when the economy is booming, the most rapid growth in demand will be for durables such as cars, electrical goods and other durables.

ACTIVITY **1**
....

Table 13.1 shows the number of new car registrations for the period 1985–96, the period which covers the Lawson boom, the recession which followed and the subsequent slow recovery of demand. Also shown in the table is the *overall* level of consumer spending (in real terms) for the same period.

First calculate the percentage decline in the volume of sales of new cars in the recession of the late 1980s. Now compare this with the percentage decline in the overall level of consumption during the same period.

table 13.1

Volume of new car registrations and consumers' expenditure, 1985–94

	New car registrations (000s)	Consumers' expenditure (£bn, 1990 prices)
1985	1,842	276.7
1986	1,883	295.6
1987	2,016	311.2
1988	2,211	334.6
1989	2,304	345.4
1990	2,005	347.5
1991	1,600	339.9
1992	1,599	339.5
1993	1,776	348.1
1994	1,906	358.9

Sources: *Economic Trends; UK National Accounts.*

Check with answers/suggestions at the back of the book.

13.2 The volatility of investment
....

Cars are just one particular example of **capital assets** – things which are long lived and yield a stream of services to their owners throughout their life. Other examples of capital assets are machine tools and buildings. Expenditure by companies on purchasing capital assets such as these is known as **investment spending** or **fixed capital formation**. Like consumer spending on durable goods, this investment spending by companies is likely to be highly volatile – that is, to fall very rapidly in recessions and rise quickly in booms. Those firms engaged in producing and selling investment goods will therefore suffer greater fluctuations in the demand for their products than those producing consumer goods.

Table 13.2 compares indices of investment spending and consumer spending for the last decade. Because the figures are expressed as index numbers, it is easy to see that investment spending by firms rose more rapidly in the boom (the period up to 1989) and fell more sharply in the recession (the period 1990–92) than did consumption spending by households.

table 13.2

Indices of consumer spending and investment spending in the UK, 1985–95

	Consumer spending	Investment spending
1985	100	100
1986	106.8	102.5
1987	112.5	113.2
1988	120.9	128.9
1989	124.8	136.6
1990	125.6	131.9
1991	122.9	119.4
1992	122.7	117.6
1993	125.7	118.4
1994	129.0	121.9
1995	131.5	121.7

Source: Derived from *Economic Trends*. Both indices are based on spending at 1990 prices.

13.3 The accelerator

There is a further reason why companies' investment spending is so volatile. This results from the fact that most fixed capital assets, such as machine tools, yield a stream of services to their owner in the first year of their acquisition which is less than the purchase price of the asset. The same is true, of course, of buildings – the annual stream of services they yield, equivalent to the rent that would have to be paid to enjoy such a property, is less than the capital value (the purchase price) of the building. As both buildings and machines provide services over a period of many years, the decision to purchase rather than rent is often a sensible one. However, it has an important implication – namely, that expenditure on investment will rise and fall more than other types of spending in the economy.

Suppose that a typical machine has a purchase price which is five times the value of the annual stream of services which it provides. If a company which is currently using all its productive capacity expects that the demand for its products will increase by £10,000 over the coming months, it will have to spend *five times* this amount now – £50,000 – to install the equipment necessary to produce the extra output. Conversely, if it expects a drop in sales of £10,000, it will curtail the investment spending it would otherwise have undertaken by five times the anticipated drop in sales.

So the change in sales that the company is expecting in the near future will result in a change in its current level of investment spending, which is some multiple of the anticipated change in sales. This multiple is known as the **accelerator coefficient.** This accelerator model of investment behaviour therefore provides a further explanation of the volatility of investment spending.

We have illustrated the accelerator model in the context of spending on plant and equipment. However, roughly one-third of what we refer to as fixed capital formation is concerned with the acquisition of new dwellings, factories and other buildings. The accelerator model of investment can also be applied to spending on this type of asset. As we would expect to find, therefore, this spending behaves erratically in response to the business cycle. Consequently, the output of the construction sector is more volatile than that of other sectors.

In Table 13.3 we compare output in construction with that of the manufacturing sector. We see a now familiar pattern. In the Lawson boom, output in construction rises more rapidly than that in manufacturing. It then falls more sharply in 1991 when the recession takes hold.

PAUSE FOR THOUGHT

Suppose that in 1990 you decide to set up a business manufacturing drawing office equipment – drawing boards and other specialist equipment used by draughtsmen. What are your chances of establishing a successful business?

Your chances are poor. The building industry which you supply is itself facing recession, as can be seen from Table 13.3. In addition, however, you are manufacturing *capital equipment* (investment goods) used in that industry, so the demand for your product is likely to fall even more than if you were selling consumable items such as pencils and paper used by draughtsmen.

13.4 Exogenous spending

Table 13.4 is an index of the output of public services, and for ease of comparison the index of output of the manufacturing sector is also repeated from the previous table. As can be seen, the output of public services shows a slow but relatively steady growth. It is not affected by the business cycle in the same way that private spending is. In the boom years it grows much more slowly than private spending, but when the recession hits it continues to grow, albeit very slowly.

The reason for this is that the demand for these public services is not directly dependent on the incomes of either households or companies. Hence it is not subject to the vagaries of the business cycle – it does not automatically

table 13.3

Indices of output in UK manufacturing and construction sectors (1985 = 100)

	Manufacturing	Construction
1985	100	100
1986	101.4	104.1
1987	106.0	116.3
1988	113.5	126.4
1989	118.6	133.8
1990	118.3	137.0
1991	112.1	126.0
1992	111.2	120.4
1993	112.7	119.4
1994	117.3	124.1
1995	120.1	122.8

Source: Derived from *Economic Trends*.

	Public services	Manufacturing
1985	100	100
1986	101.8	101.4
1987	104.6	106.0
1988	107.4	113.5
1989	107.9	118.6
1990	108.3	118.3
1991	109.3	112.1
1992	109.8	111.2
1993	111.1	112.7
1994	112.4	117.3
1995	114.1	120.1

table 13.4

Indices of output in UK public services and manufacturing (1985 = 100)

Source: Derived from *Economic Trends*.

rise when income and spending in the economy as a whole rise, nor does it automatically fall when they fall. Rather the decision to purchase or not to purchase public services is planned in advance by various government departments. Although spending will tend to increase more when Treasury coffers are brim full of tax revenue, as in a boom, and will tend to be cut in recessions, it will not be dependent on current income to the same extent that the spending of private households and firms is.

To use a technical term, public spending is **exogenous** – it is not dependent on what goes on within the economy. In contrast, both consumption spending and investment spending are **endogenous** – they depend directly on the growth of income in the economy. One of the implications of this is that the growth of public spending will be more stable, and its very existence therefore helps to stabilise the economy. It smooths out to some extent the cycles in economic activity, making the booms less inflationary and the slumps less severe.

13.5 Forecasts and indicators

In discussing the accelerator model in section 13.3, we noted the importance of **expectations** of future sales prospects in determining companies' investment behaviour. These expectations are likely to be based on companies' recent experiences – in effect, they are likely to extrapolate from current trends by projecting them into the future. If they have recently enjoyed a rapid growth of sales, they are likely to expect – in the absence of any evidence to the contrary – that the growth of sales is likely to continue in the future. They will have optimistic expectations of future sales prospects. Conversely, if sales have recently been declining, the company is likely to have pessimistic expectations about the demand for its products in the coming months.

However, in addition to information gleaned from the length of its *own* order book, the company is also likely to be aware of published **forecasts** about the strength of demand in the economy in the coming months. Such forecasts are published on a quarterly basis by HM Treasury, the National Institute for Economic and Social Research, and many other official and private organisations (such as firms of stockbrokers). These will contain forecasts not just of the future course of demand and output in the economy, broken down into its constituent parts, but also projections about inflation, the exchange rate and so on, all of which may be of relevance to individual companies in assessing likely changes to the environment in which they will find themselves in the near future.

More simplistically, if the firm is solely interested in the likely strength of demand for its products in future months, it will consult a range of so-called **leading indicators**. They are known as 'leading' not because they are particularly important or major, but because changes in these variables are normally thought to *precede* changes in economic activity itself – that is, they are a few months ahead of the business cycle. The CSO issues monthly publications of both longer leading and shorter leading indicators (based on an amalgam of data).

The CBI (the Confederation of British Industry) publishes the results of monthly surveys of its members relating to things such as capacity utilisation and export orders. Some of these indicators can be quite subjective. For example, one question relates to 'business optimism' and it measures 'the balance between those who are more optimistic about the business situation than 4 months previously and those less optimistic'. Other indicators are less subjective, such as the survey of investment intentions, which measures 'the difference between the percentage of respondents expecting to authorise more expenditure over the next 12 months and those expecting to authorise less'. These leading indicators may be of some value to the firm in forecasting future trends, but they cannot be presumed always to predict subsequent events accurately.

In general, leading indicators will be less reliable (because they are more subjective) than **coincident indicators** – those variables which change at the same time as demand and output in the economy generally (or *coincide* with the business cycle). The levels of retail sales, housing starts and new car registrations are all examples of such indicators. Coincident indicators are useful because data on these variables are collected and become available sooner than data on the overall level of spending and output in the economy, which are always subject to a **time lag** of several months before they can be collated and published. Typically, data on incomes and output are subject to a lag of about three months, so that the Chancellor, and indeed any firms that listen to him, do not know what the economy is doing at the present moment, only what it was doing in the recent past.

In addition to coincident and leading indicators, economists also use **lagging indicators** to analyse what has been happening in the economy. These are variables which follow the business cycle. Useful lagging indicators are the level of unemployment and vacancies, since conditions in the labour market are normally thought to follow conditions in the market for the goods and services that labour helps to create.

13.6 Investment and the rate of interest

We have already noted how investment decisions are influenced by firms' expectations about their future sales prospects. These expectations will in turn depend upon the current state of demand for their product. Rising demand generates optimistic expectations of future sales. To meet the expected increase in demand for their product, firms need extra capacity. Optimistic expectations generate a willingness to commit resources to purchasing the capital goods which will give them this extra capacity. However, firms will also be influenced by the *price* they have to pay for the funds to finance this investment. That price is the market rate of interest.

The market rate of interest is the cost of borrowing funds. The higher the cost of funds, the less profitable will each investment project become. When the market rate of interest rises, some projects which had previously been profitable will no longer be so and will therefore be abandoned. In short, as the rate of interest rises, the amount of investment undertaken by firms will fall.

To see in more detail why this should be so, consider the process of **investment appraisal** that firms undertake to decide whether or not to invest in a particular project. This will consist of calculating the *net present value* of the project. The firm will immediately reject any project which does not appear to yield a positive net present value.

A related technique of investment appraisal is to calculate the *internal rate of return* of the project, and to compare the internal rate of return with the external cost of funds.

13.7 Net present value
....

How does the firm calculate the **net present value** (or NPV) of an investment? Suppose the investment involves the purchase of a machine for £250 which will produce an output of £100 per year throughout its three-year life, after which it will be scrapped. This is illustrated schematically in *Figure 13.2*.

In the diagram we assume for simplicity that both costs and revenues accrue as discrete 'lumps' at the beginning or end of a period. The costs are incurred at the beginning of year 1. The revenues are received at the end of year 1, year 2 and year 3.

Figure 13.2
Cash flows

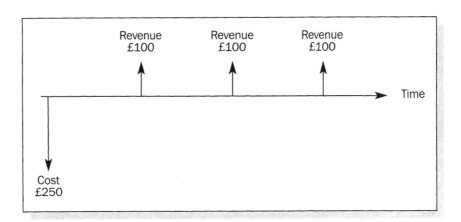

Consider the revenue of £100 which the firm receives at the end of year 1. If this had accrued earlier – for example, at the beginning of year 1 – the firm could have put the money in the bank where it would have earned the market rate of interest. At the end of twelve months, it would then have been worth

$$100 \times (1 + r)$$

where r is the rate of interest. For example, if the rate of interest is 7 per cent then $r = 0.07$ and

$$100 \times 1.07 = 107$$

That is, if the £100 had been received at the beginning of year 1, it would have been worth £107 by the end of year 1. It follows from this that the *present value* of this £100 accruing in twelve months' time is less than £100. We value it less highly than we would have done if we had received it earlier. This is the principle of **discounting**. We shall use the market rate of interest as the **discount rate**. The present value of £100 received in one year's time is therefore

$$\frac{100}{(1 + r)}$$

since this is the sum which, if put in a bank, will be worth precisely £100 in twelve months' time. That is

$$\frac{100}{(1 + r)} \times (1 + r) = 100$$

(In effect, you are multiplying and dividing by the same factor $(1 + r)$ to get back to the number you started with. If you have any difficulty with understanding this, you should check it for yourself with a calculator, using $r = 0.08$ or whatever).

By a similar process of reasoning, the present value of the £100 which accrues at the end of two years is

$$\frac{100}{(1 + r)^2}$$

and the £100 which accrues in three years' time is

$$\frac{100}{(1 + r)^3}$$

ACTIVITY **2**

Assuming that the interest rate is 8 per cent, use a calculator to work out the present value of £100 accruing in one, two and three years' time. What therefore is the present value of this revenue stream?

Now repeat this activity using an interest rate of 9 per cent to discount the future revenues.

Perform the calculations a third time using a discount rate of 10 per cent. What happens to the present value of the revenue stream?

Check with answers/suggestions at the back of the book.

In our example, the cost of the investment project (which was incurred at the beginning of year 1) was £250. Using a discount rate of 8 per cent, the present value of the income stream is £257.70, so that, at this discount rate, the project has a *positive* net present value of £7.70. The NPV remains positive if the discount rate is 9 per cent. However, when the discount rate rises to 10 per cent, the present value of the income stream is only £248.68 and therefore the project now has a *negative* net present value of minus £1.32 (that is, £248.68 − £250).

It follows that, as interest rates rise, the number of projects which yield a positive NPV will fall. As we stated earlier, firms will embark only on projects which yield a positive NPV. We can therefore conclude from this that, as interest rates rise, firms will undertake fewer investment projects. In short, investment falls as interest rates rise.

13.8 The internal rate of return

A related technique of investment appraisal consists of calculating the **internal rate of return** (IRR) of a project. We can define the internal rate of return of an investment project as that rate of discount which makes the net present value exactly equal to zero. It is the value of r which satisfies the equation

$$0 = -250 + \frac{100}{(1+r)} + \frac{100}{(1+r)^2} + \frac{100}{(1+r)^3}$$

Incidentally, this equation is *not* something which you can easily work out for yourself with a calculator. Intuitively, however, we can see that in our previous example the IRR will be somewhere between 9 and 10 per cent. If the market rate of interest at which the company can borrow money from the bank is only 9 per cent, then the project will be profitable and may be undertaken, since the estimated internal rate of return exceeds the external cost of finance. If the market rate of interest rises above 10 per cent, however, the project is no longer profitable and therefore will not be undertaken. If firms throughout the economy are making such calculations for all potential investment projects, we can again see why it is that as interest rates rise aggregate investment spending will fall.

In practice, of course, companies will not undertake all those investment projects which have an estimated IRR greater than the market rate of interest. Rather they are likely to have a range of investment projects which they rank according to the expected return, and then concentrate only on those at the top of the rank order. However, the general principle still holds – as interest rates rise, some projects which previously had a positive IRR will now have a negative one, and therefore will be shelved. Aggregate investment spending therefore falls.

Even if the firm can finance the investment entirely from its own resources without having to borrow money externally, it will still appraise the profitability of an investment in the same way – by comparing the internal rate of return of the project with the market rate of interest. To the non-economist this may seem strange. Surely if the firm has sufficient retained profits to finance its investment without having recourse to borrowing externally, the cost of those funds is zero?

A moment's thought will show that this is incorrect. Although those funds do have a *financial* cost of zero, they have an **opportunity cost** which is positive. The opportunity cost is the return the funds could yield if put to some alternative use. In this case the alternative is simply to put the money in the bank or building society or some other riskless asset which will yield the market rate of interest. Thus the market rate of interest is again the yardstick against which the firm will appraise the profitability of an investment – the firm will undertake only those investments which yield an internal rate of return greater than the market rate of interest.

DID YOU KNOW?

The concept of opportunity cost is one of the important insights that economics brings to decision making. The opportunity cost of using resources for any one particular use is what those resources could have yielded in the next best alternative use. Everything has an opportunity cost, including your time. The opportunity cost of the time spent reading this textbook is the benefit you could have derived from spending that time in the next best alternative – down the pub, shopping or watching EastEnders.

13.9 What determines market interest rates?

Economists and others often use the term 'the market rate of interest' as if interest rates offered by high street banks, building societies and other financial institutions were all identical. In practice, of course, this is not so. Households and companies with money to lend will find that some banks will offer slightly higher rates than others. But since the market is competitive, the differences will be very small – normally no more than a fraction of a percentage point.

If one bank did decide to offer a substantially higher rate to lenders than its competitors, those competitors would rapidly have to follow suit, since otherwise they would lose custom. Similarly, if one bank offered a significantly lower rate of interest to lenders, its customers would withdraw their funds for deposit elsewhere. That bank would rapidly have to come in line with what everyone else was doing. Therefore interest rates offered by different financial institutions tend to be broadly similar, and the rates offered all move in the same direction at the same time.

Moreover, as everyone knows, the interest rate which banks demand from borrowers is higher than that offered to lenders. This higher rate is partly to take account of the risks associated with lending money and partly to take account of the administrative cost of the transaction – in effect, the borrower pays the cost of administering the loan and this is reflected in a somewhat higher rate of interest than that which the bank offers to lenders. Interest rates demanded of borrowers all move up together or down together in the same way as rates offered to lenders.

The important point is that all rates move together – if interest rates to borrowers move up by one percentage point then interest rates to lenders will tend to move up by the same amount. Thus to talk of 'the market rate of interest' is a reasonable shorthand for some expression about the overall level of interest rates in the economy, taking into account differences between borrowers and lenders and the fact that some institutions will be offering slightly better rates than others at any one time.

But what then determines the market rate of interest? The short answer is that it is determined by the Chancellor of the Exchequer. The precise mechanism that he uses involves him changing the so-called **Bank base rate** (or simply **base rate**), which is the rate of interest that the Bank of England offers to those financial institutions which lend money to the Treasury by the purchase of Treasury bills. In practice – and this is the important thing – a movement in the base rate is followed within a day or two by a more or less equal movement in all other interest rates in the economy, so that it can reasonably be said that the Chancellor does in fact control the overall level of interest rates in the economy.

DID YOU KNOW?
The Chancellor of the Exchequer has regular monthly meetings with the Governor of the Bank of England, at which the main topic of discussion is interest rates. If they disagree on the level at which to set rates for the coming month, the Chancellor's view prevails.

Interest rates can be changed more quickly and more easily than any of the **fiscal instruments**, such as tax rates or government spending. Because changes in interest rates are both quick to implement and quick to take effect, they have come to be seen as the most important instrument of short-term demand management.

Frequent, small changes in interest rates have been used in order to **fine tune** the level of demand in the economy. The effect of an interest rate change spreads like a ripple throughout the economy. For example, a rise in the base rate raises mortgage interest payments by households, thus reducing their disposable income and so affecting their consumption demands.

But on what basis does the Chancellor decide to set interest rates at a particular level?

PAUSE FOR THOUGHT | *Suppose interest rates in the UK rise. What is the probable effect on each of the following? Explain the precise nature of the causal mechanism involved in each case.*
(a) the level of consumer spending
(b) investment spending by firms
(c) the current account of the balance of payments
(d) the capital account of the balance of payments.

If the Chancellor judges that demand is increasing too rapidly, bringing with it the danger of demand-pull inflation, he will increase interest rates to discourage both consumption and investment spending and bring demand in check. If he judges that demand is too low, he will reduce interest rates to encourage more spending.

However, interest rate changes also have a major – and rapid – effect in the foreign exchange market for sterling. An increase in interest rates discourages spending. This will include spending on imported goods, which now falls in line with spending generally, and an improvement in the current account of the balance of payments results, since exports from the UK are not affected. There will also be a capital account effect, however, which takes place even more immediately. An increase in UK interest rates will increase the demand by foreigners for UK securities, causing an increase in the demand for pounds to purchase them. The supply of pounds also falls because holders of UK securities will continue to hold on to them rather than sell. Thus the effect brought about on the capital account reinforces that on the current account, further pushing up the value of a floating currency or supporting the value of a fixed one.

Before concluding this section, it is worth pointing out that what has been provided here is a partial and perhaps controversial 'explanation' of the determination of interest rates. The essence of the explanation given so far is that interest rates are an exogenous instrument used by the Chancellor to influence both the domestic economy and the external value of sterling. Some economists, however, would argue that interest rates are *market determined*.

The interest rate, they say, is the price of borrowed funds and, like any other price, is determined by demand and supply. The supply of funds comes from those households and firms which have surplus cash for which they have no immediate use, and which they therefore wish to lend to others. This could be called 'saving'. In contrast, there are others who wish to borrow. There is an equilibrium interest rate, it is argued, which adjusts itself automatically as a result of market forces and ensures that the demand for loanable funds exactly equals the supply.

An assertion often appended to this explanation is the claim that, if the government has a large borrowing requirement, this will *ceteris paribus* increase the demand for funds and hence push up interest rates. High interest rates are thus sometimes seen as the result of high levels of government borrowing.

It is important to appreciate that these explanations see interest rates as *endogenously determined* – they result from what goes on *within* the economy and are not under the direct control of the policy-maker. The alternative explanation sees interest rates as an *exogenous instrument* – something which can be altered by the Chancellor at will in pursuance of certain domestic and other policy objectives. Each explanation can, of course, have some explanatory power. However, the evidence of the 1990s – and particularly those events surrounding 'Black Wednesday' in September 1992 – strongly point to an interpretation which sees interest rates as an exogenous instrument.

In the weeks and months leading up to Black Wednesday interest rates were kept at a high level in order to protect the external value of sterling. Following sterling's exit from the ERM, interest rates rapidly fell (from around 10 per cent to around 6 per cent three months later) because high interest rates were no longer required to support the value of sterling, which by this time was floating. Further evidence comes from the observation that in the 1990s high interest rates have been associated with *low* levels of the PSBR and low interest rates with *high* levels of the PSBR – exactly the opposite to an explanation which claims that high interest rates are the result of high levels of government borrowing.

Some quarterly data on interest rates and the PSBR are shown in Table 13.5. The absence of a positive correlation between the PSBR and interest rates is obvious from these data, as is the drop in interest rates which occurred after Black Wednesday in September 1992.

table 13.5

**Bank base rate and
PSBR, 1990–96**

		Base rate (%)	PSBR (£m)
1990	Q1	15.0	–1,750
	Q2	15.0	1,412
	Q3	15.0	–1,163
	Q4	14.1	–349
1991	Q1	13.5	–339
	Q2	11.9	2,689
	Q3	10.9	3,444
	Q4	10.5	3,013
1992	Q1	10.5	4,730
	Q2	10.2	6,898
	Q3	9.9	7,944
	Q4	7.6	10,697
1993	Q1	6.3	10,651
	Q2	6.0	10,462
	Q3	6.0	10,988
	Q4	5.8	11,570
1994	Q1	5.3	11,235
	Q2	5.3	9,034
	Q3	5.4	8,926
	Q4	5.9	8,031
1995	Q1	6.6	9,906
	Q2	6.8	8,890
	Q3	6.8	8,753
	Q4	6.7	7,821
1996	Q1	6.2	6,479
	Q2	5.9	..

Note: Negative values for the PSBR indicate a public sector debt repayment.
Source: *Financial Statistics*.

13.10 The impact of inflation on business

For the moment we leave aside the question of the impact of inflation on competitiveness, an issue which we discussed earlier in sections 7.7 and 8.15 and to which we return later. Considered within the context of a *closed economy*, therefore, the impact which inflation imposes on business is not very different to that which it has on households, or indeed society in general. However, firms do have to pay what are sometimes known as **menu costs** – shops periodically have to reprice their goods, manufacturers have to issue new price lists and have to recalculate their wage rates – and restaurants have to print new menus.

The so-called menu costs of inflation refer to the resources of paper, printing ink and people's time required to update price tags, issue new catalogues and so on. (Actually, the better restaurants do change their menus quite frequently anyway, I'm told.) Although seemingly fairly trivial, menu costs can be quite significant when you consider the necessity to recalibrate vending machines selling drinks and cigarettes, telephone coin boxes, pay and display parking meters, and all the other coin-operated mechanisms.

Similarly, buyers of goods, and that includes firms as well as households, have to spend time and money searching around for the best prices available. The costs of so doing are known – equally fancifully – as **shoe leather costs**.

If the rate of inflation were very high, this would impose significant menu costs *on retailers such as Argos. Explain why this should be so. How might they reduce these costs?*

In inflationary times, households and firms are also said to be confused by **white noise**. A radio telescope pointed out to space can detect millions upon millions of radio signals. Within this apparently random and meaningless hiss, known as white noise, may be communications from intelligent beings in some far distant galaxy. But it is impossible to separate out such signals, even if they did exist, from the background of white noise.

In a similar way, the price mechanism functions inefficiently in inflationary times. Prices are also signals. They broadcast information about *relative scarcity*. A rise in the price of a particular good is an indication that it is becoming increasingly scarce; a fall in price, that it is becoming increasingly plentiful. In inflationary times, *all* goods and services are increasing in price and against this background it is difficult for economic agents to distinguish **changes in relative prices** from the **change in prices generally**. Therefore they cannot correctly interpret changes in relative prices as meaningful signals about which goods are becoming more scarce and which more plentiful. The background of white noise confuses economic agents, causing them to act inappropriately.

These information costs resulting from inflation can be significant. However, when inflation is fairly low, as it has been in Britain in the last decade, shoe leather costs and menu costs can be considered to be fairly trivial, as can the problem of white noise. Moreover, developments in computers and communications have improved the speed and ease with which information on prices can be sent, received and updated, so the burden of these information costs has been reduced.

13.11 The exchange rate and business
....

In addition to the information costs discussed above, inflation may affect the ability of UK firms to trade profitably with the rest of the world. However, the outcome will depend crucially on what happens to the exchange rate. It is helpful here to distinguish between the **nominal exchange rate** and the **real exchange rate.**

We define the real exchange rate for sterling as equal to the nominal rate adjusted for the difference between the rate of inflation in the UK and that overseas. Suppose that over a certain period the movement in the nominal exchange rate is such that it fully compensates for the difference between the rate of inflation in the UK in comparison to that in the economies of its competitors. For example, if UK domestic prices rise 10 per cent a year while competitors' prices rise by only 7 per cent, UK goods become 3 per cent dearer in relative terms each year. However, a compensating fall of 3 per cent in the nominal exchange rate will neutralise this difference in inflation rates, leaving the real exchange rate unaltered.

The notion of the real exchange rate is similar to the notion of *price competitiveness,* which we discussed in section 8.15, and similar considerations apply. We cannot, for example, talk about the *level* of the real exchange rate at any particular time, but only about *movements* in the rate between one point in time and another. Although the concept of the real exchange rate is not synonymous with that of competitiveness, it is nevertheless correct to say that a rise in the real exchange rate is always associated with a loss of competitiveness. Similarly, a fall in the real exchange rate brings with it an improvement in competitiveness.

To illustrate this further, consider the following hypothetical example. In year 1 the value of the fixed exchange rate between sterling and the French franc is £1 = 10 francs. A British product, say a pullover, sells for £10 in the UK and 100 francs in France. Suppose that inflation is 5 per cent higher in the UK than in France – assume for simplicity an inflation rate of 5 per cent in the UK and zero per cent in France. In year 2, therefore, the price of the pullover will be £10.50 in the UK and, if the price of the pullover in France is set by simply multiplying the UK price by the fixed exchange rate, the price in France will be 105 francs. This UK-produced export will therefore have become less competitive – it has risen in price relative to locally produced substitutes, whose price will have remained unchanged.

If, however, the value of the pound were not fixed, but were to float down by 5 per cent to offset the relatively higher rate of domestic inflation in the UK – to a rate of approximately £1 = 9.5 francs – then the French price of the pullover would remain at 100 francs and competitiveness would be restored.

ACTIVITY **3**

In this example the new exchange rate would be only approximately £1 = 9.5 francs. Using a calculator, work out the new exchange which would ensure that the French price of the pullover remained at exactly 100 francs.

Check with answers/suggestions at the back of the book.

It follows, therefore, that the impact of inflation on the competitiveness of UK firms depends very much on whether there is a fixed or a floating exchange rate in operation. Moreover, even if the exchange rate is floating, this does not automatically ensure that the rate will move in such a way as to exactly offset a relatively higher rate of domestic inflation. The movement in the exchange rate may be less or more than that required to re-establish the status quo ante, since, as we have seen, the value of a floating currency goes up and down in response to buying and selling pressures, some of which have little if anything to do with trade.

We can summarise the discussion as follows:

➤ In a fixed exchange rate regime, if inflation in Britain is higher than that abroad, the real exchange rate rises and competitiveness declines. As a result, the profitability of exporting from the UK will be reduced and the volume of exports may also fall.

➤ If the exchange rate is floating and moves in such a way as to offset exactly the relatively higher rate of domestic inflation, the real exchange rate and competitiveness are unaltered.

➤ Movements in floating rates may either undercompensate or overcompensate for the difference between the UK rate of inflation and that abroad. Competitiveness may therefore either decline or improve.

Of course, UK firms that are in the business of *importing* goods and services into the UK will have a different perspective. For them a *rise* in the real exchange rate is beneficial, since it makes it more profitable to sell imported goods in the UK, or makes it possible to sell more of them by reducing their price. British holiday-makers travelling abroad are in a similar position – for them the higher the real exchange rate, the more attractive foreign holidays become.

A further consideration, independent of the question of the level of the real exchange rate, is the question of its stability. As we know, fixed exchange rates – by which we mean fixed *nominal* rates – are in theory more stable than floating rates. Fluctuations in rates can themselves make it difficult for firms to plan and to price their foreign contracts consistently.

However, firms can protect themselves against the uncertainties caused by exchange rate movements by using forward currency markets. For example, they can take out a contract to buy dollars in three months' time at a price which is fixed today. But firms will always have to pay a premium for the privilege of protecting themselves against exchange rate risk – in effect, they are paying someone else to take on the risk for them.

13.12 The single European currency

We end this chapter by considering the question of a single European currency. Undoubtedly the issue of whether or not Britain should join this currency bloc, if it is created, will be the major question facing the British economy in the next few years. As already noted in section 12.6, the completion date for the moves towards a single European currency is 1999. At the time of writing (autumn 1996) it is unclear whether it will in fact come into being at that time and, if it were to do so, whether Britain would join.

DID YOU KNOW?

*The name chosen for the single currency is 'euro'.
Readers with a knowledge of other European languages will realise that, in choosing this name, politicians have, ironically, hit upon a word which is pronounced differently in almost every one of the different European languages.*

The decision about membership of this currency union will be of fundamental significance for UK businesses because of the probable effect in the long term on the real exchange rate and hence on competitiveness. In assessing the probable effects of the adoption of a single currency, it is helpful to think of it as being equivalent to the imposition of fixed nominal exchange rates between those European countries which take part. However, these rates would be immutably fixed – it would not be possible to change them at some future date, unless of course a country were to quit the single currency area and re-establish its own national currency, which would be difficult to do, though not impossible. Getting divorced takes longer than getting married.

We have shown that a fixed *nominal* exchange rate does not necessarily imply a fixed *real* rate. The real rate will depend upon what happens to domestic inflation rates within the individual countries of the currency area. As we saw in section 7.7, there are strong arguments for supposing that the rate of domestic inflation will tend towards equality for all those countries in a single currency area, at least within the tradables sector of the economies concerned.

The purchasing power parity theorem suggests that the external value of a currency will be equal to its internal value in the long run. If the external value is fixed, as in effect it would be in a single currency area, then any discrepancy between internal and external values will be eliminated by movements in *internal* values. In other words, forces would arise to ensure that domestic inflation rates will be the same in all those countries that have the euro as their currency. This is an application of the Law of One Price, which we discussed in section 7.7.

However, as we also demonstrated in that section, the Law of One Price does not hold very strictly – there can be substantial divergences between the external value of a currency and its internal purchasing power. When we discussed inflation in Chapter 5, we saw that there were basically two contrasting models of what determines inflation – a demand-pull model and a cost-push one. Whichever of these models we believe is the 'correct' explanation of the causes of inflation, it does not follow that demand pressures and cost pressures will be the same, or even similar, in all countries within a single currency area.

For example, cost pressures will be influenced by the rate of productivity growth – the slower the rate of productivity growth, the less the downward pressure on prices and hence the higher the rate of inflation is likely to be. Countries which have a lower rate of productivity growth are likely to find that their domestic inflation rate is higher than that of their neighbours and, if they are locked in by a fixed exchange rate, they will experience a rise in their real exchange rate and a consequent loss of competitiveness. Moreover, this loss of competitiveness cannot be made good by devaluation. Opponents of British membership of a single currency area have argued that Britain might suffer this fate – a loss of competitiveness in the longer term which cannot be offset by devaluation. However, although it is difficult to measure satisfactorily, the growth of productivity in Britain in the last decade appears to have been on a par with European levels, so that such fears may be unfounded.

The other costs or benefits for Britain of joining a single currency are equally uncertain. Proponents of a single currency argue that once it has been achieved interest rates will be lower. This, they claim, results from the fact that the euro will be an international currency equivalent in status and strength to the dollar. It will not be subject to the sort of speculative attacks that national currencies are prone to, so there will be less need to prop it up with high interest rates. Moreover, they add that the currency area will be heavily influenced if not dominated by Germany, where interest rates have traditionally been low.

Whatever the final outcome, the path towards monetary union will be hazardous. To reach the goal of a single currency, countries will have to go through a transition stage, which involves fixed exchange rates between national currencies, and at this stage there may be rich pickings for speculators. Like lions attacking a herd of antelope, speculators will try to single out the weakest member of the group. At the moment, sterling is not the weakest member – strictly, it is not a member at all because it has a floating exchange rate. Moreover, the value of sterling has fallen considerably since 1992 and therefore in the run-up to 1999 there may be other currencies which are more vulnerable to attack than sterling.

Within Europe, at least at governmental level, the political wish for a single currency is strong. President Chirac and Chancellor Kohl are enthusiastic supporters, and if they proceed with the plan, as seems likely, they will take the Benelux countries with them. More surprisingly, perhaps, Italy and Spain, which have economies not noted for their low inflation rates and financial rectitude, also seem to regard the single currency as a game which they wish to join.

Since 1992 the value of sterling against the mark (and perforce against the franc) has fallen by about a quarter, bringing with it an improvement in competitiveness. Before the depreciation, the arguments *against* Britain joining a single currency were overwhelming. Moreover, on the supply side, competitiveness may also have been improved by the structural changes which have taken place over the last ten years and which were discussed in Chapter 11. Therefore the argument in favour of Britain joining a single currency area is now more finely balanced. By the time you read these words, the situation may be clarified – or indeed the decision to join may already have been taken.

Summary
·············

The macroeconomic environment affects the firms operating within it. They need to have an appreciation of the issues involved in order to respond appropriately, since there are no easy decision rules which can be mechanistically applied.

Economic activity is subject to cycles of irregular duration and magnitude. These fluctuations in demand within the economy will impact on the demand for the goods and services produced by each individual firm. Investment will be more volatile than other types of spending, particularly those, like government spending, which are exogenous.

In addition to being affected by fluctuations in activity, investment will also be influenced by the level of interest rates. This is not necessarily related to the economic cycle, since changes in interest rates are used by the Chancellor to influence both domestic demand and the demand for sterling on foreign exchange markets.

Firms appraise the future profitability of investment projects by calculating the internal rate of return and comparing it with the external cost of finance. Increases in interest rates reduce the profitability of investment and hence reduce the amount undertaken.

The impact which inflation has on firms' competitiveness will depend upon what happens to the exchange rate. If the exchange rate is fixed, and the rate of inflation in the UK is higher than that elsewhere, then competitiveness will be eroded. This will reduce the demand for UK exports, causing trade imbalances and reducing growth rates.

REVIEW QUESTIONS

1 Consider the components of total final expenditure shown in table 13.6, where:
   C = consumers' expenditure
   G = government spending (public authorities' current spending on goods and services)
   I (GFCF) = fixed investment spending (gross fixed capital formation)
   I (stocks) = inventory investment (value of the physical stock change)
   X = Exports
   TFE = total final expenditure.

table 13.6
Components of total final expenditure, 1986–95 (£bn)

	C	G	I (GFCF)	I (stocks)	X	TFE
1986	295.6	106.8	83.7	1.2	114.0	601.4
1987	311.2	107.6	92.3	1.6	120.6	633.7
1988	334.6	108.6	105.1	5.1	121.2	674.7
1989	345.4	110.1	111.5	2.7	126.8	696.6
1990	347.5	112.9	107.6	–1.8	133.1	699.4
1991	340.1	115.8	97.4	–4.6	132.2	680.9
1992	339.6	115.7	96.0	–1.7	137.7	687.3
1993	348.0	115.9	96.6	0.3	142.4	703.3
1994	356.9	118.2	99.4	2.9	155.6	733.0
1995	364.0	119.7	99.3	3.2	166.8	753.0

Source: *UK National Accounts.*

Which of the components of total domestic expenditure is the most volatile and which is the least volatile? Why is this?

2 Which of the following variables are endogenous to the UK economy and which are exogenous?
   ➤ consumers' expenditure
   ➤ government spending on goods and services
   ➤ government spending on transfer payments
   ➤ spending on imports
   ➤ export demand.

3 Use a calculator to work out the net present value of an investment with an initial capital cost of £2,600 which produces an income stream of £1,100 per annum for three years. Assume the income accrues at the end of each year. Use a discount rate of 9 per cent. What happens when the discount rate (the rate of interest) rises to 12 per cent?

4 Suppose you have £10,000 for which you have no immediate use. You decide to invest it all for a period of one year in the National Lottery and do in fact win a number of £10 prizes totalling £400. Use the concept of opportunity cost to calculate the return from this investment.

5 Consider two countries which you know about which share a common currency – say, England and Wales. What does the Law of One Price predict about the price level, and the rate of inflation, in those two countries? Is this borne out by your experience? What are the implications of this if Britain were to adopt the euro, the planned single European currency?

Key concepts
....

The following key concepts have been introduced in this chapter. Make sure you understand the meaning and significance of each of them. They are listed here in the order in which they first appear, and the page number where they appear is also given. You will find these key concepts in section headings or in **bold** in the text. Each chapter contains a list of key concepts and you may find these particularly useful for revision purposes.

business cycles	(p. 218)
boom	(p. 218)
recession	(p. 218)
volatility of investment	(p. 220)
capital assets	(p. 220)
investment spending	(p. 220)
fixed capital formation	(p. 220)
accelerator coefficient	(p. 221)
exogenous spending	(p. 222)
endogenous spending	(p. 223)
expectations	(p. 223)
forecasts	(p. 223)
leading indicators	(p. 224)
coincident indicators	(p. 224)
time lag	(p. 224)
lagging indicators	(p. 224)
investment appraisal	(p. 225)
net present value	(p. 225)
discounting	(p. 226)
discount rate	(p. 226)
internal rate of return	(p. 227)
opportunity cost	(p. 228)
Bank base rate	(p. 229)
fiscal instruments	(p. 229)
fine tuning	(p. 229)
menu costs	(p. 231)
shoe leather costs	(p. 232)

white noise   (p. 232)
changes in relative prices   (p. 232)
changes in prices generally   (p. 232)
nominal exchange rate   (p. 232)
real exchange rate   (p. 232)

Answers to activities and review questions

Chapter 1

Activity

1 The current account deficit in 1989 works out at about 4.4 per cent of GDP.

Review questions

1 GNP per capita works out to be slightly less than £10,000 per annum, since

$$\frac{567,000,000,000}{58,000,000} = 9,776$$

You can compare the answer with your own income to see if the *order of magnitude* of the answer is sensible. Your own income as a student is likely to be considerably less than £10,000 per year, but you can readily see that the answer we have obtained is at least sensible. If we had obtained an answer of £10 per year, or a million pounds per year, this would clearly not be sensible.

2 About £25,000. Note that this is roughly two and a half times the per capita income, implying that the 'average household' contains two and a half persons.

3 The best way of doing this is to express your own income as a fraction of per capita or household income. As a student your income is likely to be much less than the average.

4 You should express Cedric Brown's income as a multiple of average earnings. Average annual earnings work out to be in the range £21,580 (in Greater London) to £13,780 (in Cornwall). Mr Brown's income is therefore roughly 22 times greater than average earnings in London (and $34\frac{1}{2}$ times greater than earnings in Cornwall).

Chapter 2
. . . .

Activities

1 (a) They more than doubled.
   (b) The increase in prices is 170 per cent.
   (c) After 1991 prices fell by about 6 per cent.

2 Implicitly this gives a weight of 1 (or 100 per cent, if you like) to Mars Bars and a weight of zero to everything else.

Review questions

1 Although it could be argued that all the statements are 'correct' in an arithmetic sense, only (e) correctly describes the change in relative prices.

2 A 'Ford Escort' is not the same now as it was in 1971. Quality changes mean that, although something may be *called* the same as it was 25 years ago, it actually represents quite a different product.

3

	1971	1994	% reduction
Minutes of work to buy one unit of			
1 lb back bacon	47	22	53
250 g Danish butter	20	8	60
1 lb old potatoes	3	3	0
1 lb oranges	12	2	83
1 lb cod fillets	37	27	27
Chicken	30	10	66
Pint of beer (draught)	20	15	25
20 cigarettes (king size)	33	25	24
Hours of work to buy one unit of			
Ford Escort	3259	2119	35
Colour TV licence	29	15	48
Return rail ticket London to Edinburgh[a]	31	10	70

[a] Standard return in 1971. Supersaver in 1994.

4 The footnote shows that the comparison is between a standard return in 1971 and a 'Supersaver' in 1994. The Supersaver is a heavily discounted fare the availability of which is heavily restricted. Thus you are not really comparing like with like.

5

	Weight in the basket	Percentage increase
Food	one-half	10
Housing	one-third	30
Clothes	one-sixth	3

Overall increase = ($\frac{1}{2}$ x 10) + ($\frac{1}{3}$ x 30) + ($\frac{1}{6}$ x 3) = 15$\frac{1}{2}$ per cent

Chapter 3
. . . .
Activities

1 The velocity of circulation of milk bottles is 6 times per month. Why are you being asked this question? Because it is easier to understand something highly abstract (like the circular flow model) by using the analogy of something more concrete and more mundane and with which you are more familiar. The daily sale of milk – which is a flow – corresponds to the flow of national income. This is serviced by a stock of bottles (stock of money) and the ratio between the two is the velocity of circulation.

In bad winters the velocity of circulation of milk bottles will slow down because people will not return them so quickly and the milk deliverers will be unable to find them under the snow. The dairy might find it has insufficient bottles to service the sales of milk.

2 Initially equilibrium income will be 250. If investment rises to 110, the new equilibrium level of income will be 275. The value of the multiplier is 2.5 and there are two ways to work this out. Either

$$\text{Multiplier} = \frac{\text{Change in income}}{\text{Change in injection}} = \frac{25}{10} = 2.5$$

or

$$\text{Multiplier} = \frac{1}{mps} = \frac{1}{0.4} = 2.5$$

Note, however, that the second method only works in a simple model where there are no leakages other than savings.

Review questions

1 (a) Injection.
 (b) Withdrawal.
 (c) Withdrawal.
 (d) Injection.
 (e) Withdrawal.

(f) Injection.

(g) Injection. In this simple model it makes no difference how the spending is financed. The important thing is the extra spending – the first-round effect.

2 (a) This will reduce the demand for UK-produced goods and services.

(b) The initial personal allowance is that part of income which is free of tax. An increase in the size of this allowance will mean the individual will pay *less* tax and hence have more disposable income. Spending will rise.

(c) Since consumers are spending more on imports, the demand for UK-produced goods and services will fall.

(d) This is an injection (investment). Hence spending will rise.

(e) Additional export demand increases the demand for British goods.

3 Both natural and man-made disasters usually lead to an increase in demand. It was the increased military expenditure in the late 1930s which finally brought the Great Depression to an end. Some of the hurricane damage in Florida will be paid for by the Federal Government, and some will be covered by insurance (with insurance companies in New York and London). Hence funds will flow into Florida. The overall effect is likely to be an increase in demand as households and firms spend money repairing the hurricane damage.

4 The large amount of saving done by Japanese households would lead to a shortfall of demand in the Japanese economy were it not for the fact that Japanese firms spend large amounts on *investment*, utilising the savings of households. The Paradox of Thrift applies everywhere, but what is important is the *overall* level of demand in the economy – which depends on the balance between total injections and total withdrawals.

5 We can calculate the *mpc* for the entire period 1985–94. This is

$$\frac{\text{Change in consumption}}{\text{Change in income}}$$

which is

$$\frac{(358.9 - 276.7)}{(395.5 - 309.8)} = \frac{82.2}{85.7} = 0.96$$

so that the *mpc* is just less than 1.

However, for some individual sub-periods the rise in consumption is *more* than the rise in income, and this is obviously not sustainable. For example, for the period 1985–86:

Rise in consumption = 295.6 – 276.7 = 18.9
Rise in income = 323.6 – 309.8 = 13.8

Similarly, in 1993–94:
Rise in consumption = 10.5
Rise in income = 3.2

Conversely, in 1990–91:
Fall in consumption = 7.6
Fall in income = 0.5

So the *fall* in consumption was much *more* than the fall in income. This again is not consistent with the simple model of the consumption function.

Chapter 4
••••••••••••

Activities

1 The degree of openness depends upon the size of the economy, other things being equal. Therefore the United States, with a population of about 260 million, is comparatively 'closed', in the sense that foreign trade accounts for a smaller proportion of output than in the other two countries – only about 12 per cent of output in fact. The Netherlands is the smallest of the three countries (population about 15 million) and is therefore the most open – foreign trade accounts for nearly half of output (about 46 per cent, in fact). Britain, with a population of about 58 million, is comparatively open – foreign trade accounts for about 27 per cent of output. That is, in Britain slightly more than one pound in every four is spent on imports (and exports account for slightly more than a quarter of total output).

2 The data on income per head are measured in real terms. The footnote to Figure 1.1 explains that they are 'at constant 1990 prices', which is another way of saying that they are in real terms. It would not have been meaningful to measure them in money terms – to measure income in 1995 at 1995 prices, income in 1969 at 1969 prices and so on – because the fall in the value of money over the period would have made valid comparison impossible.

Review questions

1 The national accounts would look as follows:

Consumers' spending	115
Government spending on goods and services	90
Gross domestic fixed capital formation	45
Value of physical increase in stocks and work-in-progress (stockbuilding)	–4
equals total domestic spending	*246*
plus Exports of goods and services	75
minus Imports of goods and services	–81
equals Gross domestic product	*240*
plus Net property income from abroad	–6
equals Gross national product	*236*

2 (a) The balance on the current account of the balance of payments:

Trade balance (visible plus invisible)	–6
Interest, profits and dividends (net property income)	–6
Current account balance	*–12*

(b) The fiscal stance (budget balance):

Government spending on goods and services	90
Tax revenue	85
Budget deficit	5

Note: privatisation proceeds are excluded from the calculation of the budget deficit (this is explained in a later chapter).

3 Consumption increased by 188 per cent
Government spending increased by 170 per cent.

These estimates are in *money* (or nominal) terms. We can deflate them to convert them to *real* terms as follows:

	Consumption (nominal)	RPI	Consumption (real)
1981	155.4	79.1	196.5
1982	170.6	85.9	198.6
1983	187.1	89.8	208.3
1984	200.3	94.3	212.4
1985	**218.9**	**100.0**	**218.9**
1986	243.0	103.4	235.0
1987	267.5	107.7	248.4
1988	302.1	113.0	267.3
1989	330.5	121.8	271.3
1990	350.4	133.8	261.9
1991	367.8	141.1	260.9
1992	383.5	146.9	261.1
1993	406.4	149.3	272.2
1994	427.3	152.9	279.5
1995	447.3	158.0	283.1

The figure for 1981 is

$$\frac{155.4}{0.791} = 196.5$$

and so on. Notice that the figure for 1985 (the base year of the index) will, of course, remain unchanged.

Thus in real terms the growth of consumption is 44 per cent : that is,

$$\left(\frac{283.1 - 196.5}{196.5}\right) \times 100 = 0.4407$$

We can calculate a series for government spending in real terms in a similar way. The growth works out to be about 43 per cent over the period.

These estimates are more meaningful than the estimates of growth in money terms, which will be swamped by the effect of inflation.

Notice that the growth of private consumption is much more than the growth of public spending, which reflects a decade of right-wing policies designed to 'roll back the frontiers of the state'.

4 Trident, the Newbury by-pass, video games ... insert your own list of things you think society should not be spending its money on.

5 (a) and (b) are false because they fail to take account of the fact that prices also increased over the period.

(c) is correct.

(d) is also correct, though again it fails to acknowledge the fact that the prices of the things that people spent their money on also increased.

6 People choose to spend money on insurance and choose to spend money on gambling. In the same way, they may choose to spend money on foreign holidays or buying plants for their garden. All of these things constitute part of the output of the economy.

In contrast, black market activities are by their very nature not recorded, so they do not form part of GNP.

Chapter 5
∙∙∙∙∙∙∙∙∙∙∙∙∙

Activities

1 OPEC – the Organisation of Oil Exporting Countries – is a cartel formed to protect the interests of its members. This it did by restricting the supply of oil coming on to the world market, hence keeping the price high. However, by the mid-1980s OPEC became increasingly unable to police its members and the cartel broke down. A worldwide glut of oil brought the price tumbling down.

This is an example of the old adage that in the long run 'market forces will out': in other words, price will ultimately be determined by relative scarcity.

2 (a) Raising income tax would reduce disposable incomes and consumption spending would therefore fall. A reduction in government spending on unemployment benefit (the Jobseeker's Allowance) would reduce the incomes of the unemployed, who would therefore reduce their spending.

There are many other types of deflationary fiscal policy – government spending on defence, health care, education and so on could be cut, and this would reduce incomes and reduce demand. Similarly, there are lots of other tax measures which can be used to similar effect.

Note that the term 'fiscal policy' relates to any action taken by the Chancellor of the Exchequer in his annual Budget. It stands in contrast to monetary policy, which can be enacted at any time by the Chancellor acting in collaboration with the Governor of the Bank of England.

(b) Anything which affects the availability of money or credit, or its price (the rate of interest) can be described as a monetary policy. Thus cutting interest rates will boost consumer spending and investment by firms, since such policy makes it cheaper to borrow money.

Review questions

1 (a) Houses in Wembley are a *substitute* for houses in Ealing. A fall in prices in Wembley will cause some people who would have bought a house in Ealing to switch to the cheaper substitute. This will therefore lead to a *fall* in demand for houses in Ealing, so the effect will be to cause prices there to drop.

    (b) A reduction in interest rates will encourage more people to borrow money for house purchase. The demand for houses including those in Ealing, will rise, and prices will rise. This is a demand-pull effect.

    (c) This will increase the supply of houses, depressing prices *ceteris paribus*.

    (d) The cost of building will rise, so prices will go up. The mechanism this time is of the cost-push type.

2 The rate of inflation did indeed fall from 20 per cent to 5 per cent, but it would be wrong to attribute this entirely – or perhaps even partly – to Mrs Thatcher's policies. Just because one event follows another event in time, we cannot establish that the first event *caused* the second event.

    Most other countries experienced a similar rapid decline in inflation rates in the early 1980s.

3 *Wages* are not the same thing as *wage costs per unit of output*. Only if *productivity* stays constant is an increase in wages synonymous with an increase in wage costs per unit of output.

    Labour productivity is defined as the ratio of output to labour input. It reflects a transformation process whereby inputs are converted into output. If there is an increase in the efficiency with which this transformation takes place, we say that labour productivity has increased. Any increase in productivity will offset, partly or wholly, an increase in wages.

    Even if wage costs do rise, the firm will not automatically pass on these increased costs in the form of higher prices. If doing so would result in a loss of market share, the firm may decide to absorb some or all of the increased costs in the form of lower profits. Its decision will largely depend upon the sort of market the firm is operating in. In a highly competitive market, any increase in prices which is not matched by the firm's rivals will lead to a loss of market share and is therefore likely to be avoided. If, on the other hand, there are few if any rivals (the firm enjoys a monopolistic position), it is likely to increase prices if costs increase.

4 We can calculate the growth of real earnings for the UK as follows:

	Indices (1987 = 100)		
	Money earnings	Prices	Real earnings
1984	80.2	87.6	91.5
1985	86.3	92.9	92.9
1986	93.3	96.1	97.1
1987	**100.0**	**100.0**	**100.0**
1988	108.2	104.9	103.1
1989	117.8	113.1	104.2
1990	129.0	123.8	104.2
1991	139.7	131.1	106.6
1992	147.7	135.9	108.7
1993	153.2	138.1	110.9
1994	157.6	141.5	111.4

The figure for 1984 is calculated as

$$\frac{80.2}{0.876} = 91.5$$

and so on.

Thus the growth of real earnings over the period was about 22 per cent (about 2.2 per cent per annum): that is,

$$\frac{111.4}{91.5} - 1 = 0.217$$

Since there are ten *changes* (in eleven years), we can divide this by 10 to give us the average annual rate of growth.

By a similar method, the average annual rate of growth of real wages in Germany is about 1.5 per cent and that in France about 1.3 per cent. It may have surprised you to find that the growth of real earnings was higher in Britain than in Germany or France.

Chapter 6
. . . .

Activities

1 The stricter reserve requirements mean that *less* credit money can now be created from a given amount of high-powered money. The ratio will in fact be 5 to 1. That is, only £500 of credit money can now be created from £100 of high-powered money.

2 You will find that the velocity of circulation of narrow money increased from about 25 in 1985 to about 31 in 1994. This is explained by the fact that transactions are increasingly taking place without the need for cash – for example, by the use of cheques and 'plastic money'.

3 Because the growth of M4 has averaged about 17 per cent per year whereas the growth rate of money GDP has only been about 10 per cent per year, the ratio of M4 to GDP would reach about 1:1 by 1997 if past trends were to continue. Projected increases, calculated by this very crude method, are shown below.

	M4	*GDP*
1985	215	357
.	.	.
1994	560	669
1995	*655*	*736*
1996	*767*	*809*
1997	*897*	*890*

Review questions

1 To act as a medium of exchange, a unit of account and a store of value.

2 That it should be durable, portable and divisible, but above all, acceptable and scarce.

3 (a) Cigarettes are used as money in prison. They have all the desirable characteristics of a good money substance and in addition they have a *value in use* – you can smoke them – and this is the ultimate assurance of their acceptability.
  (b) Cattle were used extensively as money in primitive societies before the invention of coins.
  (c) Pieces of precious metal (and at one time all metal was precious) became the first coins. They had the advantage of also being *homogeneous* – one coin was exactly like another, unlike cattle which were all different.

4 The correct answer is (e). Credit cards are a means of payment (a medium of exchange) but they are not a store of value or a unit of account – 'This piece of land is worth three Barclaycards and an Access'? Statements (d) and (f) are also true, but do not answer the question.

5 If forged notes were to fulfil the three functions of money and possess the desirable attributes of good money substances, then, yes, they would be money. However, the most important of the 'desirability attributes' is acceptability. Precisely because they are forged, such notes are not acceptable.

6 It appears from this news report that the amount of cash (notes and coins) in the economy is demand determined. The monetary authorities simply print as much money as people require for transactions purposes. That is, the money supply is *endogenous*. If the money supply were truly *exogenous*, it would be under the strict control of the monetary authorities, rather than being influenced by the level and the type of spending in the economy.

Chapter 7

··············

Activities

1 You would expect world trade to grow faster than world output. This is confirmed by the figures. Over the period for which you have figures (1984–95) world output (or at least the output of the OECD which constitutes about three quarters of world output) grew by about 32 per cent. World trade increased by 90 per cent.

2 The demand for francs will fall as a result of the fall in the demand for French goods. This will be illustrated by a *leftward* shift of the demand curve for francs. The supply curve will remain unchanged, since the supply of francs comes from imports of foreign products into France, which will not be affected by the boycott of French goods.

   As a result of the shift in demand for francs, there will be an *excess supply* of francs at the official exchange rate. This excess supply will have to be bought up by the Banque de France. If it is unable to do this, the value of the franc will fall.

   The intersection of the reduced demand for francs and the unchanged supply represents the new (lower) equilibrium value of the franc.

3 (a) There will be an increase in demand for imported Japanese motorcycles. The supply of pounds to foreign exchange markets will increase. These imports will be recorded on the current account.

   (b) This will be an 'invisible import'. It will add to the supply of pounds on foreign exchange markets, as British tourists convert pounds into peseta for spending in Spain. The transactions will be recorded in the services section of the current account.

   (c) Kronor are no use to the British novelist, so she will convert them into sterling (or they will already have been converted into pounds before the prize is awarded). Thus there is an increase in demand for pounds. This transfer will be recorded on the current account under the 'invisibles' category.

   (d) This is a capital account transaction which increases the demand for pounds (since Deutschmarks are converted into pounds). Remember that BMW has acquired an asset, and it is the act of acquisition that gives rise to the increase in demand for pounds.

   If subsequently BMW makes a profit on its UK operations and these profits are repatriated to Germany, then this will give rise to an increased *supply* of pounds on foreign exchange markets as pounds are converted into Deutschmarks, and this will be shown on the *current* account.

   (e) As we saw in March 1996, most continental European countries banned the importation of British beef. This resulted in a reduction in the demand for pounds (current account).

4 (a) Turkey obviously offers good value for money. Prices in Greece, perhaps surprisingly, do not seem to be particularly low.

   (b) A British visitor to Japan who converts sterling into yen will find that prices in the shops in Tokyo seem about 65 per cent higher than those in

London, as Table 7.4 shows. This is because the yen is a very 'hard' currency – its external value (its exchange rate) is much higher than its internal value. A Japanese visitor to London will, of course, find the reverse – that prices in London seem very low. Hence this Japanese visitor seems to have, and indeed *does* have, lots of money – lots of purchasing power in sterling.

Review questions

1 An increase in foreign sales of British steel will *ceteris paribus* increase the demand for pounds on foreign exchange markets. If the value of the pound is market determined, it will therefore move *up*. This means that the value of the pound has *appreciated*.

2 Statement (a) is true. Statements (b) and (c) are false.

3 (a) This too will add to the demand for pounds. It is a current account transaction.
  (b) This too will add to the demand for pounds. Current account
  (c) Adds to the demand for pounds. Current account.
  (d) He will have to convert francs into pounds. This therefore adds to the demand for pounds. This will be shown on the capital account.
  (e) The dividends will be paid in sterling, which the footballer will have to convert into dollars. This adds to the supply of pounds. Current account.

4 (a) True. The internal value is falling, but the external value is fixed.
  (b) True. Danes who have converted kroner into sterling will find that prices in the shops in Britain seem cheap in comparison to Denmark.
  (c) False. It does stay the same in nominal terms, but in real terms it will be worth *more*, because what you can buy with it in the shops in Britain is more than you could buy in Denmark.

5 (a) False. They are unchanged by the devaluation of sterling.
  (b) True. They do *seem* to be higher to the visitor from the UK, though in fact they have not changed.
  (c) False – unless the visitor from the UK only looks at the DM prices and does not think about what things cost in sterling terms.

Chapter 8
· · · · · · · · · · · ·

Activities

1 Since the trade deficit will include invisible trade as well as visible trade, it will be larger than the visible trade deficit alone. Similarly, the current account deficit will also include a deficit on IPD and on transfers, so it will be larger still. The balance of payments deficit will include the capital account deficit as well, so it will be the largest of them all. In ascending order of magnitude they will be: visible trade deficit; trade deficit (i.e. visible plus invisible trade); current account deficit; balance of payments deficit.

2 Part of the cost of employing labour is the employer's National Insurance Contribution, which together with general taxation finances the range of welfare benefits available to employees – such things as unemployment benefits, pensions, maternity benefit and sickness and invalidity pay. The more parsimonious these benefits become, the lower will be the cost of employing labour in Britain. As a result, Britain will be able to compete more effectively with the 'low-wage' economies of the Far East and other countries (including the USA) where welfare benefits are not so generous.

The opt-out from the Social Chapter is a deliberate attempt to lower the wage costs of British employers by reducing the social benefits available to British employees.

Review questions

1 Response (d) is true and so, arguably, is (c).

2 If the US resident buys francs directly, it will cost him $2 to buy 10 francs. If, however, he buys sterling first, he need only pay $1.80 to acquire £1, which he can then use to buy 10 francs, thus saving 20 cents. Everyone will realise this, and no one will buy francs for dollars directly. As a result the demand for francs will fall and the value of the franc (*vis-à-vis* the dollar) will fall until there are no longer profits to be made by going through a third currency. This will be at an exchange rate of 5F = 90 cents.

3 The reduction in German interest rates will cause capital to flow out of Germany and some of this will flow into Britain. That is, investors will now prefer to buy UK securities because they are offering a higher return. To acquire these UK securities, investors will first of all have to acquire pounds. This increase in the demand for pounds pushes up the value of the pound.

The German government may wish to keep interest rates high as a counter-inflationary measure. High interest rates reduce demand for goods and services in Germany, helping to reduce demand-pull inflation.

4 Raising interest rates is an expenditure reducing policy.
Deflation (by fiscal means) is also expenditure reducing.
Tariffs aim to switch spending away from imports and towards domestically produced goods. Expenditure switching.
Devaluation aims to change relative prices and hence is expenditure switching.

5 (a) False. Export revenues will stay the same because the elasticity is (−)1.
   (b) True.
   (c) True.
   (d) True.

6 (a) True.
   (b) True. Import prices will rise and this will tend to feed through into higher prices generally.
   (c) True.
   (d) False. They will do the reverse.

7 To some extent they do try to hold DM and yen because these are 'hard' currencies. They tend to appreciate, since Germany and Japan normally have balance of payments surpluses. But for central banks to hold these currencies they must be *available*. If a country has a balance of payments *surplus,* there is *already an excess demand* for the currency. If individuals or central banks wish to hold them, this will further increase the demand, which can only be satisfied if the central bank in Germany and Japan supplies extra DM and yen to the foreign exchange market. This they may be unwilling to do for fear of the inflationary effect of so doing.

8 Statement (a) is true, but (b) is not. The profit made by speculators is the difference between the price at which they sold sterling and the cheaper price at which they subsequently bought it. Remember that speculators can sell things that they do not own because they have a few days to acquire the things that they have contracted to sell. If the price drops in the meantime, they make a profit. If sterling fell by 10 per cent, the profit they would have made is approximately 10 per cent of £15 billion, which is still a considerable sum. You can work out (in statement (d) how many hospitals this is equivalent to. This in effect is the value of the resources that were 'lost' to speculators.

Chapter 9

Activities

1 There is no definitive answer to this but a possible ordering would be as follows:
(e) to make Trade Unions more accountable to their members
(d) to improve TU democracy
(c) to reduce the monopoly power of the unions
(b) to reduce the market power of the unions
(a) to emasculate the unions.

2 (a) You would expect infant mortality and income per capita to be negatively correlated. Richer regions will tend to have lower infant mortality.
(b) With the exception of Greater London, it does seem to be the case that richer regions have lower infant mortality.
(c) Greater London has the highest income per capita (index = 122), but the 'quality of life' as measured by infant mortality is among the worst in the country (only the West Midlands, another large conurbation, has higher infant mortality). This illustrates that although, in a statistical sense, income *influences* infant mortality, it does not *determine* it. Other variables also have an important influence.
(d) Figure 9.7 shows the scattergraph you should obtain. The observations do tend to fall into the top-left and bottom-right quadrants. There is clearly an association between these variables – they are negatively correlated – but the association is not a strong one. Moreover, note that we have already excluded Greater London, where there is a *positive* relationship between the two variables.

Figure 9.7

Infant mortality and income per capita (by region)

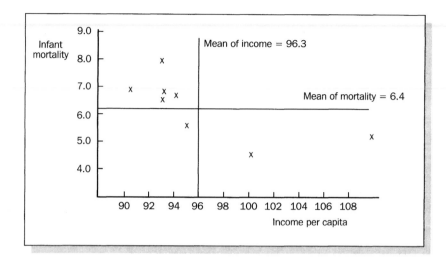

(e) One expects that 'richer' regions will have lower unemployment rates. Where the labour market is more buoyant (that is, the demand for labour is higher), earnings and therefore incomes will be higher and unemployment will be lower.

(f) If we again exclude Greater London, there does seem to be a general tendency for richer regions to have lower unemployment.

(g) Greater London, the 'richest' region, has the highest unemployment, as well as very high infant mortality. East Anglia also has rather high unemployment (but exceptionally low infant mortality).

(h) Figure 9.8 shows the scattergraph you should obtain. There is a weak negative correlation, since the majority of points fall into the top-left and bottom-right quadrants. However, East Anglia has somewhat higher unemployment than might be expected on the basis of income alone, and the East Midlands and South West somewhat lower unemployment.

Figure 9.8

Unemployment rate and income per capita (by region)

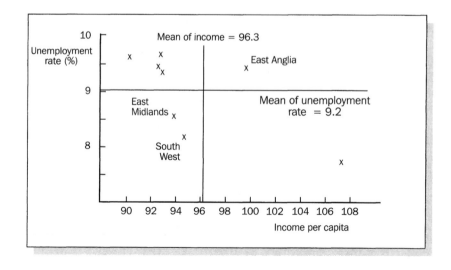

Review questions

1 The activity rate measures the proportion of the population of working age who are in the labour force (either working or seeking work). The reason why the activity rate is low in Italy is probably to do with the role of the Catholic Church in influencing social attitudes about the role of women.

2 If you are a full-time student with no paid employment, you will be classified as economically inactive, since you are neither working nor available for work.

If you are a part-time student in paid employment or registered as unemployed, you will be classified as economically active.

Finally, if you are a 'full-time student' but you also have a part-time job, you pose something of a problem for the statisticians at the ONS. To avoid double-counting you have to be classified as either active or inactive, but to classify you simply as one or the other would not be correct. The government statisticians are aware of the problem and if you want more information you can phone them on 0171-270 3000

3 This is something of a paradox. Northern Ireland has the highest unemployment rate and the South East has the lowest. However, within the South East region, Greater London itself has a very high unemployment rate – the highest, in fact, in the entire country. The following table shows the rates in 1995.

Unemployment rates by region, 1995 (by ILO definition, %)

North	10.8
Yorks. and Humberside	8.7
East Midlands	7.5
East Anglia	7.1
South East	8.6
Greater London	11.5
Rest of South East	6.8
South West	7.8
West Midlands	9.0
North West	9.1
Ireland	11.0

Source: *Regional Trends 31*, 1996.

However, it does depend to some extent on how unemployment rates are measured. The table above shows the rates calculated according to the International Labour Office (ILO) definition. The picture which emerges when national definitions are used is slightly different, but the same general impression emerges.

4 It is somewhat simplistic to equate frictional unemployment with unemployment of a short-term nature. However, as the figures show, slightly fewer than half of those registered as unemployed had been without a job for less than six months – a rough indication of the extent of 'frictional' unemployment.

5 (a) The Phillips curve suggests that inflation rates and unemployment rates will be negatively correlated – high inflation will be associated with low unemployment and vice versa. This is the so-called 'trade-off'. However, if we investigate the relationship, we find that the correlation is not particularly high. In the 1970s in the UK, the Phillips curve is said to have 'broken down' – that is, the expected statistical relationship was no longer apparent. It seems to have reappeared in the 1980s, but more recently there have been years when the two variables have moved in the *same* direction – not the opposite direction, as predicted by the Phillips curve.

(b) The growth of money wages will be highly correlated (positively) with the growth of prices. If money wages increase, this will *tend* to increase wage *costs* and this increase in costs will tend to be passed on in the form of higher prices. Moreover, the higher the rise in the cost of living, the greater will be the rise in money wages needed to maintain the real value of employees' earnings – hence the greater their wage demands. This is the 'wage-price spiral'.

(c) The faster the rate of growth in the economy, the higher the demand for labour and therefore the lower the level of unemployment. We therefore expect these things to be negatively correlated.

(d) Consumption spending will be highly correlated (positively) with disposable income. Higher incomes lead to higher spending. But since one man's spending is another's income, it follows that higher spending will also lead to higher incomes. So the two things rise (and fall) together. They both affect each other.

Chapter 10

Activities

1 The key to the answer lies in the fact that these are projections or forecasts of spending in the future. The actual level of spending which occurs will depend to some extent on the state of the economy. If the economy is in recession, it will experience higher levels of cyclical unemployment. There will therefore be more spending in total on unemployment benefit simply because more people are unemployed. In contrast, at the opposite point in the business cycle, a booming economy will produce a fall in unemployment and therefore less will be spent in aggregate on unemployment benefit. This will happen even though the level of benefit per person remains unchanged.

Cyclical social security payments therefore refer to those payments – particularly of unemployment benefit – that are related to the business cycle. Similarly, the amount that the government pays in debt interest will depend upon the level of interest rates in the future – and these are not known for certain when the spending projections are drawn up. The control total therefore excludes those expenditures which it is impossible to forecast with complete accuracy. It includes only those expenditures which, in theory at least, should be under the complete control of the government.

2 Individual A (income £20,000)

Taxable income = 20,000 – 3,525 = 16,475

Tax payable

20% on 3,200	= 640
25% on remaining 13,275	= 3,318.75

Total tax   = 3,958.75

Percentage of income taken in tax $= \dfrac{3,958.75}{20,000} = 19.8\%$

Individual B (income £40,000)

Taxable income = 40,000 – 3,525 = 36,475

Tax payable

20% on 3,200	= 640
25% on 21,100	= 5,275
40% on remaining 12,175	= 4,870

Total tax   = 10,785

Percentage of income taken in tax $= \dfrac{10,785}{40,000} = 27\%$

Thus we see that the proportion of income taken in tax rises as income rises. Note also that the *average* rate of tax (the proportion of income taken in tax) is always lower than the *marginal* rate of tax. Very few people will have worked out what their average tax rate is, but most will know what their marginal rate is.

3 Low income groups devote a larger *proportion* of their income to heating their homes than high income groups do. Hence a tax on domestic fuel can be seen as regressive – it would result in the poor paying proportionately more of their income in tax than the rich.

4 Defence of the realm is the classic public good, being both non-rival and non-excludable.

Street lighting is *non-excludable*, in the sense that all who use the road can be assumed to benefit from the fact that it is lit, whether or not they contribute towards the cost of provision. In a given location, it is also a *non-rival* public good because the utility that I derive from the lighting does not reduce the amount of light available to you. However, if resources are used to light the street in front of *my* house, those same resources cannot be used to illuminate the place where *you* live. In this sense, it is a rival good.

In contrast, TV and radio broadcasts are definitely non-rival – if I tune in to watch my favourite programme, this does not reduce the strength of the signal available for you. Broadcasts are non-excludable, unless of course they are *scrambled* broadcasts, such as TV programmes broadcast by satellite, in which case you would have to buy a decoder – and pay a monthly fee – to receive them.

As a delivery medium, the Internet is similar to a broadcast. 'Surfing the net' is like fiddling with the tuning dial on your radio to try to find something which interests you. Incidentally, it does not matter whether the material is regarded as being pornographic or wholesome. Public 'goods' can be bad, at least in the opinion of some people. I may not want to be defended by nuclear weapons, and hence will regard this part of the defence of the realm as a 'bad'. I may also dislike street lighting because I feel deprived of darkness and regret that I cannot see the stars at night.

Public parks are non-excludable – unless you have to pay to get into them. They are non-rival – unless, of course, the presence of other users detracts from the enjoyment you get from them.

Sea defences along the coast, and structures like the Thames Barrier, are classic public goods, being both non-excludable and non-rival. Cedar fences in gardens (pun intended) are private goods. But they do also confer benefits on your neighbour, which he can enjoy free of charge.

Review questions

1 A tricky one this. If you see Grant's grant income as something designed to ensure that his income does not fall below some minimum acceptable level, then it should be treated in the same way as retirement pensions or social security benefit – that is, as a transfer payment. In contrast, if the grant is thought of as an *award,* then it constitutes part of the expenditure on education – that is, it should be classified under 'spending on goods and services'. I do not actually know the answer, but you could try contacting the Central Statistical Office, Great George Street, London SW1P 3AQ, telephone 0171-270 6363.

2 Ordinary roads are non-excludable, in the sense that you can use them whether or not you pay for the privilege of so doing. But access to motorways is restricted to the designated junctions and it therefore becomes feasible to collect money from those who wish to use them. If you do not pay, you cannot use them.

France and Italy have toll motorways, and probably other European countries do as well. Britain does not as yet have toll motorways, but it does have toll tunnels and bridges.

3 Television broadcasts are a non-rival good – if they are supplied to one person, there is no additional cost involved in supplying the broadcasts to everyone. Moreover, like suburban roads they are non-excludable – it is difficult to collect the money from those who refuse to pay.

Since TV broadcasts are a pure public good, it might be better to pay for them out of general taxation, in the same way that we pay for defence. Or perhaps defence should be sponsored by commercial promoters. There is quite a big space on the side of tanks and armoured personnel carriers for notices such as 'This tank is sponsored by the Nationwide Building Society' or 'Coke is it'.

4 If infertility treatment produced social benefits, it would be logical for society as a whole to subsidise it. But infertility treatment seems to produce purely private benefits to the couple in question. We would therefore have to rely on some other argument to justify state provision – such as the merit good argument.

5 The term 'public good' is a technical term which relates to the non-excludability and non-rivalness of the good in question. Some 'goods' might actually be 'bad' – that is, some people would argue that spending on nuclear weapons is morally wrong.

6. External defence (that is, defence of the realm) is a pure public good, but defence of individual property is not. The existence of private security companies is evidence of this.

Chapter 11
. . . .

Activities

1 The number of people in part-time jobs increased by 25 per cent. The increase in temporary working was about 13 per cent.

   The evidence as to whether people took on part-time/temporary work because they wanted to work in this 'flexible' way or because they had the choice forced upon them is inconclusive. Among those working part time, a slightly higher percentage stated that they did so because they could not get a full-time job, but more also stated that they did not want a full-time job. The evidence is difficult to interpret because of the large number of 'other reasons' in 1984. Among those in temporary employment the picture is clearer – more and more people were forced to take a temporary job because they could not get a permanent one.

2 The data in Table 5.7 give information on average earnings and prices, and this can be used to verify that earnings normally increase at a faster rate than prices. Linking state pensions with prices rather than earnings would therefore have the effect of reducing the growth of state pensions below what they would otherwise have been. The purchasing power of the pension will remain unchanged, but pensioners' incomes will fall relative to those in employment. Pensioners will thus become *relatively* impoverished.

3 If you are a full-time student not in paid employment, your original income is likely to be very small, if not zero, since you have no income from employment and probably no investment income. The maintenance grant which you receive from your local authority will be your main source of income. Your *gross* income will be much higher than your *original* income. If you are not in employment, you will not pay income tax, so your *disposable* income will be the same as your gross income. You do, however, pay sales taxes (customs and excise duties and VAT) on most of the items that you buy, and typically students spend quite a high proportion of their income on highly taxed items such as alcohol and tobacco. Your *post-tax* income will therefore be less than your disposable income. However, you will benefit from free health care – and as a student you will not have to pay prescription charges, or charges for eye tests or dental care. The value of benefits-in-kind of this type will increase your *final* income.

If, on the other hand, you do not receive a maintenance grant and you do have a job, full time or part time, the situation will be different. You will have some original income (from employment) and this will be equal to your gross income. You may pay income tax, in which case your disposable income will be less than your gross income, although if the job is part time, you will probably fall below the income tax threshold and therefore pay no income tax.

Review questions

1 The rationale for the deregulation of bus services was to introduce competition as a spur to efficiency – that is, to drive prices down and improve services for consumers. The results of this policy have been mixed, but in at least some areas commercial companies have tried to eliminate competitors, thereby securing a monopoly position for themselves. For example, in 1995 the major bus operator Stagecoach Holdings was found guilty by the Monopolies and Mergers Commission of repeated 'predatory action' which was 'against the public interest'.

2 The provision and maintenance of the track would appear to be a natural monopoly – hence the establishment of a single firm (Railtrack) responsible for this aspect of the railways. The operation of trains on that track similarly appears to give little scope for effective competition. The government's plans are to issue franchises to commercial companies which would run the trains in each region for a specific number of years (probably seven), after which time the franchise comes up for renewal. The existing firm can then bid for renewal of the franchise, but other firms also have the right to bid.

3 Economic indicators are things which give clues to what is happening in the economy. Changes in *lagging indicators* occur *after* the changes in the economy that we are trying to monitor. Changes in *coincident indicators* occur at the same time.

Structural changes in the labour market appear to have shortened the time lag between an upturn in economic activity and the resulting fall in unemployment. That is, unemployment appears now to fall more quickly in a recovery than it did previously. But – and this is the bad news – unemployment also rises more quickly as the economy enters a recession because the removal of employment protection legislation has meant that firms now seem to be more willing to fire employees rather than retain them.

4 You could use bar charts to present these data, but line graphs are more straightforward and probably better. It is not a good idea to put all four series on to one graph, so you have to decide how you wish to combine them for maximum effect, and to bring out the trends you wish to highlight.

These trends are:

➤ the decline in full-time male employment
➤ the large proportionate increase in part-time male employment
➤ the increase in female employment, both full time and part time
➤ the large increase in total female employment and the small increase in total male employment
➤ the fact that there are still more males in employment than females, but that females now form a larger fraction of the workforce than previously.

5 Figure 11.9 illustrates that since 1971 all groups have increased their incomes. However, the richest quarter of all households have increased their incomes *faster* than the rest of the population. You can tell this both by the *steepness* of the line (for the 75th percentile) and also the *gap between* the lines (which is now larger than before). It illustrates the growing inequality in the distribution of household incomes. Moreover, the diagram shows that the growth in inequality is a trend that has occurred only since the early 1980s.

Chapter 12
....

Activities

1 No. A distinction is made between speculation and *hedging*. Your transaction is related to trade, since tourism constitutes an invisible export for the American economy. By buying forward currency, you are essentially paying a premium (that is, a higher price) in order to reduce the uncertainty to which you will be exposed. This is rather like taking out an insurance policy, where you pay the insurance company a fee to take on some of the risk on your behalf.

2 Non-tradable goods would include things such as houses and other real property. Many services are also non-tradable – the services of the local builder, window cleaner, gardener, garage mechanic, osteopath, hairdresser and so on.

Cars are an example of a tradable good. If cars were significantly cheaper in one part of the country than another, it would be possible to buy up cars where they are cheap and resell them where they are expensive, and this action would tend to eliminate the price differences. This buying for resale elsewhere cannot take place in the non-tradables sector, however, because such goods are by definition non-tradable.

3 If you borrow from the German bank, you will be borrowing DM22,000. You will have to repay the capital plus interest: that is,

$$22,000 \times 1.06 = DM23,320$$

If the value of sterling falls as expected, then in twelve months' time to acquire this number of marks it will cost you

$$\frac{23,320}{2} = £11,660$$

Had you borrowed from the British bank, you would only have to find £11,000 to repay the loan. Hence you calculate that it is more expensive to borrow from the German bank even though interest rates in Germany are considerably lower. The expected fall in the exchange more than eliminates the advantage of borrowing on the German market.

This analysis also ignores the effect of uncertainty. Even if your calculation appeared to make it cheaper to borrow on the German market, you might have feared the possibility that the pound would fall even more than your best estimate of what was likely to happen – say, to only £1 = DM1.90. If you were *risk averse*, you might have preferred the relative certainty of borrowing on the British market.

Review questions

1 The convergence criteria relate to:

➤ inflation
➤ interest rates
➤ the budget deficit
➤ outstanding government debt
➤ exchange rate stability.

Refer back to section 12.11 for the precise terms of the criteria.

With the exception of Luxembourg, *none* of the fifteen EU countries listed in Table 12.1 is likely to satisfy all the convergence criteria. According to the figures given, Germany would meet all the criteria, but its budget position has deteriorated somewhat since September 1995, when these figures were collected.

2 Countries with high inflation rates tend to have high interest rates. These high *nominal* interest rates are necessary to compensate savers for the fall in the value of money. *Real* interest rates can be thought of as being equal to the nominal interest rate minus the rate of inflation.

3 The franc has been tied to the DM by the exchange rate mechanism. Because the pound has fallen *vis-à-vis* the DM, this means that the pound has also fallen *vis-à-vis* the franc. This, however, is only a partial explanation – it does not explain *why* the pound has fallen in value against the DM.

4 The price of tradable goods would be more or less the same, but non-tradables – such as houses and the services of the local garage – would be cheaper in Wales (see also the next question).

5 Shoes, mineral water and computers are all tradable goods and therefore we would expect their prices to be similar in France and Germany. Houses, hairdressing services and motorway tolls are not tradable, so there would be no mechanism by which large price differences between the two countries would be eroded.

6 (a) In some Latin American countries, and in Russia, the national currencies are not readily acceptable because they do not fulfil the three functions of money – in particular, they are not a good *store of value* because inflation rapidly erodes their value both domestically and on foreign exchange markets. Traders prefer dollars and Deutschmarks because they feel that these currencies are not going to lose their value.

(b) This gives seigniorage to the United States and Germany. They could if they wished run balance of payments deficits and pay for those deficits in their own currencies.

Chapter 13

Activities

1 From the peak of 2.3 million vehicles in 1989, new car registrations fell by about 0.7 million, a reduction of about 30 per cent. In contrast the fall in consumers' expenditure was only about $1\frac{1}{2}$ per cent.

2

	$r = 8\%$	$r = 9\%$	$r = 10\%$
Present value of £100 received in one year's time	92.59	91.74	90.91
Present value of £100 received in two years' time	85.73	84.17	82.64
Present value of £100 received in three years' time	79.38	77.22	75.13
Present value of the revenue stream	257.70	253.13	248.68

As the rate of interest, which we are using as a discount rate, rises from 8 to 9 to 10 per cent, the present value of the income stream falls.

3 This is similar to the many examples we have done with index numbers, which involve putting one number *over* another rather than *subtracting* one number from another. The correct answer is that the new exchange rate will have to be £1 = 9.5238 francs. Demonstrate this for yourself with a calculator.

Review questions

1 Inventory investment is the most volatile. In some periods it becomes negative, meaning that stocks of raw materials and finished goods were being run down. Investment in fixed capital formation is also highly volatile – it increases rapidly in the boom period up to 1989, but then declines.

Government spending is the most stable magnitude. It is the least affected by cycles of activity in the domestic economy. This is because it is autonomous (or exogenous)

Exports are not part of domestic expenditure, although they are of course part of final expenditure. They will not be much affected by what goes on in the domestic economy, being dependent on demand in foreign markets rather than demand in the domestic UK market.

2 A variable which is endogenous to the UK economy varies with the level of activity therein. Thus consumers' spending and spending on imports are endogenous. Exports and government spending on goods and services are exogenous. However, government spending on transfer payments (such as unemployment benefit) is endogenous because the total amount of money spent will depend upon the total numbers of unemployed and this varies with the business cycle.

3 Construct a table as follows:

	r = 9%	r = 12%
Present value of £1,100 received in one years' time	1,009	982
Present value of £1,100 received in two years' time	925	877
Present value of £1,100 received in three years' time	849	783
Present value of the revenue stream	2,783	2,642

If the discount rate is 9 per cent, the NPV of this investment is £183. At a higher rate of interest (12 per cent), the investment yields a return of only £42.

4 This was a very bad investment indeed. Had you put the money into an alternative such as a building society account, you would have earned a lot more than 4 per cent.

5 The Law of One Price states that, if the same good is sold on two different markets, it is not possible for them to be sold at different prices if trade is possible between the two markets. This implies that, in the tradable goods sector, prices in Wales will be the same as those in England, if we ignore differences due to transport costs. The rate of inflation in this sector will also necessarily be the same in the two countries. However, the non-tradable sector consists of goods which by definition cannot be traded, and therefore the Law of One Price does not apply here. The cost of services such as car repairs and hairdressing could therefore be higher in London than in Swansea, and the rate of inflation in things like house prices could be different.

If Britain, France, Germany and the Benelux countries all had the same currency – the euro – then prices in the tradables sector of all those countries should be the same, or at least similar.

A guide to statistical sources

This is a brief guide to those statistical sources which you will find most useful. Not all of them will, of course, be available in the library that you use, but some, such as *Social Trends* and the *Monthly Digest,* are usually available even in small public libraries.

Statistical sources can be divided into three types:

➤ those relating to the UK only, most of which are published by the Office for National Statistics (ONS). This was formerly the Central Statistical Office (CSO).
➤ statistics relating to European Union countries
➤ international statistics covering not only the UK and Europe, but also the rest of the world.

They are listed below in that order.

UK National Accounts (formerly known as *National Income and Expenditure*), more normally referred to simply as the **Blue Book**. Published annually in the autumn by the ONS, it is the most important source of data for the UK economy. Most of the data presented are annual and the tables usually cover a twenty-year period. As with all ONS publications, recent editions have become more user-friendly and the latest (1996) contains useful notes explaining how to interpret the accounts.

UK Balance of Payments (known as the **Pink Book**). The sister publication to the Blue Book. Published annually by the ONS.

Economic Trends is published monthly by the ONS. Most of the data are quarterly, extending back over, perhaps, five years. It covers a range of areas including output, prices, employment and trade. The **Economic Trends Annual Supplement** is particularly useful for obtaining long series of both annual and quarterly data, some series going back to 1945.

Regional Trends is published annually by the ONS. It includes economic and social indicators, broken down by the various regions of the UK.

Social Trends, published annually by the ONS, is more like a 'coffee table book'. It uses statistics to 'tell a story' about how people's lives in Britain are changing. *Social Trends* can genuinely be described as 'a good read'.

Annual Abstract of Statistics. An amalgam of topics are covered. Annual data.

Monthly Digest of Statistics. As the name implies, an amalgam of statistics published monthly. It covers a wide range of topics, including economic, social and demographic.

General Household Survey. The results of a sample survey of households are published annually in the GHS. Five core topics are covered – education, employment, health, housing, and population and family information.

Family Expenditure Survey. Primarily a survey of household expenditure on goods and services, the main purpose of which is to provide data on spending patterns for the Retail Price Index. Information published about every six months.

Key Data. A variety of official sources are drawn on for this compilation published annually by the ONS.

Guide to Official Statistics. A definitive reference work, published most recently in 1996.

Employment Gazette. A monthly publication covering labour market issues and offering detailed information on wage rates, productivity, hours worked and so on for various sectors of the economy. It also includes articles about the labour market. It formerly contained information relating to the Retail Price Index (and other indices), but this is now contained in *Business Monitor* (see below).

Business Monitor MM23. The responsibility for the compilation of price indices has been removed from the Department of Employment and now rests with the ONS. Hence this *Business Monitor* is now the source of detailed information on prices.

Financial Statistics. Monthly publication of the ONS relating to financial indices such as interest rates, exchange rates and the money supply.

Bank of England Quarterly Bulletin. Published by the Economics Division of the Bank of England, containing a number of articles and statistics about the money supply and the financial sector.

National Institute Economic Review. Unlike all of the above, this is *not* an official Government publication. However, it does contain a statistical appendix which is a very useful compilation of UK and international data on a wide range of economic issues. Published quarterly by the National Institute of Economic and Social Research.

Eurostat. Published monthly by the Statistical Office of the European Union, this contains comparative data on various aspects of EU countries. There are also annual publications under the Eurostat heading covering specific issues.

OECD Main Economic Indicators. Published monthly by the Organisation for Economic Co-operation and Development, this contains annual and quarterly data on OECD countries. Very useful for purposes of comparison.

International Financial Statistics. Published monthly by the IMF it covers a larger number of countries than *OECD Main Economic Indicators*. Statistics relating to all member countries of the International Monetary Fund (IMF) are included. The data are annual, quarterly and monthly where appropriate.

Index

accelerator 221
accommodating transactions 114
active, economically 132
activity rate 132
adaptive expectations 69
adjustable peg system 202
adjustment problem 203
aggregation problem 193
appreciation (of exchange rate) 99
autarky 95
autonomous increases in costs 59
autonomous transactions (on balance of
    payments) 114

balance for official financing 113
balance of payments 6
balance of payments deficit 114
balance between private and public sectors 7
balancing item 115
bank multiplier 78
Bank base rate 229
barter transaction 27, 74, 76, 201
basket of goods and services 14
benefits in kind 186
benefits trap 183
Big Bang approach (to monetary union) 213
bilateral monopoly 141
billion (defined) 10
black economy 51
Black Wednesday 104, 209, 230
Blue Book 115
boom 218
Bretton Woods system 202
broad money 80
budget 33
budget deficit 33
budget surplus 33
burden of adjustment 203
business cycles 218

capital account 102

capital assets 220
capital consumption (depreciation) 48
cash base 79
cash economy 51
cash ratio 77
casual observation 8
causal mechanism 143
central bank 76
ceteris paribus 34
change in official reserves 113
child benefit 158
child tax allowances 158
circular flow of income 29
claims (money as) 74
classical view (of determinants of
    unemployment) 136
closed economy 27
closed shops 179
coincident indicators 224
command economies 45
commercial banks 76
comparative advantage 98
competitiveness, price 122
    measures of 124, 125
concentric circles (approach to EMU) 213
confidence problem 203
conflicts in objectives 3
conjuncture 3
constant price estimates (compared to
    current prices) 49
consumer durables 34
consumption function 38
contracting out (of services) 192
convergence criteria (Maastricht) 211
correlation 143
cost-push inflation 59
credit money 77
credits (on balance of payments) 111
crowding out hypothesis 39, 213
current account 102
current account deficit 114

current price and constant price estimates 49
cyclical (Keynesian) unemployment 135

debits (on balance of payments) 111
debt interest (on National Debt) 154–5
deflating (of current price estimates) 49
deflationary budget 33
deflationary policy (demand reducing
    policy) 62
deflator 49, 52, 61
demand curve/demand schedule 99
demand deficient unemployment 135
demand-induced (demand-pull) inflation 58
demand-side policies 143
depreciation (capital consumption) 48
depreciation (of exchange rate) 99, 118
desirable characteristics of money 76
devaluation 118
direct tax 162
discount rate 226
discounting 226
disposable income 32
distribution of income 7, 163, 188
distribution of earnings 189
division of labour 27
double coincidence of wants 27, 74
double entry bookkeeping 77

earnings, distribution of 189
economic growth 5
economically active 132
economically inactive 132
economies of scale 96, 176
effective marginal rate of deduction 183
elastic/inelastic (defined) 118
elasticities approach (to devaluation) 118
elasticity coefficient 119
endogenous 85, 223, 230
endogenous spending 223
equation of exchange 80
equilibrium in the circular flow 30
European currency unit (ECU) 208
European Coal and Steel Community 206
European Monetary System 103, 204,
    206, 208
exchange rate mechanism 103, 174, 206,
    208, 211
exogenous instrument 85
exogenous spending *see also* endogenous 222
expectations 223
expenditure method (of calculating
    output) 46
export profit margins (measured competi-
    tiveness) 124
exports 47
external purchasing power 105
externalities 168

factor cost adjustment 48
factor inputs 29
fiduciary currency 201
fine tuning 40, 229
fiscal instruments 229
fiscal policy 32, 66
fiscal stance 33
fixed capital formation 47, 220
fixed exchange rate 103
flexible (floating) exchange rate 103
flexible labour market 179
forecasts 223
fractional reserve banking 76
frictional unemployment 134
Friedman, Milton 66, 89, 152
full capacity level of output 58
full employment 3
functions of money 74

gains from trade 98
GATT 118, 176, 202
GDP 48
    at market prices 48
General Theory (Keynes) 86
Gini coefficient 187
globalisation 95, 175
GNP 48
    per capita 50
Gold Standard 201
government spending 47
Gross Domestic Product (GDP) 48
Gross National Product (GNP) 28, 48
growth (defined) 5

high–powered money 78
homogeneous (factor of production) 139
hyperinflation 56

IMF 202
IMF Drawing Rights 202
imperfections in the labour market 135
import price competitiveness 125
inactive, economically 132
income, definitions of 184
    disposable 186
    final 186
    gross 185
    original 185
    post-tax 186
income, distribution of 7, 163, 188
income in kind 169
income maintenance programme 7, 169
income method of calculating output 46
income per capita 5
index numbers 14
indirect tax 162
inelastic (defined) 118

inflation defined 14
inflation 4
   cost-push 59
   demand-pull 58
   pure wage-push 59
initial tax allowances 163
injection 32
instruments 3, 117, 128, 229
interest profits and dividends 113
internal purchasing power 105
internal rate of return 227
International Monetary Fund (IMF) 202
internationalisation 95, 175
intervention currency 202
intervention in foreign exchange market 103
investment appraisal 225
investment spending 220
invisible trade (trade in services) 100
invisibles 113
involuntary unemployment 137

J-curve effect 120

Keynes 86
Keynesians 39, 40, 86, 136, 196

labour market imperfections 135
lagging indicators 224
Law of One Price 106
leading indicators 224
leakage (withdrawal) 32
liberalisation 190
liquidity problem 203
liquidity spectrum 89
living standards 5
local pay bargaining 141
long-run Phillips curve 68
Lorenz curve 187

Maastricht 206
Maastricht convergence criteria 211
macroeconomics (defined) 2
male/female activity rates 132
manufacturing productivity 193
marginal propensity to consume (mpc) 37
marginal propensity to save (mps) 37
marginal rates of tax 163
market clearing wage 136
market power 139
medium of exchange 74
menu of choice 66
menu costs 231
merit good 169
microeconomics (defined) 2
minimum wage 138
model of the economy 26
monetarist view 39, 40, 66, 85, 86, 89,
   136, 178, 213

money (a stock) 28
   broad definition 80
   functions of 74
   high powered 78
   narrow definition 79
monopsonists 139
multiple credit creation 76
multiplier 36

narrow definition of money supply (M0) 79
National Debt 155
national expenditure 28
national income 28
national output (national product) 28
national pay bargaining 141
natural level of unemployment 67
natural monopoly 190
neo-classical view 136
net national product (NNP) 48
net present value 225
net property income from abroad 48
neutral budget 33
nominal exchange rate 232
nominal output and real output 46
non-bank financial intermediaries 87
non-durables 34
non-excludable 166
non-rival 166

objectives 3
open economies 95, 175
opportunity cost 98, 228
output method 46
output measured in money terms 45
output measured in value terms 45

par value (parity) 103
paradox of thrift 37
parity 103
parity grid 208
participation rate 132
per capita GNP 50
perfectly competitive market 99
performance indicators (PIs) 192
Phillips curve 64
Phillips curve (long–run) 68
Pink Book 115
portfolio balance 89
positive science contrasted with normative
   science 116
price competitiveness 122
price index 14
price maker 121
price taker 121
private cost/social cost 168
privatisation 189
productivity, manufacturing 193

productivity 192
progressive tax 163
proportional change 15
proportional (neutral) tax 164
PSBR 155
public good 166
public sector borrowing requirement
    (PSBR) 155
public sector debt repayment 156
public spending 32, 152
pure wage-push inflation 59
purchasing power parity theorem 106

quality of products (changes in) 22
quota 118

ranking of objectives 7
rate of inflation 14
rational expectations 69
real earnings 59
real exchange rate 232
real terms 5
rebasing an index 62
recession 218
Red Book 34
reflationary budget 33
regional imbalance 7
regional multiplier effect 135
regional unemployment 135
regressive tax 164
relative export prices (measured competi-
    tiveness) 123
relative prices 19
relative profitability approach (to devalua-
    tion) 121
relative unit labour costs (measured com-
    petitiveness) 124
replacement ratio 183
reserve requirements 78
revisions to the data 11

savings and investment 35
Say's Law 81
scale, economies of 96, 176
scarcity 57
SDRs 203
secondary picketing 179
seigniorage 203
shoe leather costs 222
simple average contrasted with weighted
    average 21
Single European Act (Single Market) 206
single European currency 207, 211, 234
Smithsonian Agreement 204
'snake in a tunnel' analogy 207
social security spending 152
Special Drawing Rights (SDRs) 203

specialisation 97
specialisation and exchange 27
speculation 205, 206, 209
spending on imports 47
standard of living 50
statistical data 8
statistical regularities 143
statutory minimum wage 138
stockbuilding 47
stocks and flows 28
store of value 74
structural change 174
structural unemployment 135
supply curve 99
supply–side economics 143
supply–side policies 177

targets 3
tariff 118
tariff reduction 176
tastes (globalisation of) 177
taxation 32
    direct 162
    indirect 162
    neutral 164
    progressive 163
    proportional 164
    regressive 164
taxes on expenditure 162
taxes on income 162
telecommunications 176
terms of the trade–off (Phillips curve) 66
time lags 224
tokens (money as) 74
trade balance 112
trade credit 88
trade deficit 114
tradeable/non-tradeable goods 212
trade–off between inflation and employ-
    ment 65
transfer payments 152
transfer of technology 96
transfers 113
transmission mechanism 80
transnational corporations 176
Treaty on European Union (Maastricht) 206
Treaty of Rome 206
two-sector model 29
two-speed Europe 213

unemployment
    cyclical 135
    demand deficient 135
    frictional 134
    involuntary 137
    Keynesian 135
    natural level 67

regional 135
structural 135
unit labour requirements 97
use of money 27

value in use 76
value judgements 3
value of the output of the economy 47
value terms (output measured in) 45
velocity of circulation of money 28
vertical Phillips curve 68
visible trade 100
visible trade deficit 114
volatility of investment 220

wage cost per unit of output 67
wage-price spiral 59
Wages Councils 138
wealth portfolio 89
weighted average 21
welfare state 7
Werner Report 206
white noise 232
wider margins (Smithsonian) 204
wider definition of the money supply (M4) 79
withdrawal (leakage) 32
WTO (World Trade Organisation) 118